THE CREATIVE ARTS

The Creative Arts

MALCOLM ROSS

Lecturer in Education
University of Exeter
School of Education

with contributions by

BEN BRADNACK

ANNE COLE

DAVID JOHN FARNELL

LEN JENKINSON

SUSAN MORRIS

JOHN WOOLNER

HEINEMANN EDUCATIONAL BOOKS

LONDON

Heinemann Educational Books Ltd
LONDON EDINBURGH MELBOURNE AUCKLAND TORONTO
HONG KONG SINGAPORE KUALA LUMPUR IBADAN
NAIROBI JOHANNESBURG LUSAKA NEW DELHI KINGSTON

ISBN 0 435 80780 3

First published 1978

Published by
Heinemann Educational Books Ltd
48 Charles Street, London W1X 8AH
Printed and bound in Great Britain by
Cox & Wyman Ltd
London, Fakenham, and Reading

Contents

Acknowledgements

The author, contributors and publishers wish to thank the following for permission to reproduce copyright material: East Anglian Examinations Board for an extract from the Art and Craft syllabus; Associated Lancashire Schools Examining Board for CEE and CSE Mode III examinations in Modern Educational Dance; Southern Regional Examinations Board for a CSE Mode III examination in Drama and Theatre Arts, a (Revised) CSE Mode III Drama syllabus, and CEE Communication Working Party modules; Associated Examining Board for the GCE A-level Outline Syllabus in Theatre Studies.

In addition, Anne Cole wishes to acknowledge her indebtedness to Miss J. V. R. Gregory, Headmistress, and her former colleagues at Wakefords School, Havant, and Susan Morris her special gratitude to Mr Ernest Goodman, CBE, Headmaster of the Manchester High School of Art.

Foreword

Of all the high aims that schools have, those concerning the arts perhaps more often than others wither in a frustration of well-meaning effort pitted against practical limitations. Malcolm Ross sees the difficulties as lying not merely at the surface level of classroom activities, but more fundamentally in the failure of the profession to think out the 'idea of the role of the creative arts teacher'. In giving us such a thoughtful and logical account of the underlying concepts, and through them the organizing systems, Malcolm Ross has written with tough-minded sensitivity a deeply practical book, one that will be useful not only to teachers of the Arts subjects and Heads of Arts Departments, but Headteachers and Deputies anxious in their curriculum planning to work out the true 'educational function of the arts', which is described in this book as 'through the expressive use of media to further the development of intelligent feeling'.

As Malcolm Ross says early in his account: 'We need organizational structures geared to facilitate human interaction.' His book is an important addition to the *Heinemann Organization in Schools Series*, which is a systematic attempt to help schools improve the quality of the school experience by a methodical study of ways in which they can be organized. Each book is written by a different author and from a different point of view, out of his or her observation, experience, and conviction. The titles will show the scope of the series, and the way that aspects of school organization, certain kinds of jobs in schools, and certain kinds of schools are each covered. This is one of the books in the series that will explore sectors of the curriculum itself.

The author is especially well placed to write on this subject, not only because of his extensive experience as a teacher of pupils and, on in-service courses, with teachers of the arts, but also because of his experience directing the Schools Council's Arts and the Adolescent project for four years. He provides, with modesty but passionate conviction, a rationale for creativity, an interpretation of the function of the arts, a definition of the role of the arts teacher, and (with the aid of six specialist contributors) a review of practical school possibilities.

MICHAEL MARLAND

The world is too much with us: late and soon,
Getting and spending, we lay waste our powers:
Little we see in Nature that is ours:
We have given our heart away, a sordid boon!
This sea that bares her bosom to the moon;
The Winds that will be howling at all hours
And are up-gathered now like sleeping flowers;
For this, for everything, we are out of tune;
It moves us not. – Great God! I'd rather be
A Pagan suckled in a creed outworn;
So might I, standing on this pleasant lea,
Have glimpses that would make me less forlorn;
Have sight of Proteus rising from the sea;
Or hear old Triton blow his wreathed horn.

                                William Wordsworth

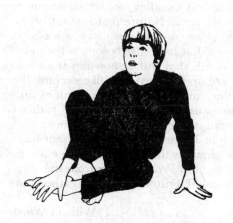

Introduction

This book draws extensively upon the fruits of my original partnership with Robert Witkin and, although he has had no hand in it, it nevertheless owes a very great deal to him. My personal debt to him will be life-long and I shall always think of that period of close and intense collaboration as one of the most exciting and rewarding of my working life. Our Schools Council project (1968–1972) culminated in the publication of two books: Witkin's *The Intelligence of Feeling* (Heinemann Educational, 1974), and my own Working Paper 54, *Arts and the Adolescent* (Evans/Methuen Educational, 1975).

When the original project was wound up, my immediate concern was to see that development and dissemination followed the research and here I was very fortunate in obtaining grants from the Michael Marks Charitable Trust which enabled me to launch the 'Arts Curriculum Project'.

My contributors – all experienced teachers – and I have written this book in an attempt to convey something of the impact of the original research upon a group of practitioners. We are aware that the arts are in a vulnerable and isolated position in schools and that the ideals of arts teachers need defending today more vigorously than ever. We believe that children need the arts *throughout* their school lives, as an essential and unique way of knowing. Arts teachers are expert in nurturing a creative approach to living: in particular, a creative approach to the developing life of feeling. Their special skills deserve to be more widely appreciated and better supported. For their own part, and in their own interests, arts teachers must get together in a determined effort to secure a legitimate status for their work. If they are to do so their claim must rest upon a clear understanding of the primary purpose of education through the arts, and a determination to maintain the integrity of their work at all costs. We hope that they will find our book useful.

In Part I, I suggest a way of conceiving of arts education: essentially I try to suggest why arts teachers should concentrate their efforts on developing children's creative self-expression. Part II provides a number of insights into arts education in practice; each chapter is written by an experienced teacher. The section is completed by two further chapters of my own. In Chapter 13 I discuss Creative Music; it is offered, I should admit, with many misgivings and was made necessary only by my failure to attract a suitable piece for the book from a specialist musician. In Chapter 14 I try to pick my way through the minefield of assessment and examinations in the arts – I leave the reader to judge whether I made it or not. In case I didn't, I asked my contributors to give the subject some thought and we have included some specimen papers as appendices.

In conclusion I should like to pay special tribute to my friends Edna Cross and Alma Craft both of whom have been of the utmost help in the preparation of this book. Perhaps our greatest debt is to our students.

MALCOLM ROSS
Exeter

PART ONE

A Theoretical Framework

1 Creativity in Education

The Creative Person

Studies of the characteristics of so-called creative people have tended to take the exceptional or distinguished individual as subject, and in consequence there is little information on what might be called general or universal creativity as a normal feature of intelligent behaviour. However, study of the factors isolated as significant in investigations of the personalities and performances of creative writers, scientists, architects, etc. would suggest that the creative person is endowed with what most of us would regard as the usual attributes of a lively mind: sensitivity to problems, fluency of ideas, flexibility of mental strategy, originality, the capacity to redefine situations and sustain penetrative mental processes. *What seems to distinguish the creative from the merely effective or competent individual is not so much special intellectual ability as certain traits of personality.* If creativity is the capacity to break away from habitual thought processes into novel and original ones, it is generally felt that the roots of such a capacity lie in the effects of 'environment' upon personality development – particularly in terms of the relationship between parent and child in the early years.

Most researchers point out the incidence of psychic tension and mental conflict in the lives of the creatives they have studied. Liam Hudson (1966) has said that creativity 'if not born of unhappiness is born certainly of unease'. Everyone is of course subject to tension and mental conflict but the creative person seems to be better able to resolve such conflicts rewardingly, to sustain the high levels of anxiety involved and turn them to advantage.

This tendency to pit himself against himself (rather than participating in inter-personal competition) is born, so it seems, of belief in oneself. Such basic self-confidence allows him to put himself at risk in ways that prove to be conclusively inhibiting in less secure personalities. So we find the investigators reporting high levels of independence, stubbornness, self-sufficiency, autonomy, and social selectivity where creative persons are concerned. Allied to such characteristics – and presumably emanating from confidence in their own powers – creative people are also found to be capable of indefatigable industry, diligence, and self-discipline in their work, of achieving high levels of technical and mental accomplishment in their chosen field and of becoming totally absorbed in the work in hand.

The educational lesson drawn by Barron from studying the research, and from his own experiments, is this: 'To stimulate creative change, we must begin with the psycho-dynamics of the individual.'[1]

We shall be considering this statement fairly closely when we turn to examine the teacher's role. Meanwhile here is Barron again.

> In the creative process there is an incessant dialectic and an essential tension between two seemingly opposed *dispositional tendencies* (my italics): the tendency towards structuring and integration and the tendency towards disruption of structure and diffusion of energy and attention . . . . The expansion of consciousness requires the temporary abandonment of certain ego structures. (ibid.)

He concludes that this 'restless view of the creative process' is, normally, under entirely rational and healthy self-regulation. Openness is a characteristic implicit in everything that has so far been said. By openness I mean both the propensity for seeking out new experiences (essentially the problematic element in such experiences) – opening up – and the capacity for deferring judgement, postponing closure, resisting the urge to draw conclusions, to interpret, to tie up (or down). One essential requirement for creative action is a capacity for tolerating tension. Conflict and unease attend the open-hearted and the open-minded – they are inherent in the creative process of 'making grow' (to create literally means 'to make grow') and have to be suffered and endured in the hope and for the sake of eventually achieving *a unique personal response*.

The Development of the Creative Response

Before looking more closely at the role of conflict in the creative process I think we need to remind ourselves of the developmental process which, as has already been suggested, gives us in the first place either our predominantly *creative* or our *imitative* characteristics. One of the books which I have found particularly relevant on this subject has been D. W. Winnicott's *Playing and Reality*, and this would seem to be the right moment to draw him into this

[1] Barron, F., *Creative Person and Creative Process*, Holt, Rinehart and Winston, 1969.

discussion. Dr Winnicott expresses his own position on the subject of creativity:

> Assuming reasonable brain capacity, enough intelligence to enable the individual to become a person living and taking part in the life of the community, everything that happens is creative except in so far as the individual is ill, or is hampered by on-going environmental factors which stifle his creative processes.[1]

Dr Winnicott's purpose is to persuade his readers to take the *playing* of children and adults seriously – for him the individual is most creative when he is playing. People who cannot play cannot be creative and do not achieve the wholeness and satisfaction that comes to the creative ones, for whom life has personal meaning and is intrinsically worth living.

Critical in the development of the creative attitude to life is the early experience of the infant in his or her relation with the mother (or mother figure). Whereas Piaget's model is essentially biological Winnicott's is cultural, for he suggests that the creative potential of the individual – leaving aside the questions of personal endowment, growth and development – is absolutely dependent upon the mother's capacity to develop the child's capacity to play in an atmosphere of trust and reliability.

> We find either that individuals live creatively and feel that life is worth living or else they cannot live creatively and are doubtful about the value of living. This variability in human being is directly related to the quality and quantity of environmental provision at the beginning . . . of each baby's living experience. (ibid.)

To clarify his conception of play Winnicott proposes three areas of experience, three related worlds or realities in which people act and have their being, as opposed to the more usual and simple distinction that is made between the inner and outer realities – the complementary worlds of subjective and objective experience. Winnicott postulates an intermediate area of experience in which he locates playing and indeed the whole field of cultural experience. This area he calls 'the potential space' between mother and child. It is described as 'potential' because it is culturally or experientially determined. Its development is entirely subject to the quality of mothering at the critical period when the infant begins to distinguish between 'me' and 'not-me' – as separation is effected.

Implicit in the notion of the 'potential' space is the optional nature of the experiences that take place within it. Whereas in practice few children are so chronically deprived of maternal affection that they never learn to play and remain bound throughout childhood to the crushing wheel of their own overwhelming anxieties, the potential space that is developed in trust and love by the mother for her child

[1] Winnicott, D., *Playing and Reality*, Tavistock, 1971.

is very much an individual phenomenon, and will become more or less important to the development of the particular child as he or she feels able (i.e. secure enough) to make use of it. *It is an allowed, a privileged and unchallenged area of experience within which compelling and in their own way 'serious' actions and encounters are entered into.* Initially it is the world of mother-baby playing. The mother creates the play space between herself and her child. Into this space the child draws objects from the environment that stand symbolically for the separated, and occasionally absent, mother. These 'transitional objects' as Winnicott calls them are neither strictly subjective nor objective in character – they are subjective objects, significant for their capacity to organize the infant's feelings of separateness (separate being). The potential space affords the child a kind of half-way house on the road towards individuality. The transitional object is the first possession. The potential space that the 'good enough' mother creates for her child provides an opportunity for the child to interact with and give substance to his expressive drives.

Each developmental change in himself, each new manifestation or organization of environmental events, requires that the child remake his own world picture, refashion his sense of his own identity, since each change in the environment sets up disturbance in his inner world. For the infant, outer reality is the Mother. Gradually the horizons fall back and his own separateness is born in upon him. He learns to master his own experience of separateness through play – using this magical space conjured by the mother out of love for her child. It is an area of experience memorably represented in this famous and beautiful passage from the writings of Rabindranath Tagore:

> They build their houses with sand, and they play with empty shells. With withered leaves they weave their boats and smilingly float them on the vast deep. *Children have their play on the seashore of worlds.* They know not how to swim, they do not know how to cast nets. Pearl fishers dive for pearls, merchants sail in their ships, while children gather pebbles and scatter them again. They seek not for hidden treasures, they know not how to cast nets.[1]

Eventually, Winnicott suggests, transitional objects give way to real objects and play-with-mother opens out, if all goes well, into independent, social and symbolic play. *Ultimately the potential space survives as the site of all creative and cultural experiences* – Winnicott mentions in this connection 'adult play, artistic creativity and appreciation, religious feeling, dreaming, the arousal and loss of affection, imaginative living and creative scientific work'. As teachers of the creative arts it is precisely into this area of the potential space that we should be prepared to draw our pupils and step ourselves. It is precisely here that the conflicts of creative living are resolved. Winnicott says:

[1] Quoted in Barron, op. cit.

It is assumed here that the task of reality acceptance is never completed, that no human being is free from the strain of relating inner and outer reality, and that relief from this strain is provided by an intermediate area of experience which is unchallenged (arts, religion etc.). This intermediate area is in direct continuity with the play area of the small child who is 'lost' in play.[1]

We are of course talking about control – self-control and self-determination. Separation is the fact that precipitates all learning: it is the basis of psychological development and from it spring the roots of personal integrity. It is at once the greatest threat the individual has to face: it is also the source of every opportunity to realize or actualize oneself. In the infant consciousness no distinction is drawn between separation and destruction, and we retain, buried deep within our adult consciousness, the paradox that the destruction of the object is both necessary for our survival (and this includes of course the continual destruction of the self as object), and at the same time is critically threatening to it since we are essentially dependent creatures, intimately and absolutely bound to the object world for our very survival. We learn to manage both the flux of subject-object-relations and, if we are lucky, the anxiety attendant upon it.

The importance of play in developing the individual's own powers of self control has also been appreciated by Otto Fenischel. Here he is writing about play in an illuminating essay on acting:

> Playing is a process of learning while developing the ability to master the outer world. The primitive game is repetitive. It serves the purpose of achieving a belated mastery of highly cathected impressions. What was endured passively is done over again in play in an active manner until the child has become familiar with the qualities and quantities involved. The more highly developed game is anticipatory. It makes tensions which might occur, but at a time and in a degree which is determined by the participant himself, and which therefore is under control. Such play is an anti-surprise measure.[2]

This is a key passage for us since it adds significantly to the model we are trying to put together. Not only are the tensions of play – and of course play has its own 'allowed' or 'test' tensions – regulated by the player, but the learning is self-directed, self-motivated, presumably self-rewarding and certainly self-validating. There could hardly be a more comprehensive system of intrinsically determined behaviour to set against the picture drawn a moment ago. It is in this world of play, set in Winnicott's potential space, that personal creativity is born, nurtured and flowers into maturity.

Separation then, though fraught with potential disaster, must be perceived by the child as, in the final reckoning, strongly rewarding,

---

[1] Winnicott, op. cit.
[2] Fenischel, Otto, *Collected Papers*, Routledge and Kegan Paul, 1955.

so that attendant anxieties and frustrations may be used creatively as a spur to learning – ultimately as the motive force to full symbolic operation. It is in this early experience of play that the confidence and appetite for such self-regulation is developed. The potential space is an illusion, but, if Winnicott is to be believed, it is an illusion that may not be challenged since, within the magic circle that the mother draws about herself and her baby, a unique creative flame is kindled. Too few alas survive as vigorous and unquenchable flares in the desert of adulthood.

> The searching (for the self) can only come from desultory formless functioning, or perhaps from rudimentary playing, as if in a neutral zone. It is only here, in this unintegrated state of personality, that that which we describe as creative can appear. This, if reflected back, *but only if reflected back*, becomes part of the organised individual personality, and eventually this in summation makes the individual to be, to be found; and eventually enable himself or herself to postulate the existence of the self.[1]

Winnicott's reference to what he calls 'desultory formless functioning' echoes a point made by Barron and quoted earlier. It was this: 'The expansion of consciousness requires the temporary abandonment of certain ego structures.'[2] He spoke of 'disruption of structure' and 'diffusion of energy and attention'. It is hereabouts that a lot of people reach for their hats and make their excuses. What is being suggested is that *the self*, so carefully, so painstakingly and indeed so painfully put together over the years and designed precisely to defend the individual against surprise attack and immunize him from paralysing bouts of anxiety, should be voluntarily dissolved and a condition of 'formless functioning' entered upon. The threatened loss of face, and the fear that, having left the organized ego behind, it might somehow disappear altogether leaving no trace and so be quite irrecoverable, assume horrendous proportions for many, perhaps most adult Westerners.

If every creative action requires as its *sine qua non* such abandonment – albeit on a limited scale and under conscious control – one can perhaps guess why creative action is so feared and so rare. And yet the testimony of creative people (some of whose statements we have already cited) and of the psychologists who have investigated the subject, very strongly affirms the essential role of diffusion and of what, under other circumstances and in a different context Coleridge called 'the suspension of disbelief'. That the fears of many people are well founded is probably true enough – and there is of course a pathology of identity-loss or breakdown to underscore the dangers. However, perhaps a closer, rather more technical, look at the phenomenon of 'adaptive regression' will help us to a more balanced view of the problems involved and may suggest ways in which such

[1] Winnicott, op. cit.
[2] Barron, op. cit.

regressive behaviour may be both encouraged and supported in the interest of the full development of an individual's creative potential. For this technical help I shall draw on one book in particular, *Ego Functions in Schizophrenics, Neurotics and Normals*, by L. Bellack, M. Hurvich, and H. K. Gediman. The authors begin their discussion of regression with this account of creativity – and I quote it because it is entirely in line with the view I have tried to develop:

> In the broadest sense, creativity – the ability to meet life's demands with other than previously learned solutions – is the essence of adaptation. It is not a quality or a process relevant only to the arts and sciences, in which the end product is cultural or technical success; it can be observed in more diverse and private sectors of living as well.[1]

The authors concur with Winnicott in equating creativity with the adaptive principle itself. This is what they have to say about regression – it is an extremely measured statement and repays study.

> ... a brief, oscillating, relative reduction of certain adaptive functions of the ego in the service of the other, specifically the 'synthetic' ego functions. What happens is that cognitive, selective, adaptive functions are decreased; this weakens the sharply defined boundaries of figure and ground, of logical, temporal, spatial, and other relations, and permits them to reorder themselves into new configurations with new boundaries, under the scrutiny of the again sharply functioning adaptive forces. (ibid.)

The authors associate regressive behaviour with 'wit, humour, art, productive fantasy and imagination, problem solving, the capacity for orgastic experience, ego-building identifications, motherliness, love and therapeutic processes'. They recognize however the threat implicit in such behaviour in this important statement – one that again echoes other writers we have referred to.

> Only if a firm structure is established can one permit oneself the regression in the service of the ego necessary for adaptive creative acts. (ibid.)

Winnicott in particular stressed the importance of play within the potential space created by the mother as a means of establishing basic self-confidence and security and a creative style of dealing with tension, anxiety and frustration. The infant that learns the scope as well as the limits of its own powers of self-determination is likely to develop ego structures strong enough to allow the kind of relaxation and diffusion described above – adaptation then becomes an organic rather than an imitative or purely accommodatory process.

When we speak of regression in this sense we mean the capacity to relax certain attentive modes of behaviour and allow consciousness to flow and expand fully. In practice this means allowing possibly childish forms of behaviour and certainly childhood feelings,

[1] Bellack, L., Hurvich, M. and Gediman, H. K., *Ego Functions in Schizophrenics, Neurotics and Normals*, Wiley, 1973.

memories, fantasies and images to revive and energize the restructuring process. Regression is literally a going back to earlier experience and modes of organizing experience – to the source of creative energy. Not so much to earlier, simpler structures as to the naïve dynamics of the structuring process. Fortunately this process is intrinsic and natural to everyday living though generally undervalued – we all dream, some of us daydream, moon, become wrapt and lost in thought and in play. *If such processes are not to be lost or distorted, homes and schools have a vital responsibility to endorse and sustain them.* At the social level recreative pursuits serve the same function when they remain true to their original impulse. The professionalism of sport is of course a distortion of the recreative principle. Our innate creativity does not depend either upon therapy or schooling; however, and this is my point, teachers and therapists professionally concerned with the creative responses of their pupils and patients must appreciate the nature and the significance of what Winnicott calls 'formless functioning'.

The earlier quotation continues as follows:

> This gives us one indication for therapeutic procedure – *to afford opportunity for formless experience, and for creative impulse, motor and sensory, which are the stuff of playing* (my italics). And on the basis of playing is built the whole of man's experiential existence. No longer are we either introvert or extrovert. We experience life in the area of transitional phenomena, in the exciting interweave of subjectivity and objective observation, and in an area that is intermediate between the inner reality of the individual and the shared reality of the world that is external to individuals.[1]

Something John Cage said in an interview catches exactly the 'desultory' quality of the activity Winnicott describes as play – and incidentally mirrors other, earlier references in this book.

> What we need is to fumble around in the darkness because that's where our lives (not necessarily all the time, but at least some of the time, and particularly when life gets problematical for us) take place: in the darkness, or as they say in Christianity 'the dark night of the soul'. It is in those situations that Art must act, and then it won't be just Art, but will be useful to our lives.[2]

Of his own creative processes Cage says, 'My purpose is to remove purpose'; and then the marvellous image in this piece from his book *Silence*:

> . . . the way to get ideas is to do something boring. For instance composing in such a way that the process of composing is boring induces ideas. They fly into one's head like birds. (ibid.)

Do we have heads the birds fly into – or are we merely scarecrows? I hope the point of all this is becoming clear. Creativity involves

[1] Winnicott, op. cit.
[2] Cage, J., *Silence*, Calder and Boyars, 1971.

conflict – conflict between what we know ourselves to be and the unknown that we would become. This conflict is resolved through an 'act of regression' into a privileged or allowed realm that permits the untidy processes of creative activity to proceed unchallenged. This regressive manoeuvre entails the diminishing of the sharply focused 'attentive' mode of functioning so that there may be free and unconstrained interaction between conscious and unconscious experience. Essentially it allows the adoption or recovery of primary or *aesthetic modes of structuring experience* – the play of feeling and the adaptive operation of what Witkin calls 'the intelligence of feeling'. Poincarré, the French mathematician, wrote: 'More generally, the privileged unconscious phenomena, those susceptible of becoming conscious, are those which, directly or indirectly, affect most profoundly our emotional sensibility . . . and which are capable of developing in us a sort of aesthetic emotion.'[1]

Such experiences almost invariably evoke some sensation of discomfort or dis-ease since we naturally feel some anxiety in such a formless and unstructured condition, and may well be apprehensive of our capacity to deal effectively with whatever demands are made upon us to effect a viable reconstructuring of the self. There must come a new structure – we know well enough the insistence of the drive towards balance and stability that is the basis of Piaget's work on cognitive development. In adopting the regressive mode, in risking ourselves in the potential space, we withdraw from the pressure of reality and pin our faith on the vigorous character of our own innate personality. In the process, anxiety may trigger a premature closure – the abortion of a particular enterprise. But not every enterprise will suffer the same fate. Frustration there will certainly be and once again the negative feelings associated with it may jeopardize the work in hand. *But the process we commit ourselves to is a wholly natural and a healthy one though we may have lost faith in it or have forgotten it and need to find our way back to it again.* Upon it depends self-knowing and the continuous remaking of self all our lives long. If anxiety is the underlying motive of all our actions in the world (as has been suggested by some writers), and boredom the bottom of the sine curve in terms of man's neurology of experience then the capacity to create new worlds out of his own private chaos is man's perennial means of self-redemption. Such redemptive action is and has to be, by definition, self-propulsive. Mental conflict and psychic tension are essential and invariant features of the creative – adaptive process. The temptation to sabotage one's own integrity – to deny or to compromise one's commitment – can be very strong.

I suggest that the second developmental crisis for individual creativity occurs at adolescence (the first is very much, as we have seen, a question of 'good-enough' mothering) since full creativity requires full mental and full emotional maturity. Only when regres-

[1] In Vernon, P. E. (ed.), *Creativity*, Penguin, 1970.

sion is optional – when there is a past to be accepted or rejected and when the choice is one's own – only when there is a felt risk attaching to the shift in realities, and the realm of the possible suddenly expands seemingly to infinity, can the creative crisis be undergone. *It is arguably a teacher's most important – and certainly his most difficult – task to help the adolescent boy or girl negotiate this threat to autonomy, self-determination and full self-realization.* Loss of the kind of aesthetic – affective control that we have been discussing will inevitably be critically damaging to continuing emotional adaptation. It is vital for the teacher to stay with the adolescent as he swings now this way, now that, under the often conflicting charges of his impulses. To stay with him and not endorse either 'fixing' (withdrawal of commitment) or 'faking' (a spurious conformity to ready-made solutions to his problems). *He must be encouraged not to avoid the tensions of experience but to master them in his own terms and for his own purposes.* The adolescent needs his teacher every bit as much as Dante needed Virgil, and in much the same way. He can so easily become overwhelmed at this time by what Maslow calls 'deficiency needs', and never recover from the trauma of adolescence sufficiently to move into the higher modes of self-expression and self-actualization.

The Agonistic Principle

The creative individual enters into a contest which certainly involves some pain – the negative feelings associated with diffusion, loss of conscious control, frustration in the face of one's own unknowing. *His is a contest with himself that requires that he should hazard what he is, for what he might become.* As Barron says, it can be a punishing experience since there is no way of guaranteeing a successful outcome:

> Looking backwards from end to start point of the creative process we are inclined to say 'Ah yes, it had to be so; the chance had to be taken . . . But facing forward in time we see only risk and difficulty, and if we have not the courage to endure diffusion we cannot achieve the new and more inclusive integration.[1]

The 'agonistic' principle, which I take to be an essential of the creative process, means simply this: if I am to remake myself, I must take issue with myself first. Everyman wrestles with his angel – in the dark and alone until the dawn. In following Winnicott I have suggested that what some writers have called the critically 'unconscious' processes of creativity involves regression to primary modes of perception. The self-contestant resolves the problem in the course of what Arthur Koestler in his great book *The Act of Creation* calls 'underground games'. Adaptive regression becomes, paradoxically, adaptive aggression.

The period of incubation represents a *reculer pour mieux sauter*. Just as in

[1] Barron, op. cit.

the dream the codes of logical reasoning are suspended, so 'thinking aside' is a temporary liberation from the tyranny of over-precise verbal concepts, of the axioms and prejudices ingrained in the very texture of specialized ways of thought. It allows the mind to discard the straitjacket of habit, to shrug off apparent contradictions, to un-learn and forget – and to acquire, in exchange, a greater fluidity, versatility and gullibility.[1]

The contest is resolved in the perception of a new truth. Every creative act is an intuitive leap that short-cuts the tortuous path of logic. Koestler again:

> The moment of truth, the sudden emergence of a new insight, is an act of intuition. Such intuitions give the appearance of miraculous flashes, or short circuits of reasoning. In fact they may be likened to an immersed chain, of which only the beginning and the end are visible above the surface of consciousness. The diver vanishes at one end of the chain and comes up at the other end, guided by invisible links. (ibid.)

The interplay of conscious and unconscious processes in the contest is summed up by Koestler thus:

> Habit and originality, then, point in opposite directions in the two-way traffic between conscious and unconscious processes. The condensation of training into habit, and the automatization of skills constitute the downward stream; while the upward traffic consists in the minor, vitalizing pulses from the underground, and the rare major signs of creation. (ibid.)

Perhaps we are now in a position to begin to draw the threads of our discussion together and examine the pattern they make. There does seem to be an impressive concurrence of opinion about the nature of the creative process. In an essay entitled 'The Conditions of Creativity' in his book, *On Knowing – Essays for the Left Hand*, Jerome Bruner defines the creative act as producing 'effective surprise' – he describes the activity itself as 'combinational', a matter of placing apparently disparate things in new relationships, an idea very close to Koestler's own theory of 'bisociation'.

Bruner explains:

> The triumph of effective surprise is that it takes one beyond the common ways of experiencing the world. Or perhaps this is simply a restatement of what we have been meaning by effective surprise. If it is merely that, let me add that it is in this sense that life most deeply imitates art or that nature imitates science. Creative products have this power of re-ordering experience and thought in their image. In science the reordering is much the same from one beholder of a formula to another. In art, the imitation is in part self-imitation. It is the case too that the effective surprise of the creative man provides a new instrument for manipulating the world – physically as with the creation of the wheel or symbolically as with the creation of $e = mc^2$.[2]

[1] Koestler, A., *The Act of Creation*, Hutchinson, 1964.
[2] Bruner, Jerome S., *On Knowing – Essays for the Left Hand*, Harvard University Press, 1962.

Summing up what he sees as the conditions of creativity, Bruner makes use of a series of paradoxes: detachment and commitment; passion and decorum; freedom to be dominated by the object; deferral and immediacy. For Bruner too the process is agonistic: 'It is in the working out of conflict and coalition within the set of identities that compose the person that one finds the source of many of the richest and most surprising combinations.' (ibid.) Creativity is the capacity to realize new forms, new cognitive structures, new products – they may be actual or symbolic. Creativity means making grow and the struggle to go on growing. The process of creativity itself is still essentially mysterious since the moment of insight or resolution cannot be forced. Certain features of the creative process however do seem to emerge from the evidence as 'constants' – and certain prior conditions appear to be necessary:

1. Considerable knowledge of the field of experience in question – and a propensity to seek out new problems – to venture beyond the edge of the known.
2. Certain qualities of character as they apply to a specific situation make a creative response more likely: independence, self-confidence, playfulness, indefatigability, tenacity – most of these characteristics being developed under the right conditions of early childhood. And a readiness to take risks.
3. The capacity to allow some diffusion of attention; to regress to primary modes of cognition; to allow unconscious and intuitive forces to play upon the problem; and to defer closure – to wait.
4. A strong drive towards integration and equilibrium once the resolution of the problem becomes feasible.

While some people are culturally and genetically more especially inclined towards creative action than others, the capacity for creative behaviour is an invariant human characteristic and lies at the root of the adaptability of the species. We have to recognize however that each of us tends to behave differently in different circumstances, and that significant creative experiences, like Maslow's 'peak experiences', occur rather infrequently, and then within fairly specific areas of our lives. To invoke Maslow again, the relation between 'deficiency needs' and 'being needs' is a shifting rather than a constant condition of human experience, and when D needs predominate then there is little or no prospect of a creative response. Creativity is not merely the capacity for certain kinds of 'productive' action – it is a quality of being, a mode of cognition. Creativity can be nurtured, can be reinforced, can be recovered.

2 Creative Teacher

In his book, *Music Education, Psychology and Method*, Eric Franklin gives two illustrations of music teaching taken from a biography of Edward Grieg by J. G. Cederblad. The passage cited by Franklin is worth quoting in full.

No doubt the dramatic, hot-tempered Edward Grieg felt like running away from the whole business after he had had his first piano lesson. Was it to get this experience that he had been sent away from home by Ole Bull?

Close to the piano was a stout and bald-headed man with his right fore-finger under his ear didactically repeating:

'Immer langsam, stark, hochheber, langsam, stark, hochheber. . . .'

(Ever slow, strong, lift high, slow, strong, lift high . . .)

It was that occasion that started the bitterness that Edward Grieg always felt towards the conservatory at Leipzig. We hear it from his lips several times. Once he writes to his friend, Julius Rontgen, complaining about his lack of technique in composition: 'For this however I have not only myself to blame but above all the damned Leipzig Conservatory where I definitely learned nothing at all. . . .'

The one teacher who got Edward Grieg's devotion and love was the old Moritz Hauptmann. The young man, transplanted into foreign ground, was always longing for kindness. From the moment that Hauptmann said to Edward Grieg that they were to be good friends Grieg was willing to die for him.

Charming and of tender humour is the picture that Edward Grieg gives us of his old master, who, because of his illness, gave his lessons at his home, the Thomas School, the old lodgings of Bach. He was sitting on his sofa in dressing-gown and skull-cap, spectacles on his nose, and, while the yellow-brown sap of snuff dropped from his nose down into Edward Grieg's practice book, he made his delicate comments bearing witness to the power of his mind. The sixteen-year-old boy was composing and when Hauptmann nodded his old head and said: 'Sehr schön, sehr musikalisch' ('Very beautiful, very musical'), Edward Grieg knew that he had made a good start on the way that is the road of the arts. [1]

[1] Franklin, Eric, *Music Education, Psychology and Method*, Harrap, 1972.

I want now to consider the relationship between teacher and pupil in the creative enterprise. It is a vexed, difficult and controversial subject. My own thoughts and suggestions, such as they are, are prompted by deep misgivings over the idea that the arts may be 'taught' – misgivings I know many arts teachers share. My work, in recent years, has taken me into a great many arts 'lessons' – in nursery and first schools, in secondary and further education, in colleges and university departments. Each phase of education has its own characteristic problems and constraints which, though incidental to the arts curriculum as such, nevertheless bear upon it with more or less effect. For the moment I do not wish to be drawn into that particular discussion. I wish to consider the problem of 'teaching' creative writing, or reading, or art, or science at a more general level: to examine the possible relationship of the teacher to the process described in the preceding section. *How are we to conceive of the creative teacher, and of creative teaching? Can 'creativity' itself be taught?*

I cited the Grieg illustration because I feel it helps to pin-point the dilemma of the arts teacher – or of any other teacher for that matter whose concern is to nurture the creative talents of his pupils and students. And it raises some critical issues. We could begin by saying that the 'curriculum' of the damned Leipzig Conservatory was subject-based and that of old Moritz Hauptmann student-based, and there would be some justice in the observation. At the conservatory Grieg encountered the public world of music, a world governed by its own laws and generating its own set of values. The teachers at the conservatory were indeed conservationists where music was concerned; their duty lay in bringing the uninitiated into conformity with received practice and in giving them access to received knowledge. They were assiduous in tracking down and penalizing all forms of deviation and heresy, and confined their teaching to what could be publicly taught, and so, publicly assessed. Essentially such a curriculum would have a strong factual and technical emphasis, and would imply for the learner an alignment with publicly recognized and esteemed modes of musical behaviour, and for the teacher, a thorough knowledge of the legitimate modes and the capacity to impose them upon the student's practice. This may seem a rather harsh account but I dare say it will be recognized, in essence, by many who have suffered similar experiences to Grieg's in the conservatories of their own day.

I wish to extend this point briefly. The arts, the sciences, the humanities may all be taught as bodies of knowledge or codes of practice – all human experience may be reduced to rule, and the rules may be publicized and, with more or less rigour, enforced. There are, understandably, skills of all kinds that the young of a particular society need to learn, both for their own good and for that of the society to which they belong. In our schools we teach children mental and manual skills – we help them to interpret and make use of the complex world of symbolic interaction, and we equip them in various ways technically to manipulate their physical environment. *Instruction* is the keynote of such teaching – all teaching would seem to imply some degree of instruction whether we are speaking of the learning of manual skills, languages, history, good health practices, or exercises designed to deepen and refine the spiritual life. Art, music, dance and drama may be taught in this sense – instruction in 'the way' is possible, even essential, since a corpus of knowledge exists to be transmitted, and culturally refined techniques for controlling artistic media are available to the learner. And of course there is no inherent reason why 'instruction' in either of these two aspects of the arts should be either boring or stultifying. That Grieg found his experience at Leipzig so unhelpful may of course have been simply because he could not get on with his teachers there. On the other hand one recognizes in his expression of frustration the alienation and exasperation of many pupils in school and students in college with a curriculum for which the teacher seems to care inordinately strongly, and for which they have no use and in which they see little point. The reason for such disaffection, I would suggest, lies in the fact that the 'conservatory' style curriculum begs the question of pupil motivation; put another way, it rests upon the assumption that the pupil is either already intrinsically motivated or may be rapidly coerced into accepting that he needs as urgently what his teachers urgently wish to teach him. There are of course many school children – and music, art, drama students – who readily, if not always happily, acquiesce. The awkward customers will be those who, for one reason or another, do not buy it. And it is hard to see why they should. If you live within walking distance of shops, your work and the local football ground, you may not be easily persuaded to buy a motor car and to pay to learn to drive it. The law of diminishing returns can be brutally uncomfortable for teachers offering instruction in useless or unwanted skills. And a skill is useless if it will not be used by the person who pays in blood, sweat, tears or hard cash to acquire it.

The question of the usefulness of the arts we must leave until later. Suffice to say for the moment that many people find music, art and drama intensely rewarding experiences *in their own right*, and where they do, there is rarely any question of balking at whatever price has to be paid for instruction that will extend command of the chosen medium.

But to return to Grieg for a moment. He found the conservatory at Leipzig mortifying because the teacher referred to had reduced music-making to a mechanical exercise – almost a matter of routine. Essentially the music curriculum was *what could be taught* – and we do not have to look far in education today to find the same principle at work. Teachers frequently complain that the curriculum is dictated by the requirements of the examination boards – that is to say, they complain that they must teach what may be examined and, with reasonable objectivity and reliability, certificated. No doubt there is truth in this, though it is also only fair to add that what may be most readily examined and assessed is also, usually, easiest to teach (in the sense of giving instruction in). This brings us close to the heart of the dilemma facing the teacher of creative art, science or whatever. Since the creative process is essentially subjective, how may objective standards of evaluation be applied? Indeed, since, as we have seen, the process is also essentially private and mysterious – requiring unconscious as well as conscious action – how is the teacher to involve himself at all? Many arts teachers have responded to this problem by eschewing 'intervention' of any kind and limiting their contribution to the provision of materials and technical advice as required.

Was that old Moritz Hauptmann's way? From the extract I have quoted there is no way of knowing exactly but there are significant hints, I think. In the first place we hear of the young Grieg's 'devotion and love' for his master, and of the warm feelings of the old man for his pupil. The implication is of a deep, mutual attachment growing out of their shared interest in music but embracing the two of them as separate and whole personalities. The contrast with the cold detachment of the earlier instructor could not be more striking. Grieg, we are told, was lonely – but his need for the kind of companionship that Hauptmann offered stemmed, I would suggest, at least as much from the strain of pushing back his creative horizons as from his being far from home. We are told that his comments on the boy's composition were 'delicate', and when he says 'very beautiful, very musical' one senses not simply his recognition of the composer's need for encouragement, but also – and I do not think this is to strain the scene too much – his capacity for listening and responding in a way that is at once sensitive and authentic.

Clearly, however he conducted himself, the old man had a profound influence on the *creative* work of the young Grieg, and we can all probably think of individual men and women, not necessarily, but perhaps, teachers of ours, who have made a similar impact upon our own development. We are now speaking not of wise instructors, necessary though they may be, but of those whose devotion for us and confidence in us have given us the courage to know ourselves and to be. As I said earlier, I have misgivings about the idea that the arts may be taught. I fear that much that goes on in the name of arts education, even where it is specifically concerned with learning and not with the hundred and one other things school teachers and college lecturers are expected to take upon themselves, is dictated by what *can* be taught and merely qualifies at best as instruction or informed supervision. The teacher may fulfil this role with kindness, concern and even devotion, and it is a well-established fact that arts activities are often felt to be among the most enjoyable experiences children have at school. But – and this is the point I wish to make – we do not have at the present time a satisfactory idea of the role of the *creative* arts teacher; we desperately need a model for the teacher that will allow a proper reconciliation of the pupil's need on the one hand for sound instruction and on the other for emotional 'cover': we need to know, paraphrasing Winnicott, what we mean by 'good-enough teaching'. The creative teacher must have a role in relation to the pupil's creative process if his task is to be more than merely an instrumental one. Many arts teachers, recognizing the inadequacy of the instructor model, have opted for kinds of companionship and partnership with their pupils, but frankly find themselves at something of a loss as to the legitimacy of such a role, and frequently have to suffer their own lack of self-definition reflected back to them from the children they are 'teaching' – reflected back as disturbed or disruptive behaviour. In seeking a new role for the 'creative' teacher we must find one that has a *necessity* about it, a necessity that is recognized by both the partners to the educational encounter, the teacher and the pupil. Pupils tend to respond to useless or unnecessary teachers in much the same way as they respond to what they regard as useless or unnecessary teaching.

I now want to reconsider some of the questions raised in the preceding section in the discussion of Winnicott's notion of the 'good-enough' mother – in particular I want to take another look at the function of the 'potential space' between the child and the environment, and of the mother's role in creating that space and in leading her child to accept his or her separateness.

Essentially what I hope to be able to develop from his argument is the kind of model we are looking for as the basis of creative teaching, much as he develops a model of the creative therapist – our companion has to become a 'good-enough' creative arts teacher.

It will be remembered that Winnicott proposes a third area of experience, a potential space located between the world of inner subjective experience, and the outer world of objects – the environment. Here, in the potential space between subject and environment we find located all an individual's cultural experience, including play, which is the beginning of creativity. 'Good enough' mothering depends on the mother's natural capacity to meet the infant's needs, both for the illusion of omnipotence (the child feels that it creates the breast it seeks – the breast exactly reciprocating the urge to suck) and for ultimate disillusionment and the survival of frustration. The space in which the child plays – testing, assimilating, and preparing for experience – is created experientially, as a result of the infant's trust of the mother. From that sense of trust grows an increasing self-confidence in terms of the relationship with the environment as a whole. Winnicott describes how gradually the infant moves from play with mother to play with transitional objects (objects that stand for the absent mother), to play with objects objectively perceived, alone but in the presence of the mother, and ultimately to mutual playing, the assimilation of the mother into the child's play and the accommodation of the child to the play of the mother.

> This intermediate area of experience, unchallenged in respect of its belonging to inner or external (shared) reality, constitutes the greater part of the infant's experience, and throughout life is retained in the intense experiencing that belongs to the arts and to religion and to imaginative living, and to creative scientific work.[1]

Winnicott continually emphasizes the importance of trust in the establishing of this intermediate area, and when he comes on to consider the theory in terms of the psychotherapeutic situation – 'psychotherapy has to do with two people playing together' – he insists that the first duty of the therapist is to give the patient *the confidence to play*.

> The person we are trying to help needs a new experience in a specialised setting. The experience is one of a non-purposive state, as one might say *a sort of ticking over of the unintegrated personality*. (ibid., my italics)

He goes on to suggest the following sequence of activities in the therapeutic encounter:

> (a) relaxation in conditions of trust based on experience;
> (b) creative, physical, and mental activity manifested in play;
> (c) the summation of these experiences forming the basis for a sense of self. (ibid.)

In other words it may be necessary for the therapist to *substitute for the mother* in creating a potential space that has either never existed effectively before or for whatever reason seems to have become unavailable to the patient. Once established, the space becomes the place of healing, of creative relationship and creative action, experiences that hopefully will provide the basis for a new sense of self.

One further point is of interest to us here: having suggested that both the therapist and the patient must be able to play, Winnicott distinguishes between the complementary roles of therapist and teacher:

> Here in this area of overlap between the playing of the child and the playing of the other person there is a chance to introduce enrichments. The teacher aims at enrichment. By contrast, the therapist is concerned specifically with the child's own growth processes, and with the removal of blocks to development that may have become evident. (ibid.)

His distinction is a useful one since it will help us steer clear of the trap of confusing the role of the teacher with that of the psychologist. I see it as no part of the teacher's role to attempt to deal with chronically disabling psychological disturbance – rather I see the

[1] Winnicott, D. W., *Playing and Reality*, Tavistock, 1971.

creative teacher as assisting the full flowering of the creative potential of the developing and maturing child. An enriching of experience, a strengthening of possibly weak signals – essentially encouraging the extension of creative capacity by structuring an appropriately stimulating and responsive environment: a creative 'curriculum'.

Whereas the therapist may be necessary to correct abnormal development or release what has been arrested, the teacher works with healthy vital forces and nurtures them into fully mature functioning. It is essentially a difference of emphasis: the roles are closely linked and inevitably, at times, overlap.

If we are to accept Winnicott's model of good-enough mothering as the basis of our consideration of the pupil–teacher relationship, and that is what I am proposing, then we have to recognize that what counts before everything else is the *emotional quality* of that relationship. I say 'before everything else' and that is precisely what I mean. The implication of this model when extended into teaching is that nothing is possible outside a relationship of trust and devotion between teacher and pupil or student, qualities that are generated through the experience of personal interaction. As teachers, we know the truth of this very well, and in thinking of those whose teaching most affected us we recognize these qualities in them too. It has recently become fashionable to knock the idea of charisma in teaching, and most recent developments in the curriculum field have been more or less guilty of thinking of curriculum as somehow infinitely transferable from teacher to teacher and circumstance to circumstance, irrespective of the teacher's personality, the personalities of his or her pupils and the chemistry of their personal interaction. Teaching, the effectiveness of which is said to rely upon the personality or charisma of the teacher, is not readily researchable, nor is such teaching easily packaged and distributed among the chain stores of the great educational marketing enterprise. So curriculum has been reduced to a particular concoction of content and method that has come, in the trade, to be described as 'teacher proof'. That such a cynical conception of education has gained currency at all is an alarming and an appalling commentary on the direction some so-called educational studies have taken in recent years. The model we are here trying to develop is built, not upon the notions of curriculum as content or methodology, but as, in the first place, the wholly useful relationship of the teacher with the individual child or group of children for whom he or she is responsible. And we have established, as the *sine qua non* of that relationship, the twin character of *mutual trust and devotion*.

Educational change at the moment is mechanical rather than organic in its mode; the models currently being applied to the educational process, being mechanistic, are wholly inappropriate. There is widespread talk of educational organization and management as if education could – on the principles of mass production and intensive plant utilization – legitimately be modelled on industry. The failure of the system both to motivate the young and to provide adequate emotional support for their development has led to a number of equally suspect developments.

I do not wish to enter here upon a detailed critique of the problem but would suggest that two such developments, the drive towards the so-called individualization of learning and the proliferation of remedial and pastoral 'services', are significant examples of expensive and only partial solutions to what are now being called the 'survival' problems of the schools, derived from a failure of understanding of the essential nature of those problems. In the case of the examples I have given, it seems to me that the root causes of pupil disaffection – and this I hold to be the difficulty that has given rise to these two developments – has not been at all understood, and that the answers are as predictable as they are doomed to be inadequate.

Individualized learning means trying to match so-called individual interests with a curriculum that meets them as exactly as possible, the curriculum here meaning essentially 'content'. The hope is that such a curriculum will be found meaningful by the individual student and that deep levels of motivation and engagement will be immediately tapped. That such an arrangement removes learning more and more from the field of human interaction and continuity of personal relationships, and in doing so also drastically reduces much if not most of the affective framework necessary for learning, will gradually be found to be progressively counter-productive as the battery student begins to display all the tensions of the battery hen.

It is partly to meet the need for 'affective structures', now seriously missing from much of contemporary schooling, that the guidance and counselling service has come into being. The demands for such a service will go on growing at an ever-increasing rate until such time as someone dares to point out the essential bareness of the enterprise – dares to attempt an evaluation in essentially educational terms. To provide the schools with trained therapists capable of significant remedial work is one thing but the counselling service is doomed if it is nothing else but an attempt to institutionalize aspects of normal human intercourse in the absence of such intercourse. We are used to being 'serviced', much as we service the technology that we have come to use as extensions of ourselves. With the delegation of individual care and concern – of the many supportive features that can be expected of a relationship characterized by mutual trust and devotion – to 'the teacher in the counselling room' the teaching staff may safely leave more and more of their own personalities and feeling lives outside the classroom and concentrate their powers on the managerial and mechanical aspects of learning – the production of resources, work-cards, materials, assignments and so forth. Organization is the watchword; the great white hope of education is the administrator. He is, as one would expect, the most highly paid member of the profession – and the teacher, for as long as he remains a teacher and refuses administrative responsibility, inevitably the lowest paid. And we all suspect in our heart of hearts that all his timetabling and planning, his faculty boards and departmental infra-structures, are a waste of time. The schools become more and more sick, the kids sickening and the teachers sickened.

And the reason is to be sought in a fundamental misconception concerning the nature of the educational experience. We have assumed it is essentially product oriented, and so best regulated as one would organize other object manipulating, by organizational procedures. However, education is essentially a cultural matter, and there is no definition of culture that excludes human relationship, human communication and human interaction.

'Education' takes place in the overlap of two mutually experiencing human beings; its effectiveness depends upon the social viability of that relationship, and that includes the sense of mutual obligation or contract, one with the other. Instruction or training arguably requires no such overlap, only contiguity. Any study of the educational process, of aims and objectives, of content and method, must take place within the context of the human relationship obtaining between the essential participants. Education has to mean partnership, or nothing, since education, I believe, implies meaning as well as information, and personal meaning grows in mutuality.

Many of the ills and anxieties of schooling today can be seen as the outcome of the impoverished nature of the personal relationship between child, student and teachers. Many recent developments (the asylum or 'sanctuary' unit for instance) are in practice contributing to that impoverishment. In considering the idea of an education in or for 'creativity' we have to begin by defining the conditions of a good-enough relationship between the participants to the educational encounter itself. Essentially we are talking about *devotion* both ways.

We know that the natural relationship between mother and child has a lot going for it – the mother is motivated to adapt to the needs and demands of her baby by the love that grows between them. Love may have instinctual roots but it develops experientially, as the mother holds, handles, fondles, grooms, and feeds the baby. We all call upon certain instinctive drives to establish a basis for loving, for trusting and caring for others as, assuredly, love grows and deepens with the experience of mutuality. No teacher can be expected to care for his pupils as a mother might. In some cases love may certainly grow, but by and large the affection between the adult teacher and the younger student will have more of parental friendship and good companionship about it than, strictly speaking, parental love. It is not a peer friendship, however – the teacher is always felt to be more experienced and, in a very important sense, 'beyond' the pupil. It is not normally a partnership of equals either, in an affective sense any more than in a cognitive sense: mutuality there is to be sure, but the relationship is coloured by the albeit temporary dependence of the pupil upon the teacher, and the sense both partners have of the responsibility of the teacher for the pupil. The trustworthiness of the teacher is associated with some feeling of and for the teacher's authority. For very young children that authority derives from physical as well as mental stature, but even at the level of higher education the student–teacher relationship still implies a respect for and the maintenance of the teacher's authority (deriving as it does from a variety of sources, some of social investment in him, some of essential personal validity). The teacher, for as long as the relationship with the child or student remains an authentic one, is likewise aware of the student's dependence and vulnerability and of his own responsibility.

It is these undeclared understandings that provide the framework in feeling – the special relationship – that allows teacher and pupil *to play together*. In their play certain modifications of the relationship are 'allowed' – we shall return to examine this subtle transformation a little later – and are essential if mutual play is to take place. But such a development or transformation is only possible if the relationship itself is firmly and reliably established in actuality. The mother and child play together only when the actual relationship between them in terms of their mutual interdependence of role has been established, tested and found secure.

The establishing of the intermediate world of the educational encounter is something that has to be worked for. Given the correct or sufficient degree of trust and devotion between the partners, the natural tendency to play together may be exploited, and so the area for cultural playing opened up between them. Most parents know this as a gradual process and will certainly have recognized (a) the differences between the responses of their children in the extent and character of the 'playground' available between them (i.e. between siblings and parent as distinct from siblings and each other) and (b) the differences in this respect between their own children and other people's. Some children – like some animals – seem to learn the rules of play (the difference for instance between romping and real fighting) very quickly and very early. Others seem never to be quite sure where the understood line between play and actuality runs. It is a critical distinction since without it there can be no playing. We talk of knowing where to 'draw the line', of knowing 'how far to go' and of 'going too far'. Where there is some confusion on the part of one of the partners as to where the line runs then the mutual play between them is constantly threatened. Play always implies licence: we speak of taking a liberty with someone and what we mean is that we are presuming they will not invoke the full actuality of the situation in responding to our crossing the line into playing and playful-

ness. Real confusion and distress arises on occasions when we take
liberties we are not invited or licensed to, or that are not given to us,
and we hastily try to reclaim the situation by pointing out that our
behaviour should be allowed, granted some kind of social immunity
since we were only 'fooling' or 'teasing' or 'joking'. These are all
perfectly acceptable practices if *mutually licensed*. When we do not
grant such licence or when our partner deliberately abuses playing
by acting as if it were actual – by presuming upon what was allowed
by the protected nature of play – then we feel we have been 'taken
advantage of'. That is to say we are treated as though we had no
licence or liberty to grant, and the principle of mutuality is therefore
unilaterally denied. Some of us grant such licence more readily than
others – we only do so, however, when we feel fairly sure of our
ground with the person we have decided to play the fool with.
People lacking what we sometimes call a sense of humour, or lacking
in natural playfulness, find the prospect of the licensed playground,
and actual invitations to draw a magic circle and enter into it with
someone else, profoundly disturbing. Basically such people find the
behaviour of others confusing and untrustworthy; they have no
experience of a safe conduct or passage between the related worlds
of actuality and play, and so cannot tolerate the anxiety provoked
by the possibility of drawing a line and stepping beyond it. Where
this is a chronic condition of arrested personal development the
individual needs a therapist; but every relationship that goes beyond
mere information processing and develops into mutuality comes up
against this problem, and it matters not whether we are talking of
friendship in general or of the teacher pupil relationship in particular, there will be line drawing and, if all goes well, a mutual stepping
out into the protected world of shared 'playing', *a world guaranteed by
the trust and devotion that cements the relationship in actuality*.

As I have already mentioned, individualized learning programmes
are based on the assumption that if the kids are allowed to select a
group of subjects from a wide range then motivation, and so reasonable behaviour, will no longer be problematical. What seems much
more important for education as culture (as distinct from education
as instruction) is for the pupils and teachers to select each other. Now
this is, of course, what in practice they are very often doing, and in so
far as a programme of options allows students and teachers to
gravitate towards one another on the basis of a mutually acceptable
social and cultural contract, they are to be welcomed. However,
options are rarely drawn up along these lines and there must be very
few occasions indeed when decisions as to who teaches whom take
personal relationships into account. There is an unwritten law in the
profession that any teacher should be able to teach any child (this
often boils down to some kind of respect for those who can keep their
classes quiet and contempt for those who cannot). It is, by the same
token, commonly assumed that any child should be able to learn

from any teacher (worth his or her salt). It is upon some such set of
assumptions that the whole basis of teaching professionalism rests –
there is a similar, equally ill-founded assumption in the medical
profession. In schools, as in health centres, the concept of the team
approach has gained ground in recent years and although the consideration of customer choice does not, I would guess, initially figure
very prominently in terms of the personal relationship involved, this
is clearly one of the most beneficial aspects of such developments. If
we are saying that teaching, like therapy, takes place in a cultural
relationship characterized by mutuality, then the social contract or
understanding between the participants has by definition to be a
mutual one, freely entered into and sustained by choice.

Perhaps the apparent difficulty of this proposition – if one admits
that there is a difficulty – may be eased again by reference to
Winnicott. He speaks of good-enough mothering. It is a term I like
because it knocks on the head the awful spectre of the 'ideal'
mother. Perfection is not the name of the game. As he frequently
insists, mothers are human and fallible and a baby's development
depends upon recognition and acceptance both of the mother's
'failings' and of responsibility to and for oneself. Winnicott's
emphasis is upon the minimum conditions for normal, healthy
development, not on some virtually unattainable ideal of better or
best mothering. He asks only that mothering be 'good enough' to
help the baby achieve a satisfactory level of adaptation to its
environment and to itself. I have borrowed his term and am now
trying to put together a model of good-enough teaching. That is to
say, I want to be able to conceive of the minimum conditions for
normal, healthy educational development – and mutual responsibility above all things. We must resist pressures to hive off legitimate
communication and responsibility, to increase the fragmentation of
human interaction, the progressive institutionalizing of essentially
natural human processes and the proliferation of 'services' at the
expense of self-help and mutuality. The teacher must be allowed and
encouraged to make relationships with those pupils who can reciprocate his devotion to their learning; the learning itself must occur
naturally within that kind of affective framework. To the protesters
I simply say, 'Ask yourself what in the present set-up makes nonsense
of this conception, and, having identified it, ask yourself whether it
need be so.' For my part I see no more inherent educational value in
the organization of learning on the basis of the mixture of abilities
than on the separation of abilities, given an appropriate definition of
'ability'. What is much more to the point is sociability – that is to say,
the social viability of the group (teacher $+$ 1 or teacher $+$ 30). Mixed
sociability (and I am not talking of Bernstein here but merely of the
chemistry of the social interaction of the pair or group of people) will
undoubtedly cripple any well-founded attempt at comprehensive
education and the equality of educational opportunity. It is another

instance of the failure to define the problem correctly. Every educational encounter is an instance of 'licensed' behaviour – it has to be guaranteed by mutual trust and a shared belief in its value. Where these conditions do not exist or cannot be made to exist the educational enterprise has to be abandoned.

But to return to our argument. If teacher and child are to be matched in personal terms, if the teacher is to be charged with the responsibility not merely of imparting a given body of knowledge or skills but of establishing minimum conditions in terms of personal interaction that will facilitate normal, healthy development – of entering into a good-enough relationship – then it goes without saying that the teacher must be 'good enough' for the job, however we define the good-enough teacher, and we must clearly be able to include all sorts and conditions of men and women within the terms of whatever definition emerges eventually. Every teacher will have to satisfy himself that he is at least 'good enough' for each of the pupils he accepts responsibility for; if he cannot then he must recognize the problems and, should they defy resolution, see that the abortive relationship with the child in question is quickly terminated. But of course it is not only up to the teacher. If we have to have good-enough teachers, we also have to have good-enough students. That is to say we have to have students who recognize – because they experience – the necessity of the relationship with the teacher, and are prepared to honour their side of the obligation. The adult is likely to be able to grant more liberties to the child or the adolescent than vice versa, nevertheless the student has obligations – most students recognize them (some demonstrate that recognition in deliberately contravening them) and must be able to entertain them. This presupposes that they *value the learning that is the basis of the personal relationship*. If, as I have suggested, much of what goes on in the name of education today erodes and impoverishes the personal aspect of teacher–pupil relationships, there can be little wonder if learning becomes devalued and the educational experience itself something of a blood sport rather than a cultural encounter. We have to restore personal meaning to the educational encounter by allowing those who teach to care for those who are taught, and those who learn to trust and become devoted to those they learn from.

We can go on refining and elaborating organizational solutions and providing ever more specialized services, but these will rather complicate than resolve the problem. We need to train our teachers for much more complex tasks than are currently allowed them and we need organizational structures geared to facilitate human interaction with the understanding that the teacher's first concern must be the child, and that the curriculum only has validity if it centres upon and is adapted to meet the child's needs.

The 'subject' has relevance only in relation to those needs and to the child's inherent cognitive modes or styles of learning. If we think of the total curriculum not so much as composing separate and discrete bodies of knowledge but as providing for different ways of ordering (i.e. representing) experience, different cognitive styles or ways of knowing, then it becomes immediately apparent why process is more important than product and why children should be encouraged to diversify their cognitive behaviours on the one hand and yet allowed to identify and exploit to their full potential their habitual or temperamentally appropriate modes on the other. Such a conception would perhaps help draw the curriculum back from what many people now feel is a neurotic and obsessive preoccupation with so-called 'vocation' (a cynical misnomer anyway), and towards some notion of personal growth and self-actualization. That personal and vocational or occupational demands should be conceived of as separate, even conflicting concerns seems to me to have no foundation in experience, except in so far as we see ourselves as preparing people to enter into or perform inhuman or subhuman tasks. Where such is the case, there would seem to be all the more need to meet personal needs and encourage the development of personal resources, and where such is not the case, there would seem to be no reason why one's professional or vocational training should not be treated as an intensely personal matter, since only in that way will work become personally meaningful and satisfying as distinct from being the original curse of mankind.

We come therefore to the first obligation of the good-enough teacher and that is to form a good-enough working relationship with a student or pupil, a relationship that will in due course be characterized by mutual trust and devotion to learning. The creative teacher must know the pupil well enough to discern his immediate and prognose his long-term needs; well enough to recognize when, how and to what extent a cultural 'playground' might be evoked between them which would allow the kinds of learning we are concerned with. Needless to say, I am assuming now, as I have been throughout the discussion, concern with the development of the creative responses and resources of our pupils and students, and it is solely with such a concern in mind that I am developing my concept of the educational encounter.

The precise nature of the strategies and devices adopted by the teacher I am speaking of in designing and implementing the creative curriculum will be considered in the next section of the book. At this point I wish only to sketch the model in broad outline.

The building of the good-enough relationship is the first essential. It is the relationship of one generation with another, the future and the past at their intersection in the collective present. It is a partnership of differences, essentially paradoxical in that mutuality is directed towards eventual separation, dependence resolved in independence, what is painstakingly built has to be painlessly dissolved. Like all other living and nurturant relationships the measure

of its effectiveness must be the completeness of its eventual redund-
ancy. The curriculum is an artificial and a temporary learning
environment, true and valid in its own terms, created with care and
skill – eventually outmoded and discarded but leaving its mark upon
the individuals who participated in it. The good-enough teacher, like
the good-enough mother, friend or lover, must be able to say goodbye
– 'Fare forward voyager'. The good-enough curriculum has to leave
both participants healthier, freer, more open, more capable, more
sure of themselves, more honestly expressive, more authentic, more
responsible. Happier too, perhaps, though not necessarily so:
certainly better adapted to regulate their own lives in relation to the
lives of others. I have argued that the *sine qua non* of the creative
curriculum is the initiative taken by the teacher in establishing a
good-enough relationship with the pupil or group of pupils. It
requires of the teacher that he get to know his pupil, and that he
devise experiences that will allow the development of trust and
devotion through experience. This phase of the encounter I take to
be analogous to the first two stages of Winnicott's sequence of good-
enough mothering, the object of which is the separating off of the
not-me from the me.

The sequence is as follows:

1. Holding
2. Handling
3. Object-presenting

Winnicott explains:

> A baby is held, and handled satisfactorily, and with this *taken for granted*
> (my italics) is presented with an object in such a way that the baby's
> legitimate experience of omnipotence is not violated. The result can be
> that the baby is able to use the object, and to feel as if this object is a sub-
> jective object, and created by the baby.
>   All this belongs to the beginning, and out of all this comes the immense
> complexities that comprise the emotional and mental development of the
> infant and child.[1]

We must take for granted that the teacher is able to generate a
comparable sense of confidence and trustworthiness through his
interaction with the pupil. The 'holding' and 'handling' will be more
mental than physical but the effect in freeing the child from apprehension and opening him to comprehension will be the same.
Knowing the pupil also means knowing what the pupil is ready for
in terms of problematic learning experiences. The teacher must
understand the general principles of cognitive and affective development so that the next stage may be discerned and entered upon.
When I speak of the teacher's getting to know the pupil it is in this

---

[1] ibid.

sense that I mean it: I do not at all wish to imply that a teacher needs to be aware of the intimate details of every child's life and background. I refer to the generality rather than to the particularity of a pupil's experience.

Put simply, the teacher needs to be able broadly to 'place' the pupil in terms of general classes of expressive and cognitive functioning, to know his characteristic modes of organizing experience as general behavioural strategies rather than in terms of particular events. When Barron says, 'To stimulate creative change we must begin with the psychodynamics of the individual', this is what I take him to mean. There is a sense in which biographical details are not merely irrelevant but a potentially morbid distraction: the teacher needs to ascertain the strength or weakness of significant modes of behaviour rather than the health of the family home or details of the child's dream life. The whole effectiveness of a teacher's participation in the developmental process through the curriculum will depend upon his skill in delineating affective and cognitive pupil profiles.

Knowing the pupil gives way to knowing the environment, environment here meaning the medium through which expressive or impressive knowing is to be effected. Just as it is the mother's task to provide the child with media through which the separation in consciousness of not-me from me might be effected (Winnicott's third phase – 'object-presenting') so it is the teacher's task to select appropriate representational media to facilitate particular learning experiences. The teacher must fully understand the principles of media control and the special characteristics of a medium or media in organizing experience. Curriculum design may be summarized as the conceiving of problems in environmental and behavioural media that will require the pupil to organize his experience by means of appropriate action. The medium is thus seen to serve the developmental needs of the child as he comes to command increasingly sophisticated ways of knowing. To put it more simply: the teacher provides the child with situations, experiences and materials that are appropriate to his stage of development and which, because of their essentially problematic character, set him reaching forward for fresh solutions and new understandings.

Perhaps we may be allowed to turn to Winnicott again for help in drawing together the threads of this particular section of the argument. Before dealing with the relation of our model of the good enough teacher to our picture of the creative process outlined in the preceding section, I want to take a last look at what Winnicott says of good-enough mothering in relation to the development of play, for I wish to propose it as directly analogous to good-enough teaching in relation to the development of creativity, and I take that to be the essential basis of all arts education. He describes the relationship of mother and baby as play is developed (pp. 47, 49):

A. Baby and object are merged in one another. Baby's view of the object is subjective and the mother is oriented to the making actual of what the baby is ready to find.
B. The object is repudiated, reaccepted, and perceived objectively. This complex process is highly dependent on there being a mother or mother-figure prepared to participate and to give back what is handed out. . . .

Abraham Maslow makes this point about the impact upon us of our personal environment.

As Emerson said, 'What we are, that only can we see.' But we must now add that what we see tends in turn to make us what it is and what we are. The communication relationship between the person and the world is a dynamic one of mutual forming and lifting – lowering of each other, a process that we may call 'reciprocal isomorphism'. A higher order of persons can understand a higher order of knowledge, but also a higher order of environment tends to lift the level of the person, just as a lower order of the environment tends to lower it. They make each other more like each other. Those notions are also applicable to the interrelations between persons, and should help us to understand how persons help to form each other.[1]

The good-enough teacher will always have a life-enhancing effect upon his pupil.

I think I have said enough for the moment to convey something of my idea of what creative teaching involves. Put as simply as I may, the creative teacher has to provide whatever incentive and coverage or protection the pupil needs if he is to make a match with himself to melt the 'ice mountains' of inhibition. In addition he must be sufficiently expert in the handling of media to be able to help the pupil gain ever greater personal control over the organization of his own experience. The creative process, as we have seen, involves diffusion and integration – the creative teacher has to comprehend this dual process and must be able to accompany the pupil as guide, philosopher and friend through each succeeding phase of his experience. The pupil for his part needs to feel that the teacher is there alongside him, on the inside of the experience as it were, sensitive to the pressures and tensions, ready with suggestions, with emotional or intellectual support at the right moment. Delighting in his success, beside him in his failure, devoted to his struggle with himself. The role I have in mind is a dynamic one, the elements of which are constant, but the particular form always changing as the teacher and pupil adapt to meet the changing needs of their relationship. There is nothing sentimental in their devotion to that relationship. It is strong rather than warm.

When my daughter used to say to me, 'What shall I draw Daddy?' she was asking for exactly the kind of support and companionship I

[1] Maslow, A. H., 'A Holistic Approach to Creativity' in *Climate for Creativity* ed. Calvin W. Taylor, Wiley, 1975.

have been describing. She was asking me to set her an expressive problem: to propose an image (a 'problem form') to fit her mood and help her structure her expressive behaviour. When I made suggestions that didn't fit the impulse within her she always turned me down and asked me for another idea, another 'feeling idea'.

Once I had set her an expressive problem that was 'good enough' to get her going, that was not the end of the matter. She had drawn me into the action as if I were somehow necessary to it, helping her focus her restlessness so as to engage with it, to remain present at the back of her mind, as it were, throughout the period of drawing itself. She worked alone in the 'presence' of someone else – who might actually be absent. Ultimately I am called in to comment upon what has been done but more in the spirit of sharing formally in something of which I have always, in some sense, been a part, rather than to pass definitive judgement and so give the preceding effort its reward or legitimacy. By the time she has finished she 'knows' whether it works for her or not; my feelings then meet hers where the work (play) is. In comparison with the importance of this emotional attachment or participation – giving her courage and coverage – any technical advice along the way seems of rather less consequence. I do not say it is unimportant, but its relevance and significance arise within the context of the relationship itself.

3 The Representation of Experience

Image-Making

So much then for the general field of creative education. I now want to examine ideas basic to the creative arts curriculum.

Here are two pieces of writing by Nicola – an eight-year-old. She was asked to write down what the word 'Drought' meant to her. This is what she wrote:

> a drought is when there is no enough
> watar and that means there is a
> watr shortage and that means the
> rain comes from the reservoirs and
> I would go to the council.

Following this piece of writing her teacher set up a dramatic improvisation in which the class as a whole acted out a drought situation – from the writings of her class-mates one gets a clear picture of what happened. A 'tribe' struggles to survive in a desert environment: everyone is hungry, tired, thirsty. People grow sick and develop sores all over their bodies. They smell. The ground splits open and people stumble about over the cracked earth. The cattle are starving – their bones stick out from their bodies. Then a cloud appears on the horizon – it slowly approaches, growing bigger and bigger. When it is overhead there is a great storm and down comes the rain. The people feel it falling on their parched bodies and weary faces. They revive. They leap about and, joining hands, dance for joy in the rain. As the storm passes they kneel to give thanks to God. After the piece of drama the teacher again asked the children to do some writing – here is Nicola's second piece:

> I wish there would be some
> rain and I have got droopy eyes and
> I am tired and I could cry and
> I feel terrible and sticky and
> I am not strong and I wish
> I wish oh how I wish it would rain

This kind of work is, I would suppose, a reasonably familiar occurrence in a primary school – the interrelating of the two activities of writing and drama – and it has of course its counterpart at secondary level.

There is clearly a difference between Nicola's two pieces of writing – the teacher felt that the drama had brought the experience of drought home to her and the rest of the class personally, and that this greater level of involvement had been reflected in a more imaginative quality in the writing. However, I want to use them as a way of introducing some of the concepts and some of the terminology that I shall be using in the ensuing discussion about the why's and wherefore's of arts education. So, let us look a little more closely at Nicola's writing and see what can be said of it.

Although the subject of each of Nicola's pieces is apparently the same, her orientation towards them is rather different. It is as much a question of emphasis as anything else. In the first piece Nicola is using words to represent her *thinking* about the nature of drought as an event in the world and about its objective meaning for her. She repeats the words 'and that means' as she moves from an appreciation of the situation to a perception of its actual implications. The confusion in the writing about the rain coming from the reservoirs might be conceptual – perhaps she is not too sure about the relation between the two – or it might just be a linguistic difficulty. Whatever the case, her concern is to write something sensible. In this piece, concentrating upon drought as an empirical fact, she says little about how she feels. It shows her trying to sort out and present her thoughts.

In the second piece, she uses words for a different purpose. She now describes how she is feeling. 'I have got droopy eyes,' she says. 'I could cry.' The eyes are droopy with fatigue and the weight of unshed tears. She complains, 'I am not strong.' Then come the three 'wishes', and the cry, 'oh how I wish it would rain'. The last line-and-a-half take a poetic form. When she says, 'I feel terrible', she doesn't use language *as* feeling, she uses language to lay claim to feeling. But, when she says:

> I am not strong and I wish
> I wish oh how I wish it would rain

she does much more than merely assert that she feels – she embodies her feelings in a form that *represents* them (their pulse and urgency) quite faithfully. Nicola knows that language can be given a special 'feeling-form' when her need is to express *what* she is feeling and evoke that feeling in others. The form she has chosen works for us too. She uses a heavy 'crying form' we can all recognize.

I think it is not altogether inappropriate to place this beautiful piece from the authorized version alongside Nicola's lament.

> And the King was much moved, and went up to the chamber over the gate and wept, and as he wept thus he said: Oh my son Absalom, my son,

my son Absalom! would God I had died for thee, O Absalom, my son, my son!

Nicola already knows something about the consonance between feeling and form.

Nicola's writing points up several ideas that will be central to our discussion throughout this book. The first piece of writing is *impressive* in character since it bears the impress of the object world, the world of things, people and events that Nicola must suffer, respond to, come to terms with. *When her purpose is to represent her experience of the object world then she makes her use of language as objective, as free from subjectivity, as she can.* She is using the symbolic medium of verbal language impressively, to represent the world of objective experience (including herself as object).

The second piece of writing, on the other hand, is designed to carry much more of her own feeling world into representational form. Symbolizing or representing subjective feeling is *expressive. Expressive forms of representation symbolize the world of feeling* – in Witkin's words, 'the world that exists only because we exist'.

Impressive forms mirror our experience of the world of objects; through impressive representation we comprehend and find our way in that world. Expressive forms mirror our experience of the world of subjective feeling; through expressive representation we comprehend and find our way in that world. Clearly we need to feel confident of handling both sets of experience – we need to be able to represent our experience both impressively and expressively. The languages of the sciences are characteristic of impressive representation – their essential quality being faithfulness to objective reality – objectivity. The arts are the languages of feeling. Feeling is the experience of chief concern to the teacher of the arts. *The expressive use of media to represent or symbolize feeling is the basis of the arts curriculum.*

Writing is just one of a number of *representational forms* available to us. Such is the character of verbal language that is may be used for both expressive and impressive ends.

Bruner has said that representational action is our way of coming to terms with experience – our basic way of knowing. He suggests a sequence of three different representational modes through which the growing child passes:

Enactive: the representation of experience by acting it out, using the body as the medium of representation.

Iconic: representation through depiction, through the making of pictures to represent experience. This stage is obviously related to the child's growing ability to stand back from actuality or project his thought into the future, 'seeing' in the mind's eye.
The link with the preceding stage is the gesture that depicts rather than merely expresses.

Symbolic: the use of symbolic forms which stand in the place of actuality and free the child's representational behaviour from dominance by the object.

Representational action occurs in the world of objects – as bodily action or as graphic depiction in one form or another – and in the mind through the deployment of symbols. Enactive and iconic modes are significant because they form the basis not only of our representational behaviour but of sensuous perception itself. We sense a fundamental difference between the perception of stimuli by touch, taste, smell, hearing and manipulation on the one hand – enactive (or haptic) experience felt and registered as immediate sensations – and visual perception that is somehow devoid of felt sensation, more detached, on the other. Symbolic representation, the third and last stage, invariably subsumes both the enactive and iconic modes since enactive and iconic perception are the starting points of all symboling.

We must now distinguish between symbols used for *discursive* purposes – that is to say for the representation of objective events and phenomena – and the symbols we use to stand for *subjective* events. When we wish to represent the object world symbolically we need symbols that are unambiguous and uncontaminated by feelings, such as those used in mathematics and science and in musical notation. We represent the subjective world of feelings by symbols that will carry or evoke feeling – i.e. through gestures, pictures, sounds, and, of course, words. We speak of subjective symbols as 'images'. The arts are symbolic of feeling. Images evoke and organize emotional experience. The source of all imagery is the world of sensuous experience – of sensing and seeing. The images of art work like the images of dreams. Our dreams are the purest form of subjective representation since their only meaning or significance lies in the emotional charge they carry. A dream is a composite symbol *emotionally* organized.

Actual sensory experience 'places' one in actual time and space. Images evoke feeling qualities that subjectively 'place' one within a time/space context. Since all imagery recalls our sensuous response to time and space, in creating or responding to sensuous images (subjective symbols), we are seeking to 'place' ourselves subjectively – not to place ourselves as a public person in the real world of actual time and space but to place ourselves as subjective beings in our own inner world of subjective time and space. We have many coloquial expressions to depict our inner place, which place us somewhere within a private time-space environment that is sensed as being 'inside' us. Although most of these words and expressions have an obvious space connection, the time factor is also very much implied. We say we feel 'out of sorts', 'over the moon', 'under the weather', 'beyond' or 'beside ourself'; we say our heart leaps, bounds, soars; our heads spin, turn, split; our spirits droop, drag, decline; we 'fall' in love; we are 'at a loss'; we 'go to pieces'; we are depressed or elated, up, down. We use the objective world of time and space as the model for our feeling world: we sense an affinity between emotional feeling and sensory feeling. When we say we feel at home with ourselves then we seem to know 'where we are' in an inner world of subjective time and space. In representing that world of feeling, in seeking to know that inner world through representational action, we are in fact trying to 'place' ourselves subjectively. When that inner world is confused we say we feel 'lost'.

We go in for subjective symboling – we make and seek images of our feeling life in order to represent our Being. To find ourselves for ourselves. To make our feelings about how we feel intelligible. If that inner world of feeling is indeed 'a world', a place, then it is represented in the imagination – inner space 'pictured' in the image of the outer or actual world in which sensuous experience occurs. Our sensuous perceptions of actual stimuli coming from the objective environment are structured sensuously: as we shall be arguing later, our perception of our emotional responses is structured on the same principle – sensuously. The language of perception furnishes the language of the feelings as the phenomena of perception furnish the phenomena of the imagination. *Thinking in images is thinking in feelings.*

It is sometimes said that people lose their imaginative powers as they grow older. Wordsworth repeatedly told us this was so ('The World is too much with us . . .'). When this occurs it necessarily follows that they lose their capacity to *think in feelings*. There are occasions, of course, when we need cool heads and still hearts to survive. But it is one thing to make a cool decision because you have to. It is quite another to make such decisions because you cannot help yourself, because your imaginative powers have atrophied or been blocked in some way. The causes of such imaginative blocking or traumatizing are uncertain. I am sure it is neither a natural nor irreversible process. My own guess is that the cause is essentially cultural – we learn that to 'think in feelings' is not prized or rewarded in our society. The consequences of the decline of this faculty are profound: people simply become alienated from themselves and from each other. They then become capable of atrocious actions since they do not feel those actions themselves. Such men stalk among us as 'undead'.

Image-making keeps the imagination alive. Through image-making we gain access to the world of feeling, and discover its meaning and its power to make us whole people. Arts teachers, in preserving and nourishing the imaginative life of the child, enable him to make sense of his feelings, to trust them and to trust himself with himself since he senses his own Being securely at the centre of all his actions. Since he is always at home he will always know to whom to turn. He will know his own place – where he stands.

Making sense of experience means acting upon that experience and transforming it in some way. Representation is an 'acting upon experience'. I now must make a distinction between sensation and perception.

When I sense something warm against my skin I am responding to signals sent to my brain by the nerve ends: in coming to comprehend warmth as a sensuous phenomenon I have to place the sensation in relation to other sensations – I have to structure my experience. Now I cannot structure (or perceive) a sensation by thinking about it conceptually. I can recall it by evoking the image 'warmth'. Sensations are organized sensuously, in relation to other sensations. I cannot know the sensuous quality of warmth unless I also know the sensuous quality of cool. To perceive (as distinct from sensing) warmth we need to have sensed cool. Perceptual structures (organizations of sense experiences) occur spontaneously as similarities and contrasts. So we come to make sense of different temperature levels – we become perceptually intelligent. The experience of contrast seems absolutely essential in defining our perceptions. We seem to need to know what something is not before we can begin to establish what it really is. The structuring of sensuous experience by contrasts is a fundamental adaptive strategy of the brain. Fine distinctions about the precise identity of sensations are achieved in terms of resemblance. Having sorted the experience into one of two alternative perceptual schemes – there is always an actual or implicit alternative that provides the basis of all pattern-making (me and not-me) – we grade it in terms of its likeness to similar experiences. 'Warm' is far from 'cool' and lies somewhere between 'tepid' and 'hot'.

Making sense of our feelings – here I mean emotions rather than physical sensations (though the fact that we use the same word for each is of course significant) – requires a similar 'acting upon' experience. Discrete responses *mean* nothing to us in themselves; hence we cannot comprehend them or reorganize our responses in relation to them unless we can locate them within a general feeling structure. Again, as with the perception of sensation, we structure feelings in relation to other feelings, not conceptually. Feelings feel different from some and similar to other feelings. Feelings as feelings belong in perceptual structures; as ideas they belong in conceptual structures. So we perceive the feeling of being 'far away' from something or someone by contrasting it with the feeling of being 'near-by' something or someone. The concept that relates these two feelings together is the idea of 'distance': but distance is not simply an idea, it is a feeling, and we organize distance feelings as perceptions. The feeling of emotional distance is experienced as, and can only be expressed in, images deriving from the world of actual physical distance – which is why we use the word 'feelings' for emotions and sensations. Emotional distances are 'felt' in the inner world: physical distances occurring in the world of objects provide the model for our sense of emotional 'place'.

The process of structuring (perceiving) the inner world of feeling is an intelligent one since its purpose is to give coherence to that world and to help us find our place within it. Witkin's book *The Intelligence of Feeling* explores the processes of emotional organization to make the point that arts teachers are engaged in promoting *intelligent* behaviour, in helping children make sense of, and so exploit for their own satisfaction and the immediate benefit of their fellows, their life of feeling.

Forty years before Witkin, John Dewey was also writing of intelligent feeling:

> Any idea that ignores the necessary role of intelligence in the production of art works is based upon identification of thinking with the use of one special kind of material, verbal signs or words. To think effectively in terms of relations of qualities is as severe a demand upon thought as to think in terms of symbols, verbal and mathematical.[1]

To act responsibly in feeling we must use our feeling intelligence. We develop intelligent feeling by transforming feeling into sensuous form. The threat to our intelligence of feeling is precisely the same as the threat to the life of the imagination, to thinking in feelings: the whole bias of adult experience that favours and rewards conceptual intelligence and allows the perceptual or affective intelligence to die. The only way to counter the destruction of sensibility is, as far as possible, to protect ourselves from its effects. Arts teachers have a vital and difficult role in this situation – almost alone, so it seems, among educationists they have to protect and nurture the young and maturing life of feeling. They have to keep the gorgons of the intellect at bay that would turn our children into stones.

Representation transforms sensation into perception. Perception is sensuous knowing. It is an intelligent response to feeling and feelings. We achieve intelligent feeling through the creation of feeling forms or symbols: images. Arts education deals with image-making as a means of building our perceptual faculties – our intelligence of feeling. Image-making is the means by which affective adaptation is achieved.

> I wish
> I wish oh how I wish it would rain

Subject-Reflexive Action

In *The Intelligence of Feeling* Witkin develops his theory of subject-reflexive action as a basis for education through the expressive arts. He concludes the opening section of the book with the following

[1] Dewey, John, *Art as Experience*, Minton Balch, 1934, p. 46.

account of the relation between 'subject knowing' and 'object knowing':

> To be adapted in his environment the individual must be able to act effectively as an integrated person. This involves managing the world as object and himself as object within it on the one hand, and on the other, managing the disturbance evoked within him as a consequence of his being in the world. In the former context the person can be conceived of as a Self-in-action and in the latter context as a Being-in-action. Action in the world is thus double-edged. It must be effective as a system for the organizing of object relations and at the same time it must be effective in releasing the sensate disturbance that builds within the individual and which energizes his behaviour. If the demands made upon the individual in respect of object relations and action in the world are quite disjunctive with the demands made upon the individual by the disturbance evoked within him then the integration between Being and Self will break down. This condition of disjunction between Being and Self is often referred to as 'alienation', literally the state of being estranged from oneself. Action in the world becomes increasingly difficult as the individual succumbs to a motivational crisis in which he finds himself either with behaviour for which he has no impulse, or impulse for which he has no behaviour.

Personal adaptation depends upon the individual's capacity to relate these complementary worlds of Self and Being. As we have already seen, Witkin explains that adapted or intelligent action has two aspects. 'Impressive' action involves accommodation to the environment. 'Expressive' action involves the displacement of the environment in response to feeling impulses (sensate disturbance) evoked by experience. We come to know and find our way in the world of objects by 'projecting the object through the medium of our behaviour': the infant's hand moulds itself to accommodate the squareness of a brick and so comes to know squareness as one of the properties of a brick. We come to know our feelings by projecting them through sensuous media out there in the environment. *In object knowing we use media impressively; in subject knowing we use media expressively.*

In order to grasp clearly the meaning of the term 'expressive' in the context of arts education it is important to make two distinctions:

1. There are, as Witkin points out, actions that are subject reflexive, that is actions that contain and reflect the feeling impulse back to the person who is doing the expressing, and there are actions that are subject reactive, that is to say, actions that cancel out or merely release the feeling impulse. Creative self-expression is what we are interested in and *creative self-expression is subject reflexive.*

2. There are also actions which are a mixture of expression and impression. Put another way, there are actions which, for all that they contain expressive elements, have an impressive as well as an

expressive character and therefore are open to public criteria of value. Purely expressive actions, by definition, serve the subject: they are subject-specific and essentially private. In practice most of our actions occur somewhere along the expressive-impressive continuum and partake of both expression and impression.

I shall take each of these considerations in turn since each is of the utmost importance in helping us to say what arts education is all about.

There is a very real difference between expressive responses that are creative, deliberate, controlled by the feeling impulse, and those that are merely reactive, behavioural explosions triggered by the feeling impulse: between giving form to feeling and giving vent to (airing) our feelings. The work of the artist and the work of the vandal are both in a sense expressive. They may indeed both serve significant expressive ends. But we recognize that there is an essential difference between them, and that that difference is not simply a matter of the artist's 'work' being more socially acceptable than the vandal's. It is not difficult to cite the work of well-known artists that has excited as much if not more public outrage than the work of any vandal. The significant difference lies in this distinction between expression that gives form to feeling and reflects the impulse back – and expression that merely releases the impulse, gives vent to feeling so that it is lost. Creative expression is about feelings changing and growing. Reactive expression is about the discharge of tension.

Reactive expression releases energy. Reactive expression serves to reduce an uncomfortable state of arousal to a more tolerable level. We all respond reactively to situations, to frustration, anger, anxiety, disappointment, fear, sudden surprise. We lash out physically and verbally, we run away, we run amok, we gasp, we groan, we roar with delight or rage, we flash our eyes, raise our voice, wring our hands, hide the face we have lost or are in danger of losing. Such acts are of course truly expressive in terms of our definition: they spring immediately from feeling; they are full of impulse. Indeed we say that such responses are 'impulsive'. That these reactions of ours also serve as signs or signals to those near us, and allow them to adjust their own behaviour in their encounter with us, is secondary to their primary purpose which is the manifestation of an inner state. Such signs constitute the language of non-verbal communication. However they derive not from the need to share but from the need to discharge.

What is important about reactive expression is its subjective effect. What is sought is the instant and immediate release of tension. In a way, what we are describing is a kind of catharsis – a purgation of unmanageable, of irresolvable affect. Sometimes of course this sudden flow of feeling, this rapid build-up of tension serves us well. The dramatic action that releases the tension can help us achieve

almost incredible feats of physical prowess. There are situations so
alarming, so galvanizing that we do not pause for thought, we ignore
all consideration and act with precipitate alacrity – sometimes quite
astonishing ourselves when we come to reflect upon what we have
done. Such responses have a way of overriding all consideration. We
say we do these things without thinking, and that is literally the case.
That some risk attaches to such unthinking responses goes without
saying. We are only using half the resources available to us in resolving the 'problem' with which we are confronted. We may have to pay
a heavy price for not using our head. (There are those of course at the
other end of the behavioural spectrum who use their head to the total
exclusion of impulse of any kind. We tend to look for steady people of
this kind for top administrative jobs – in education as elsewhere. All
they have to do is to demonstrate scrupulous immunity to impulse,
and the job is theirs. Their first cry was their last impulsive action.
Their feelings, like wisdom teeth, are now firmly and safely impacted.
Self-consideration, before all things. Reflection rather than reflexion
is their rule.)

Action that seeks to put as much distance between the feeler and
his feelings as quickly as possible – actions that seek release from
feeling through the cancellation of feeling – are to be sharply distinguished from self-expressive responses that are genuinely creative.
They involve some measure of deliberation. Artistic expression is a
deliberative act. It is formative. Reactive responses simply reduce
the head of steam, and although they may leave quite vivid traces
behind, the forms that are evidence of expressive reaction leave one
merely spent. There is no 'knowing' that can issue from such forms.
There can be no growth, no change, no illumination, no understanding, no resolution – in the words of the song, 'no satisfaction'. Only
the exhaustion of the impulse. Such behaviour is widely recognized
as expressive but its reactive character is not well understood, and
arts education has long suffered under the 'expressive' smear. The
implication being that self-expression, besides offending against the
social ethic in being too individualistic and self-indulgent, offends
also against the moral ethic in countenancing the abandonment of
received civilized decencies, and being an open invitation to orgy,
frenzy and subversion.

The expressive arts in school are not about reactive expression.
Nor are they basically therapeutic in the sense of compensating for or
relieving the damaging consequences of chronic emotional depriva-
tion. Nor is arts education concerned with the purging of otherwise
socially disruptive energies.

These kinds of experience are necessary and serious ones, and some
arts teachers no doubt feel drawn to them (might actually maintain,
as I would, that they have to release reactive responses before
reflexive responses become available). That is as may be. The point
I wish to make here is simply that the arts in education are concerned

with something subtly but significantly different: *with self-expression through the creative use of media in action that is a way of knowing*

Creative self-expression involves a rather special use of sensuous media. The kind of behaviour we have described as 'reactive' seeks the release of tension, and the medium is the instrument of its discharge, is the 'earth' for such energy. So the medium of an expressive reaction will probably bear the impression of that discharge of energy: the telephone booth in ruins, the skull battered in, the door torn from its hinges, the black eye, the wounded feelings, the lost face. Such actions are not creative because no resolution of the stimulus, no transformation of the impulse (the feeling problem) has been achieved. Only relief for the time being. Our experience would seem to suggest that although such responses may be unavoidable at times, even necessary and useful (they are by no means simply destructive), they do not produce new forms of perception or of behaving – and I am using the term creative quite simply here to mean just that, the production of new forms (material forms, symbolic forms, social forms, relational forms, behavioural forms etc.). The reactive cycle begins again once discharge has taken place – there follows the same steady build-up and, when the reaction is triggered, the same dramatic release. Charge-discharge-charge-discharge.

The creative process is essentially different. It is deliberative, for all that much of the process might take place below the conscious level; an act of the will and, as we shall see, a very special activity of consciousness, of perception. Reactive expression is pleasurable because it lowers negative arousal; reflexive expression is pleasurable because it consummates positive arousal. In reactive acts the impulse is discharged, lost; in creative acts the impulse is held and transformed. It, quite literally, takes form, and it finds its resolution in form. The psychological significance of such action, such a working upon experience, is the assimilation of emotional unknowing into a structure of feeling – and the significant transformation of the existing structure into a new, more elaborate, more sophisticated 'intelligence'. For that is the purpose of creative self-expression, the elaboration and development of our emotional life, of our capacity to make sense in feeling of the subjective world of feeling, our capacity to feel intelligently, to find our way among feelings by feeling. This is subjective knowing. It is not a matter of knowing about our feelings, of being able to trace and draw up our own emotional case history. Such 'knowledge' has to be firmly distinguished from 'knowing' – we speak of knowing in our bones. It is a physical, sensuous experience of ease or dis-ease in the here and now, the operation of this feeling intelligence at the cutting-edge of experience itself. It is nurtured by creative encounters, by the resolution of feeling problems through creative acts of self-expression, by the incorporation of the unknown feeling into a new emotional structure.

That is the model I want to work with. Diagrammatically we could represent Reactive Expression thus –

IMPULSE ————▶ MEDIUM ————▶ (Discharge)

and Creative Expression thus –

IMPULSE ◀————▶ MEDIUM

If this hypothesis is accepted then the educational function of the arts becomes clear; *through the subject-reflexive use of media to further the development of intelligent feeling.*

Private and Public Forms of Expression

The integrated personality feels as equally at home in the world of objects as in the world of feelings – indeed the effectiveness of all our actions in the world depends to a critical degree on the energy, the motive force deriving from the subject world, the world of feeling. The integrated person will move easily from the impressive to the expressive mode and may well find it difficult to say which predominates at any one time. He will be the kind of person, for instance, who makes no distinction between work and play in the sense that work is full of playfulness for him. As Witkin suggests, personal and social problems arise when impressive and expressive modes are out of phase. From time to time most of us experience some sense of dislocation and distortion of experience. We say we feel we have gone to pieces or come unstuck. However, under normal circumstances we adjust our stance. We put ourselves back together again and bring our subjective and objective worlds back into alignment. We find the right ratio of impressive to expressive action to meet a particular situation.

The old craftsmen – the blacksmiths, wheelwrights, saddlers, and thatchers – stamped their character unmistakably on their work, expressing themselves in the act of making. Their work was not simply self-expressive in the sense we have been speaking of, however. They did not feel themselves free to allow full rein to their feeling-impulses. In fact of course they recognized that above everything else their work had to measure up to clearly-defined and well-understood public criteria. What they did had to work and to last. There is perhaps not all that much room for self-expression when you are shoeing a horse or thatching a house. Nevertheless the craftsman depended a good deal on intelligent feeling in the executing of his skills: his senses were highly tuned and he worked as much by 'intelligent' sensation as by thought, as much by intuition as by design. As he worked the medium of his craft, his actions were directed by innumerable split-second decisions – his senses informing the making process at every point. His ear would know when the work sounded right, when the iron was ready under the hammer, when the sheaf was thoroughly packed into place. He would run his hand knowingly over the wooden shaft, knowingly and lovingly. The hedger would stand back from the hedge he was trimming and run his eye over his work with the same tender and keen discernment, the same innate appreciation of form, as a studio painter studies a canvas he is working on. And then he would take his stone to the curved blade of the old drashing bill and work the edge deftly back to hair-splitting sharpness, testing it all the time with the ball of his thumb. These men were 'lost' in their work. Their products were unmistakably theirs. They had their own ways with horses, with a plough, with needles, hooks, knives, and planes. They were inside their work and what they fashioned and what they did was an extension of themselves.

Their skill lay in the transformation of raw materials into useful 'products'. They understood both the potential and the limitations of a medium. They knew the function of the product they were to make. Their task was to 'bend' the medium to the design they had in mind. This meant understanding the limits of what a particular medium would and would not do, and then creating something uniquely useful by resolving the tension between that limit and the desired form of its object. The beauty of the things they made lay in the daring compromise they achieved between the demand for functional utility and a loving respect for the medium itself. We all respond to the mixture of beauty and strength in something hand-made, and we sense that it has a heart-felt quality about it. The principal object in such making is evident enough: practical efficiency. The craftsman lived by his work. But he would have sensed no inherent contradiction between instrumental effectiveness and beauty of finish. He would have chosen his medium for its special character and for its suitability for the job, and, in seeking to realize its potential, have managed both to reveal its inherent beauty and to celebrate his love for it. And he made no separation between his mind, his senses and his feeling for the work. He would have been as unselfconscious as he would have been unsentimental. From our point of view the work of the traditional craftsman shows a fine adjustment between impressive and expressive modes of action.

As with yesterday's craftsman so, to some extent at least, with today's designer. He may not work as directly with media or materials as the craftsman, but a good designer is likely to have something of the old craftsman's affection for his materials. He certainly needs to know their properties intimately and to have a feeling for them. Again, as with the craftsman, the designer has to produce results that will ultimately satisfy public tests. The chair must be stable and comfortable and attractive to look at: it must both support and invite 'sitting'. If he is designing a bridge it must be strong enough to bear the loads it will have to carry. And it must be robust enough to sustain the pressures and assaults of physical and elemental forces. We also ask that it be aesthetically related to its setting. Except in times of direst emergency, mere functionalism is invariably rejected. The designer, like the craftsman before him, seeks a reconciliation between medium and function in a single form that is both efficient and pleasing. Given half a chance he will stamp his own personality on his design, somewhere, somehow. All good designs reflect not just the minds but the sensibilities of the designer.

Craftsmanship. Design. Both are potentially expressive human actions. At their best the work of the designer and of the craftsman evince a unique resolution of private and public interests in a single form. But for the purposes of our discussion about the nature and priorities of arts education I want to make a distinction between self-expression and what we might call public expression. Work that is essentially self-expressive is self-specific. No public criteria whatever have to be met unless the maker wishes to publish or make public what he has said or done. The making public of self-expressive action is a matter of choice for the maker. If he does so, he may seem to be inviting a public response and so becomes subject to public criteria of value. But such criteria are not essentially relevant to work that is primarily self-expressive. There is no intrinsic claim that can be made of a piece of self-expression that it mean anything whatsoever to anyone besides the author. If self-expressive work has any meaning as communication then it can only be essentially an act of *self*-communication. If it has to 'work' then the only person it really must satisfy is the maker. No public obligation falls upon the self-express-ive act. Whatever subsequent use is found for and made of such acts they are primarily self-centred. As I have said, self-expression is self-specific.

It will be obvious why the distinction between private and public expression is so important for arts education. Both are wholly legiti-mate forms of expressive action and all arts teachers will want their children to work in ways that have both private meaning *and* public meaning. As we have seen, there is no reason why expressive action should not meet both sets of criteria – when pupils act as craftsmen and designers, such should certainly be the case. Their work, for all its public reference, should be personal. However, and this is the point, private and public forms of expressive action are not one and the same thing. They may, and indeed they must, be dis-tinguished, even if in the long run we decide to promote work that incorporates them both in work that is characteristically personal. The craftsman and the designer must produce work that will stand public scrutiny and meet public standards. The orientation of the

self-expressive artist is fundamentally different. His actions *need* only
satisfy himself unless he chooses otherwise – chooses to offer them for
others to share or use or chooses to please others with them.

Now there will be immediate cries of protest from some quarters at
this assertion. It will sound altogether too self-indulgent, too arro-
gant, too decadent a position to be allowed to art. Surely, it will
be argued, the values of art are cultural values, and cultural values
are essentially social values. The artist who doesn't communicate has
failed – failed himself and failed society.

But this is not so. Certainly any artist who, like the craftsman,
wishes to live by his work cannot expect a baffled, incensed, or simply
uncomprehending public to subsidize his esoteric utterances. If he
pleases to live he must live to please. That is a very old song. And in
the event most practising artists have to find some way of achieving
a workable compromise since most wish to live and few are happy to
settle for absolute social detachment. The danger to their creative
integrity of aiming to please is well documented and of course there
have always been those who would make no such concessions and
who suffered the consequences. Patronage has traditionally come to
the artist's rescue, and today the State, in the form of special committees of experts, has taken over the role, formerly the prerogative
of the rich and the eccentric. Whether or not State patronage is
really conducive to artistic independence is, of course, a highly
controversial issue, and the propriety of public money being dis-
bursed by such experts in this way is also open to question. The
criteria used by arts councils and arts committees are constantly
being called in question, most often of course by artists themselves.
Any form of 'commission', any suggestion that essentially private
acts of self-expression should meet predictable expectations must be
regarded as posing a critical threat to the authenticity of such acts
since by their nature, as we shall see, their outcome cannot be
anticipated. Self-expression involves the probing of unknowing, the
searching of the self in the very flux and chaos of becoming. An
artist *may* choose to work privately, to work for himself, to seek himself through his acts of private self-expression and no one can say him
nay. That is his choice. He must choose when he will make to please
others and when only to please himself.

Children in school are not – or should not be – subject to these
kinds of pressure. If we feel that it is important for them to find themselves in and through their art then they must in a very real sense be
allowed (indeed, encouraged) *to please themselves*. In fact this is not
the invitation to anarchy that it sounds. For many children the
notion that they are the only ultimate judges of the value of their
work may be disturbing. They have become so dependent upon the
authorization and validation of other people (parents, teachers,
other children) that they may have actually lost the capacity to
please themselves or indeed to know whether they are pleased or not.

Restoring (or initiating) this kind of self-confidence is one of the most difficult, and possibly one of the most important tasks facing the teacher of the arts. We really have to convince them that there are times when they actually do know best – in fact when they are the only ones who know. The meaning of their expressive work in the arts is specific to them and to them alone.

I believe that as arts teachers it is vitally important that we make a clear distinction between private and public forms of expression. Until we do the present confused state of affairs is likely to prevail, and to do so very much to the detriment of the children whose 'subject knowing' we are trying to promote. Because to confuse public expression with private expression is to invoke public criteria where only private criteria are really valid. The child who is seeking to know himself through his own self-expressive acts must be encouraged to validate his own work. He may not know where or how to begin; he may lose his way in the process and become confused as to how he should go on. As we shall see, these are all situations in which it ought to be possible for the teacher to help him. But only he will know whether the work he is engaged upon has personal meaning for him and whether the process has been brought to a satisfactory conclusion. Teachers evaluating the self-expressive work of their pupils will be trying to assess the child's struggle to know himself and to become more himself. Whether child A produces work that, as public expression, is more effective, more ingenious, more original, more sophisticated in its execution, than the work of his classmate, child B, is wholly immaterial *when we are considering private forms of expression*. They may have their place in a total scheme of arts education but that is entirely another matter. Our concern for the moment is with subject knowing, with subject-reflexive action in its purest form and the role of the 'subject' is paramount and may not with impunity be usurped.

Which means that we have to be very wary of equating arts education with arts products, with artefacts, public 'works of art'. If we accept the proposition that I am advancing here, i.e. that the basis of arts education is self-expression as an essentially intimate act, an immediate and personal way of knowing, meeting criteria determined solely by the subject of such action, then it is perhaps reasonable to make the assertion that arts education is not, in the first place, about art or the arts at all. At least not in the sense that the arts are public, cultural forms of expression. Private acts of self-expression do not require that the child should be able to please his teacher with the high level of his accomplishment with a pencil or a paint brush, as a singer, an instrumentalist, a dancer, an actor. He will undoubtedly need to master such skills – but he will do so primarily in order that he be able to achieve increasing levels of refinement in his own form making. So that he will have richer and more subtle resources available to service his private expressive needs. Arts education is not really about artists: it is about young people growing. We need to make an absolutely clear distinction between educating children *for* art (i.e. as artists or patrons of the arts) and art as an educational process. Arts teachers use the processes of art for educational purposes, for the changes in personal perception and personal functioning that such processes can bring about. So, if we ask children to produce verbal, dramatic, aural or kinetic images we do so initially not so that we can compare one child's images with another's, nor to ensure that the country will have a steady flow of artists and craftsmen and entertainers, nor that the theatres and museums and concert halls will be adequately patronized in the future. All such entirely proper aims are secondary to what must be uppermost in our minds: the full and healthy expressive development of the individual.

We seek to make the feelings grow and to help each child achieve responsibility for his own life of feeling. Like all other teachers we seek to promote intelligent behaviour: our particular expertise lies in nurturing intelligent feeling.

The public consequences – and the public relevance – of private action is, of course, one of a number of considerations that arts teachers expect to deal with. I am not saying that children should not work towards the production of public forms – far from it. Arts teachers, assured that a child is gaining confidence in the production of private forms, will wish to urge the child towards the 'applied' and 'communication' fields and allow private and public considerations to be resolved in work that is essentially personal though shareable. But subject-reflexive action must be the prime goal.

I am not saying that the children should be left to do as they please. I am saying that they must take pleasure in what they are doing and see the meaning in it, whether the work is emphatically private or public. I am not saying that their work may not be assessed. I am saying that their own assessment will be of critical importance and that we should be very wary when ascribing public (aesthetic or practical) value to their products rather than personal educational value. Our assessments will be essentially concerned with their skill in handling and managing their expressive process, since that is what we are in business to develop. I am not saying that artistic skills have no place in the arts curriculum. Very far from it. Without such skills expression cannot occur, subject-reflexive action will be still-born. I am not saying that the children should not read poetry, or listen to music, or go to the theatre, to art exhibitions or to concerts. Again, this is far from my intention, as I hope will become plain enough later in this book. What I am saying is that all these activities have to be intimately associated with the child's own expressive action, and must provide occasions for intelligent feeling on their terms and at their own level. They must respond to feeling form *with feelings of their own*. If they cannot or will not, then from the

point of view of expressive action the educational experience has
aborted and should be abandoned and thought out afresh.

Arts teachers 'teach' the creative process of expressive representation, and whatever is relevant to the process constitutes the arts
curriculum. Arts education is not merely 'knowing about the arts'.
Our concern is with the integrity of the individual's feeling life and
each child's emotional confidence and sense of self-responsibility.

As teachers of the arts we have always felt that we were concerned
with feelings. If we can accept some such formulation of the role of
the arts in education as I have outlined and shall now proceed to
develop, we have a conceptual tool available to help us plan, implement, and evaluate the arts curriculum. And we shall be able to say
something intelligible in answer to the question, 'What is arts
education about?' Arts education is about the expressive representation of a child's feelings in private and public form. Our job as
teachers of the arts may be quite simply put: to help children master
the process of expressive representation.

4 The Logic of the Arts Curriculum

Feeling into Form

We come now to the heart of the conceptual model that we need if we are to make sense of the idea of creative self-expression, and, in particular, if as teachers we are to find a legitimate practical role for ourselves in relation to the creative activities of our pupils. For this is an acute problem. As long as we are unable to visualize or conceptualize the creative process in the arts we shall have no way of knowing where the pupil is or where we are in relation to the process in which the pupil is engaged. Lacking an adequate conception of that process we lack all valid guidance for a programme of pedagogic 'intervention'. This usually means that intervention either becomes merely arbitrary, based upon some hunch as to what might be appropriate support at any particular time (but typically confined to technical assistance following some form of initial stimulus or instruction), or is more or less entirely eschewed in favour of some notion of natural or spontaneous learning in the arts, variously rationalized and defended. I do not want to minimize either the dangers or the difficulties that attend participation (I will drop the word 'intervention') in the creative processes of another – they are far too obvious to need elaborating. However, there is an active and a positive role for the teacher of the arts that goes beyond mere instruction. Lacking such a conception we cannot build, manage or evaluate curricula, even in retrospect. The articulation or organization of experience is impossible.

The conception (hypothesis) I am proposing is not demonstrable or 'true' in any objective or scientific sense – it is just one way of thinking about a process that we all experience but which remains essentially inscrutable, mysterious. The point is that as teachers we must be able to think about what we are doing and to do so we need a set of concepts, even if they have to be conjectural. We can only decide whether our model is 'good enough' by

testing it against our experience as creative individuals as well as
teachers.

There are those, as I have suggested, who argue that we can only
follow with our instincts and our intuitions the movements of the
creative spirit, the flow and counter-flow of feeling. I would not
object to that. The participation I am speaking of depends absolutely
upon such sensitivity, such perception, and doesn't at all preclude
spontaneous teaching that at the time seems to have no other justification apart from 'feeling right'. But the best of our actions arise
from the interplay of spontaneity and reflection, action and contemplation, perception and conception. And by giving proper
weight to conceptual matters we may actually gain the confidence
to back our perceptions, our instincts, when only they will help
us.

It is also rightly argued that no one can know the subjective
experience of another. We cannot see through someone else's eyes;
we cannot experience the surge and sway of another's feelings. 'There
is no art to find the mind's construction in the face': to see into
another man's heart. We cannot know what – in terms of feelings –
other people are made of: slugs and snails and puppy dogs' tails . . .!
How then can we even contemplate intruding in a world from
which by definition we must always remain excluded? The answer is
that our participation has to be at a general rather than at a particular level. *The general character or structure of the creative process is the same
for all our pupils though the particular forms that emerge from it will be
unique to each one of them.* Having a notion of the process in general our
purpose will then be to help the pupil help himself. To help the pupil
apprehend that process for himself and gain increasing self-control
over it and confidence in it, so that his self-expression may indeed be
creative, and hence both effective knowing and a satisfying experience.
We participate on the basis of a conceptual hypothesis about the
nature of the creative process as human behaviour – our particular
acts of participation are themselves creative if they are adapted to
the movements in consciousness that we seek to engage with. Our
participation will be on the one hand conceptually informed and on
the other intuitively and spontaneously achieved. This is the basis of
creative teaching in the arts.

What of the model then? How might we envisage the process by
which feeling becomes form?

We need to express ourselves when we sense that our feelings need
sorting out. They need sorting out because we are having difficulty
in assimilating them. The difficulty arises on account of some inadequacy in our feeling intelligence – essentially the schema which
should be doing the work is somehow inadequate, is not fully developed, not fully operational. The schema is incomplete. I think of
feeling intelligence as a kind of emotional sorting machine: we respond emotionally to our encounters with the world and develop

increasingly complex schemas that enable us to sort and make affective sense of those responses – to respond intelligently. When
feelings 'fit' we experience no disturbance or lack of composure –
we know how we feel about our feelings. Disturbance arises when we
have trouble sorting our feeling responses, and, with disturbance,
the urge to express ourselves. Fully developed schemas allow the
rapid processing and assimilation of feeling; immature (or unresolved) schemas call attention to themselves by giving rise to
agitation, discomposure. We feel uneasy about how we feel: essentially about our inability to sort our feelings out. The major hypothesis of this book, following Witkin, is that *we sort out our feelings
through our acts of creative self-expression*. Subject-reflexive action builds
mature affective schemas, builds our intelligence of feeling.

It follows that the first requisite of the expressive process is an
encounter with a stimulus (as we shall see, the encounter may be real or
contrived, actual or recalled) that gives rise to a feeling of disturbance within us. We feel we need to express ourselves to sort ourselves out. Such a reaction signals the presence of an unresolved
(immature) schema within our intelligence of feeling and fuels the
act of expression that will allow us to probe our own unknowing.
Through repeated probing we gradually make the schema more
effective and so advance our intelligence of feeling. What we seem
to be doing is discovering and familiarizing ourselves with the 'deep
structure' of the schema.

The activation of an unresolved schema makes us uncomfortable
and we have to *express* that felt disturbance in some way if we are to
release the tension. The urge or impulse to act expressively is our
means of re-establishing equilibrium within the affective system.
If our expressive act sheds some light, some knowing upon the unresolved schema then we shall feel it has been successful, and we shall
emerge more aware and more ourselves.

The expressive urge or impulse is one of the two partners vital to
the expressive act – the other being the medium through which it is
projected. *We experience the expressive impulse as mood*. The activation of
an unresolved schema invariably arouses disturbance within the
affective field. The point about the impulse is that it is moody, it
has a specific emotional character, positive or negative. The image
we seek through the projective act is one that will both contain and
recall the 'mood of the moment'. The expressive act is a structuring
process that renders a feeling state in a sensuous form. In order to
convert feeling into form we need an *hypothesis* about its deep structure (essentially about the possible structure of the immature
schema that has failed to assimilate it). The making process then
becomes a way of testing that hypothesis. If the image seems to
fit the expressive impulse, if the disturbance subsides and the expressive urge is satisfied, then we can say that our hypothesis
was correct. We have created an analogue for the deep structure

of the schema and by our action have advanced our knowing, our self-knowing.

To be expressive in the creative sense, the action must be subject-reflexive and the chosen medium of expression must have *reflexive capability*. To the extent that the medium falls short of full reciprocity, the expressive act is destined to be frustrated. It goes without saying that when an expressive act is deficient in impulse it will also fail, and any expressive form issuing from such motiveless action will be hollow, a fake, a sham.

We follow the to and fro of the creative process with conscious awareness and attention. We sense the act of projection; we sense too the impact of the impulsive action upon the medium, and the response of the medium to its thrust. Here we become aware of the duality inherent in the nature of representational media of expression (more precisely, here, 'media that will serve the act of creative self-expression'): yielding and resistance. Herein lies the peculiar value of media for us – by yielding to our creative thrust the medium allows us to channel our feelings into and through it; by resisting us it enables us to centre the impulse and to make a representational form. The creative use of media demands respect for both their yielding and resistant properties, for the medium must contain the impulse. The reactive use of media is merely exploitative of those qualities – the medium is abused (rather than used) to allow the discharge of too much impulse.

Let us attempt a summary and a simplification – since what we are concerned with here is not a theory of knowledge so much as a working model of the expressive process that will inform our teaching and which we can test in practice through our encounters with children.

1. The stimulus encounter arouses a mood indicating an unresolved feeling schema within us.
2. With the mood on us we must first choose between expression and repression and, if we choose expression, between reaction and reflexion.
3. Subjective-reflexive action involves the formulation and the testing of an hypothesis about the deep structure of the schema.
4. We project the impulse through a medium that allows its reciprocation, and make a form expressive of and guided by the impulse.
5. When we have finished we often, but not always, wish to share what we have done with others, as a way of celebrating our sense of new being and of eliciting evaluative information from 'beyond' the expressive act as well as from 'within' it. (This sharing 'after the event' is not to be confused with performance in the case of the performing arts, where interaction between maker and audience is part of the expressive process itself, the audience being integral to the medium.)

In conclusion we must declare that the process of creative self-expression – for all the frustrations and uncertainties along the way – is invariably a *positive* experience. Once we have our hypothesis to work with, and a medium that is responsive to our projective thrust, we become utterly absorbed in a mode of action that is immediate and self-sustaining. The final consummation when a successful reso-lution is achieved can be pure joy.

Here is a diagrammatic representation of the model:

Fig. 4.1

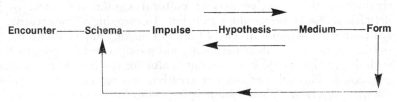

We have not just solved a problem, we have adjusted to a change in our own feeling world. We have changed our Being. We can grow emotionally only through our creative responses to feeling 'prob-lems'. Subject-reflexive action is the way, and subject-reflexive action depends upon our capacity for intelligent feeling – upon the quality and efficiency of our intelligence of feeling.

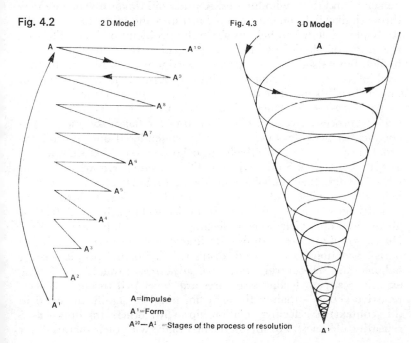

Fig. 4.2   2 D Model   **Fig. 4.3**   3 D Model

A = Impulse
A^1 = Form
$A^{10}-A^1$ = Stages of the process of resolution

Knowing Your Feelings

To know your feelings you have to engage in creative acts of self-expression, that is to say in actions that eventuate in new expressive forms – new for the agent of the action, the maker, the one whose self is being expressed. That such acts of self-expression may also sometimes be felt to be new for other people too – new for a culture as a whole – is of course important, but it is rather beside the point for our purposes. Though only some acts of self-expression may be culturally significant, all expressive acts of cultural significance must, by definition, also be personally significant. In speaking of the creative self-expression of pupils in school I am not making any claim for the public application of their personally unique discoveries – only that such discoveries should have absolute value for the individual pupil concerned. Through each of our creative acts we are reborn: we remake ourselves. This is why it is important to be clear what we mean when we use the term 'creative', and why the *creative* arts have a fundamentally vital educational role to play.

We have already said that an investigation into the history of our emotional life may help us make sense of it. We may 'understand' why we find some situations hard to take, why we cannot on any account face others. Why we seem to be trapped into repeating a profitless pattern of mistaken 'friendships'. Why we should forgive ourselves and those who hurt us. A study of human psychology may throw similar light on our personal fortunes and misfortunes – as the study of sociology can help us grasp the problems of family life, and the study of physiology the laws governing the behaviour of our bodies. But we should not expect knowledge in the abstract ('impressive' information) to bring about improved psychological or social or physical well-being. The doctor may be able to set our minds at rest and reduce the tendency of the body to inhibit its own natural healing process. Even so, chemical disorder has to be met with a chemical remedy (even if a naturally engendered one). Social disorders respond more effectively to social counteraction than to talk about such action. So too with the life of feeling. Knowledge about feeling states, their universal incidence or particular causes, may help lower anxiety and one's sense of isolation, and so liberate the beneficient influence of other, healthier feelings. But old feelings always and only yield to new feeling – never to talk about feeling. Never, simply to the analysis of feeling states and to 'the naming of parts'. Emotionally distressed, disturbed or isolated people recover balance and self-control *through acts of feeling*, through new feeling experiences. New feeling structures are developed through subject-reflexive action – mainly through 'forming' (a significant word in this context) *new* feeling relationships with others (as opposed to repeating old ones). Possibly in the first place with their therapist but then, hopefully, with a widening circle of acquaintances. This is the purpose of therapeutic intervention. Therapy may well benefit from the kind of objective knowledge (analysis and interpretation) that I have been describing; however it does not always, nor does it necessarily do so. The incidence of self-expressive action on the part of the client within the therapeutic relationship is critical.

Knowing your feelings means that your emotional life makes sense to you. It means feeling at home with your feelings. It does not mean having knowledge of feeling in the sense of having information about feeling states (your own or states in general) – knowing your feelings is a matter of how you feel towards your feelings in the here and now of your own feeling life. When we feel disturbed, uneasy, at a loss to know quite *how* we feel – towards some person, event or situation – then we have a feeling 'problem'. There are two alternatives open to us: either to ignore the problem – to suppress the disturbance – or to express it. Assuming we take the expressive rather than the repressive line, we can use the disturbance as impulse for expressive representation and seek its resolution in and through a suitable medium. That medium may be material or symbolic. The critical point is this: if the impulse (the unknowing) is to be resolved and a new equilibrium of feeling to be achieved, the action taken by the subject *must have a significant expressive* element.

It follows that the fewer the expressive opportunities available to people in their daily lives the less likely they are to find adequate means of resolving feeling problems, of developing an integrated, balanced and well-adapted life of personal feeling. It is partly to meet this deficiency in the modern world that the arts are being put to therapeutic use in hospitals, clinics, growth centres, and other such institutions devoted to problems of mental and emotional well-being. These are largely block-busting programmes. In the schools our emphasis will be different. But we are concerned with the same question: helping people to accept responsibility for their actions and to make sense of their private worlds of feeling. This is our contribution to the age-old educational quest – 'know thyself'. It can hardly have a more immediate application. When I do not know or want to know how I feel, then 'chaos is come again'.

What Precisely should Arts Teachers be Doing?

It seems reasonable to pose and face this question now. It is a 'real' one in that I once heard it asked of a tutor at a course for primary-school art teachers. The teachers on the course had been studying the 'environment' as a stimulus and source for work in art, and, working in pairs, had devised projects for themselves and then mounted an informal exhibition as a means of sharing their different experiences. There were pieces of rubbish sculpture and collage, all kinds of rubbings and impressions as well as the more obvious representations of places, objects, creatures, and events observed in the local environment. There were ingenious and colourful diagrams based on the movement of traffic through neighbouring streets and various mixed-media productions emanating from visits to the castle, the market, and the quayside. Clearly 'the environment' was a big success – the teachers had enjoyed their work and provided plenty of evidence of the sharpness of their responses and of lively imaginations. They had also discovered lots of things to do with children that involved many of the processes associated with art: observation, representation, illustration, decoration. Amidst the general excitement one pair seemed less than entirely satisfied with what they had done. They had been very busy and had enjoyed themselves – they had also made a number of genuine 'discoveries' for themselves. They were having difficulty however in distinguishing in their own minds the point where what they called 'science' ended and where what they called 'art' began. They had certainly been studying the environment, and had responded in their own way to the questions that it posed for them. But somehow this generalized activity seemed too vaguely conceived; they felt unsure of the conceptual thread that would lead them through this maze of experience. Hence the question, 'What precisely should *arts* teachers be doing?'

If we accept the particular answer I have already given, that is that 'arts education is concerned with the subject-reflexive use of representational media' then at least we can begin to look at the activities I have just been describing with some hope of sorting them out. For instance, without necessarily wishing to imply value judgements at this stage, we might wish to distinguish between the imitative forms – objective representation, illustrations, impressions, and diagrams – and the imaginative forms – the expressive 'personal' images. We might be able to discern those projects where the sorting out of data was carried through in purely conceptual terms (like things brought together with like, logical developments such as life-cycles, cause-and-effect processes), and others in which more imaginative and aesthetic relationships could be discerned. It was clear in this particular instance that very few of the teachers had responded to the environment self-expressively, had felt impelled to give expressive form to their feelings as an end in itself or had sensed the potential and the problems of using the environment as both a stimulus to expression and also as a medium of expression. One could of course argue that the projects stimulated all kinds of direct, sensory experience – of things seen, perhaps for the first time, of things touched, smelt and so forth. One could argue that in representing their experiences in a similar fashion their children should acquire important skills of hand and eye. The list of possible educational benefits is almost limitless (improved sociability, self-confidence, responsibility, elaboration of speech, writing, listening, and reading skills and so on). If the teachers were to follow up their course experiences in their schools there would undoubtedly be a lot of highly-motivated and committed work, some of which *might* be relevant to the area of experience we are concerned with. The question is – how to see that creative self-expression actually occurs? If that were what we wanted.

And this question takes us back to our model of the expressive process and carries us on to the formulation of a curriculum model for the teaching of the expressive arts. Our job as arts teachers can be summarized thus:

1. We have to help the child discover what he has to say – to find a motive in himself for his expressive act, an impulse, something to work out.
2. We have to help him focus that impulse in a way that will permit the working of it through a suitable representational medium.
3. We have to provide support and guidance through the making process so that there is a good chance that the child will find the final expressive form satisfying.

These three considerations should guide our 'participation' whether we teach art or music or drama or dance or creative writing – indeed they apply to the teaching of one and all of the arts at each and every level. If our concern is the expressive use of media, this is how, as teachers, we need to see ourselves. This is for us the over-riding concern. I would personally like to see teachers of the arts distinguished in future not so much by their differences as by what they share in common. I am suggesting that they should share a fundamental commitment to the development of children's expressive languages and, while preserving their special love for and developing their special expertise in, perhaps, one of those languages (of sound, of light, of movement, of words), should nevertheless understand and sympathize with the work of their colleagues. There seems no logical reason why this might not be so, but anyone who has tried to get musicians, writers, and painters to work together will know that there are enormous difficulties to overcome. The arts certainly exist separately – and we shall be drawing out some of those differences a little later – but they have their roots in a common human experience and, in educational terms, should serve common developmental ends. There are umpteen reasons why the expressive arts need to be considered and need to be experienced as 'solid', cohesive, and of a single mind. There is every reason why they should be, and little excuse for the perpetuation of divisive thinking, special pleading and the preservation of isolationist policies of curriculum management. The arts need each other – arts teachers certainly do. And the schools need the arts.

If the arts are to be intimately associated in schools – and this is what I shall be repeatedly suggesting – they also need to be

intimately associated in the colleges and departments of education.
Student teachers have to be brought to appreciate the expressive
potential of their own chosen medium and its relation to other media
of expression *within the context of education*. That one is forced to admit
the almost complete lack of any precedent for such an approach to
the training of arts teachers (except perhaps at infant and primary
levels) gives a measure of the enormity of the task ahead – my
suggestion will be regarded as revolutionary, even diabolical, in some
quarters. But I would insist that most of the problems of the arts in
school, if not actually deriving from the training courses, are
scarcely alleviated by them. There have, of course, been numerous
instances of departments attempting collaboration, association and
integration, but these have usually proved more frustrating than
enlightening, and generally issued in a rediscovering of the old
divisions and a falling back upon the old ways. I would suggest that
the differences have arisen principally from the lack of consensus
among the would-be partners at the conceptual level. I hope this
book may encourage some of the disappointed ones to try again, and
many more to have a go. I am not suggesting that no distinction is
to be made between the different arts, or that all such distinction
should be given up and lost in a general pot pourri of self-expressing!
Far from it. The approach I shall be arguing for will be a demanding
and a highly disciplined one – and would not in the least be tor-
pedoed by the decision of departments to maintain their separate
identities. Each of the arts should be prized for its distinctive
character. All I am asking is that this notion of arts education, as
being essentially concerned with the expressive use of media, be
allowed to act as *the basis* of all work in the arts, whether conducted
separately, collaboratively, or in a truly 'collective' way. Integration
itself is not the issue. Consensus however is. Many secondary schools
at the moment suffer a good deal from some of the worst features of
current methods of teacher education in the arts: the English gradu-
ate is too narrowly attuned to books through the lit. crit. approach
to literature; the art teacher has often spent most of his training
nursing a forlorn ambition to become a professional painter (and his
course had endorsed this all along the line); the musician is frequently an academy-oriented instrumentalist, disqualified both by
training and personal inclination from engaging with the expressive
needs of children. *There is no reason at all for supposing that the good*
oung actor or writer or painter or pianist will necessarily, or ever, make an
adequate teacher of the expressive arts. As we shall see, that demands
something else altogether.

   To come back to our question, 'What precisely should arts teachers
be doing?'. They should be encouraging children to respond to and
'reflect upon' their feelings, and to give sensuous expression to their
experiences. If they are to do so the children must be helped to find
suitable representational media since, by our definition, there can be

no expression without representation. Children's expressive modes will differ (some will prefer the enactive mode, others the iconic), and they won't all take kindly either to the same medium or the same teacher. Since every creative act (and we are of course talking here of reflexive rather than reactive self-expression) involves some element of risk, some, albeit temporary, loss of face, abandonment of the self we present to the world, then the sympathetic character of the teacher-pupil relationship will be critical to the whole process. There are going to be problems here for class and timetable organization if the mishandling of this highly sensitive issue is not to threaten the whole undertaking. Arts teachers have to match their pupils with appropriate media (not necessarily media they are already skilful in controlling but media they feel drawn towards or can be encouraged to try) and provide 'cover' for them when they feel most exposed, most lost, most vulnerable. Arts teachers must understand creative self-expression as a way of knowing, and know when to intervene and when not to; they must recognize the stresses and rhythms of the experience, and discern the direction and speed of the impulsive thrust. They should know when the impulse is too weak to sustain the formative effort; when the impulse has somehow been lost altogether in the representational action. They should be able to teach children the techniques necessary to exploit the full potential of the chosen medium while seeing to it that the nature of the medium itself is always respected, and that the impulse remains at the centre of the expressive act. Never simply teaching technique for its own sake, yet recognizing that limitations of technique are limitations of one's expressive vocabulary. Teachers of the arts must devise a means for structuring the problem-solving process and for evaluating the final 'solution' – establishing a proper balance between 'public' and 'private' criteria. They are unlikely to be able to offer a useful evaluation that is not grounded in a real understanding of the child since the object of the expressive act is that it leave the child feeling more 'himself'. Teachers of the arts should help children make personally expressive sense of their cultural heritage – of books, plays, poems, paintings, all kinds of music, films, and so forth – not as objective (impressive) information to be collected, dated, referred to, written about, but as felt experience continually available to them. That is, children must be able to perform their own acts of re-creative self-expression in respect of the images, the representational forms, of others.

It is out of some such task list as this that teachers of the arts will find their unique and legitimate work.

5 Education through the Arts

Arts Education: A Basic Statement

We make sense of our lives in two ways. We use our minds to collect and sort information and ideas. We call this kind of understanding 'conception'; its process is logical reasoning and we use discursive and conventional language when we want to represent it or communicate it. We also arrive at meaning emotionally – life makes sense (or nonsense) to us intuitively. Instinctively. We say it feels right. We represent or communicate our feelings in images. We do not have to choose between logical meanings and emotional meanings – all human beings use their reason *and* their feelings, their minds and their bodies. So it should be in education: we should train children to make sense of their experience both rationally and emotionally so as fully to understand the world they live in and themselves as individual personalities with a place in that world. So we try to avoid separating (alienating) the individual from his feelings about what is happening to him. We wish him to sense life as a whole and not as a collection of disconnected fragments, so he can keep himself together. The fate of Humpty Dumpty who fell off the wall and couldn't be put together again awaits each of us. People need to feel whole and must be responsible for their own wholeness. That means they must be helped to make their own sense of the whole of their experience, body and soul, mind and feelings.

Arts education aims to further the emotional development of children and young people in school. Healthy emotional growth is bound up with the quality of a person's expressive life: it is vital that boys and girls acquire the confidence and the skill to give form to their feelings, since without feelings life is not worth living. It is through our feelings that what we do and what we are acquire real meaning for us. Feelings can simply go sour if they do not find satisfactory forms of release – or they suddenly break out in violence and frustration that only make matters worse. The arts arose in

primitive communities as man's means of understanding and finding
a healthy outlet for his feelings. They serve the same purpose still,
both at the level of the community and for each individual. Of course
we do not all have to become artists to have satisfying emotional
lives: as adults most of us find sufficient expressive opportunities in
our work, our family relationships and our recreations, including the
arts, of course. (Though there is not much doubt that the emotional
behaviour of so-called grown-ups is often less well balanced than
young children's.) However, for adolescents growing up whose
emotions are generally understood to be going through a phase of
some upheaval there are very sound educational reasons why we
should supply *additional opportunities* that will help them to come to
terms with their feelings. The arts, by giving form to feeling, can
make a vital contribution to healthy personal development. We are
not training artists. Young people whose feelings are alive and make
sense stand a good chance of finding happiness, of getting on at work
and in their personal relationships. When feelings are confused or
frustrated we usually make a mess of our lives – and the lives of those
around us. *Education through art is education for emotional maturity.*

Arts Education: Specific Aims

The arts teacher helps children's emotional development by showing
them how to express their feelings creatively and responsibly.
Creatively in the sense that, through the kind of self-expression we
encourage, the child actually becomes capable of new feelings and of
handling feeling in new ways. Responsibly in the sense that the
expressive medium is properly respected, whether that medium is a
material one (like clay for example), a personal one (a friend –
friendly relationships provide most of our expressive needs) or a
social one. We encourage controlled expression that builds a child's
powers of self-control: mere emotionalism and self-indulgence are as
damaging to artistic expression as they are personally and inter-
personally.

We achieve our purpose by helping our pupils create and re-create
expressive forms (paintings, poems, plays, songs and so forth). This
means teaching them to master the raw materials of self-expression
in the arts – how to paint, how to read and write, how to make music,
dance, act. It also means introducing them to works of art that they
will be able to identify with, believe in, and make their own. Since
everyone's feeling world is special, and since people's emotional
needs are different, we tend to treat each of our pupils as an individual and we try as far as circumstances will allow to work with our
pupils on that basis. There will be many experiences we can share,
of course; there will be occasions when we need other people to
work with (when we sing together or act in a play, for instance);
and we can often teach particular skills or pass on information to a

class as a whole. Nevertheless our emphasis has to be upon individual work – on discovering the special needs of each child and matching that child with opportunities carefully tailored to suit his or her temperament, mood, and skills.

We aim to create an atmosphere that will encourage children to express themselves and we try to pass on to children the skills and disciplines required of work in particular media so that they will achieve success for themselves in the making of forms that express their feelings. Essentially we wish children to be confident and effective in their expressive use of media: this of course means thinking as well as feeling, knowledge as well as know-how. The point about expressive forms is that they are feelings represented in actual 'images' (images may of course be aural, verbal and kinetic as well as visual). Our work differs from that of our non-arts colleagues in that we give pride of place to the formulation of feeling-ideas, to the creation of and response to forms that must (and need only) in the final instance, satisfy strictly personal and subjective criteria.

The Content of the Arts Curriculum

Impulse is the heart of the arts curriculum. The curriculum is comprised of these four elements:

1. The education of the senses
2. Media: the languages of expression
3. Craftsmanship
4. Imagining and imagination

Problem solving in the arts means creating sensuous reciprocals for unresolved or immature feeling states. When our feelings are familiar to us we feel composed: no feeling problems are being thrown up by our encounters with the world. When something happens to disturb our being we sense it immediately and sense that we must, sooner or later, 'compose' ourselves. We must act to restore order and equilibrium, knowing. Through subject-reflexive action we are able to probe the deep structure of unresolved schemas: with knowing and resolution our general sense of well-being is restored, the mood is lifted. We feel our life enhanced by the act of self-creation: we have actualized, endorsed ourselves, turned un-being into being. Our consciousness is subtly, even radically changed. So we grow, and continue to mature in feeling. We grow through engaging creatively with our feelings and giving them healthy expression. (Which has nothing to do with making publicly acceptable images.) We 'compose' ourselves through our creative compositions.

1. The Education of the Senses
Sensation is the basis of aesthetic experience and, indeed, of what Poincarré called 'the aesthetic emotion'. We need to be sensuously

alive if we are (1) to be fully responsive to our encounters with our environment, (2) if we are to find aesthetic and emotional meaning in environmental forms, (3) if we are to make full use of the expressive potential of the media of representation, (4) if we are to guide the expressive impulse on its way to resolution in sensuous form. It follows therefore that neither we nor our pupils should shy away from sensuous experience, indeed quite the contrary: we must constantly be sharpening and refining our sensuous awareness if we are to preserve and develop our innate expressive skills. The process of creative self-expression is first and foremost a sensuous experience, immediate, felt as the intimate coupling of outer and inner worlds. The creative spirit moves intuitively, literally 'sensing' its way.

Teachers of the arts educate the sensuous responses of children: help them look and *see*, listen and *hear*, touch and *feel*, move and *sense their own moving*, encounter each other dramatically and *be aware of each other's enacting*. We may have to lift the scales from their eyes, draw the plugs from their ears, remove the muffle from that inner bell so that it will ring for them. The eye can be taught to think for itself, to sense the sensuous and affective coherence of experience directly. Perception is a creative act because it is a formative act. Our informed and informing acts of perception turn visual information into shapes, noises into sounds, surfaces into textures, motion into movement. They achieve significance, meaning. But meaning of a special kind: aesthetic, sensuous meaning. Again I am concerned with intelligent action – action that converts information into meaning. But it is not a conceptual or referential intelligence I am thinking of here, rather an intelligence of sensation: the intelligence that orders visual perceptions purely visually, that discerns texture directly through the nerve-ends of the finger-tips. We are of course talking about activities of the brain, but these activities involve no translation of percept into concept and do not call for the mediation of words. They are literally 'immediate'. Indeed the brain responds directly to sensory signals (touch, balance, hearing, tastes), and orders such signals by contrasting and comparing them, not as ideas, but as direct sensations. Such responses are non-verbal, non-conceptual. The meaning discerned in the relationship of one sensation to another is aesthetic meaning – requires no story-line, no mediation, no captions or sub-titles. No titles. We simply distinguish rough and smooth, warm and cool, soft and hard, periphery and centre, straight and curved, convex and concave, loud and quiet, shrill and muffled, rise and fall, tension and relaxation, far and near, series, interruptions, edges, endings. All felt – sensed – responded to and ordered by *intelligent sensing*. I am not concerned with the process of conceptual recognition: ah, a shell, a piano, sackcloth, spaghetti, a woman's voice, a motor accident, a dead frog, a Beethoven Sonata, chips, Olga Korbut, ammonia. I am concerned with the close attention to the character of pure sensation, and the ordering of sensation through intelligent perception. Again, not 'thinking about', not 'words for', but *sensation itself related directly to sensation.*

Children need to develop and perfect their sensing, to enjoy sensation and to explore the life of the senses; to trust their perceptual skills. Such perceiving will both provide the impulses necessary for expressive action, and, since expression takes place in a sensuous medium, will control and guide that expression. As we have seen, there are direct ties between sensuous perception and emotional response, and direct representational routes from inner response via expressive action to sensuous form. *These ties and routes do not involve any conceptual reference or intervention.* Conception, the discursive use of words, literal meanings, intellectualizing, labelling – these are all traps laid in the path of the unwary image-maker. Once you fall into one of them, your expressive hopes are lost – the aesthetic response is betrayed and the expressive process doomed.

Arts education begins with this life of the senses, and ends with it too, since the perception of sensuous meaning resolves the sensate problem. Arts education is about eye-peeling, ear-pinning, tongue-twisting, being handy, being nosey. This re-education of the outer senses and the articulating of sensation is what the practice of aesthetic education (as distinct from the theory) is all about. The opposite of being aesthetic in this sense is being anaesthetized – numbed, blinded, deafened, dumbed. No need to press the argument that schools all too often conspire in deafening and dumbing the young, making children ashamed or distrustful of feeling, and conning them into believing that all they need to get by in this world is a clear head and a thick skin. Fact and abstraction are our principal enemies; a sense of inner rhythm our great gift. Our inner and outer senses must be working intelligently for us.

2. Media: the language of expression

Teachers of the arts must help children master and control the sensuous and symbolic media of expressive representation. Media allow the release or resolution of impulse – media are used expressively when they embody feeling. When we resolve a feeling problem in a feeling form, we are creating a personal symbol, an image capable of evoking feeling, a symbol that allows us to transform experience into knowing. In order to produce personal images that embody sensate impulse, and build feeling intelligence, children must be made aware of the properties of different representational media, of their character and potential as a means of expression. As teachers of the arts this is one of our principal functions.

I have already used the term medium repeatedly: perhaps we should now pause briefly to define it. The word has a number of closely related meanings. When we speak for instance of the 'media of communication', media means simply the means of communication. We are concerned with the agency by means of which the communication occurs. By 'mass media' we mean the means of mass communication: radio, television, newspapers. We may, in the same sense, speak of the material and symbolic media of expressive representation. Clay, paint, fabrics, words, are all deployed instrumentally so that expression may take place. Since expression is a representational action eventuating in a representational form, the process essentially requires an expressive agent that provides the raw stuff of the formative act. The *Shorter Oxford Dictionary* speaks of 'any intervening substance through which a force acts . . .' In our case, material (and symbolic) media provide the element in which an expressive force acts in order to take representational form. In the discussion which follows I refer to material media as representational media since it is their instrumental function in relation to the representational act that most concerns us.

Confusion can arise when we speak of raw energy itself as media – light waves and sound waves for instance. The word is certainly appropriate since it is through the medium of light and sound that sensory information is presented to us. Although raw energy is invariably also used in the act of representation, I have designated these raw media, presentational media. Light is the medium of visual presentation; pigmented paints, carbon sticks and lead pencils are used as representational media because they enable us to organize our response to light for representational purposes. (Until photography came along it was impossible actually to draw with light itself – the literal meaning of the word, photography.)

We may also use the word rather more widely to include nonmaterial elements in the agency, for example the rules and conventions that govern form-making in the various arts. Such factors must be considered aspects of the medium since they qualitatively affect its character. Similarly we have to include in this extended notion of representational media all tools and instruments used by the imagemaker and the audience at live performances, where these qualitatively affect the form in which feeling is manifested. Whatever 'intervening substance' contributes to the character of the form, comprises the medium. Each element needs to be known, understood and controlled in the process of the resolution of the sensate problem.

All media have rules in the sense that their behaviour is characterized and constrained by certain laws (physical laws like the property of wave motion for instance). Symbolic media have symbolic rules. We usually call them conventions. In coming to terms with a medium you need to appreciate the rules governing its behaviour. You need to know its special characteristics. It is these rules, laws, and conventions which provide the resistance, essential to the ultimate resolution of the impulse. If the resistance offered by the medium is not respected – if the medium is merely abused – it will not work as the agent of expressive representation. Every medium is governed by its own rules and this means that we find some media more appropriate to our expressive purpose and some less so. Controlling media means understanding and respecting media – the best results, however, are achieved through daring as well as respect. We like to push a medium to the limit. Beyond a certain point, we merely abuse it, and at that point the expressive process aborts.

In our daily lives we are continually finding media that will serve our expressive purposes. We naturally use our bodies expressively, and our voices. Above all we use our encounters and relationships with other people. We also express ourselves through our appearance, our clothing, choice of house, car, through the dishes we prepare, the gardens we make, the friends and companions we choose. We find media because we need media. Our expressive life is mediated through everything and anything capable of registering the projection of an emotional impulse, and of either releasing it or reflecting it back. The arts occur as a cultural extension or elaboration of our natural, expressive behaviour.

All media share the characteristics of energy in action. These characteristics account for the distinguishing qualities of the different media of representation; they account for the full range of sensuous experiences generated by sensuous forms. They are these:

  intensity;
  frequency;
  distance;
  direction;
  velocity;
  duration.

These concepts define energy in action: they determine the qualitative characteristics of media.

When we look for these qualitative elements in art we find ourselves talking about stress, hue, pitch, tone, beat, accent, tempo, poise, climax, anti-climax, tension – and their affective counterparts: feelings of excitement, apprehension, sublimity, suspense, climax. It is through these manifestations of energy that feelings find their reciprocals in form. It follows therefore that we have to help children to understand, identify and exploit these general characteristics in relation to particular media. I would expect as a teacher to concentrate upon the six factors listed above that, together, determine the qualitative characteristics of the different languages of representation.

3. Craftsmanship

To express oneself effectively needs craftsmanship: a set of skills acquired probably slowly and certainly at the cost of sustained effort and application. I see no point, however, in setting our pupils learning tasks that are way beyond their powers, or the rewards of which in terms of emotional reinforcement will be long delayed. Nor do I set much store by labour and frustration as good for the soul. We teach technical skills in the context of expressive action, and accept an obligation to match the learning required (and hence the effort to be made) to the pupil's capacity to master it. The arts are a discipline and the artist-pupil must discipline himself if he is also to satisfy himself through art. In teaching craftsmanship we are careful not to sacrifice the pupil's expressive learning for the sake of 'finish'.

Given an awareness of the range of expressive languages available to them, children must be given access to them and the means of their effective control. By 'effective' control I mean, of course, control in relation to the expressive impulse. I am still arguing on the assumption that the purpose of the pupil's engagement, both with his own sensing and with the media of representation, is expressive rather than, say, merely communicative or imitative, and therefore *impulse directed*. The impulse is, as always, the *sine qua non* of the expressive act. Sensation is organized in relation to impulse, and the 'learner' seeks to master the medium so that he may be able to use it to fulfil his expressive needs and achieve his expressive purposes (i.e. the knowing of his feelings). Given the process of reciprocation between impulse and medium the only other control that the image-maker needs is technical – a mixture of conceptual know-how and manipulative or instrumental skills. So we move into the field of knowledge and co-ordination. When you have something to say you need the words and the grasp of language structures, together with adequate skills in speaking and writing, in order to achieve representational satisfaction. It follows therefore that children will need to acquire knowledge about sensuous and symbolic media – the physics of light, the 'science' of colour, the laws governing the behaviour of wood, metals, and plastics, the character of sound waves, and the dramatic values of social distance, direction, gesture, group dynamics. How to use words. They will need to learn how to control the time and space values of different media, and to distinguish their properties, behaviours and effects. They need the craftsmanship that will enable them to manipulate media and associated technology with ease and precision; without such skills they must feel themselves inhibited rather than liberated by media. Lacking effective control, they will never be carefree enough to play with media imaginatively or to improvise; both these activities are achieved only after the groundwork has been properly done. The perfection of Indian music, as with Western jazz, is to be found in the improvisation that grows out of a flawless comprehension of the traditional stock. Our children must master the representational use of media, and our responsibility in this respect is clear and simple: to teach them. To teach them to write and read expressively, to give them musicianship, craftsmanship, stagecraft – to help them master the instruments of technical control necessary to the effective realization of personal images (symbolic representation). The technical skills of voice-production, stage-lighting, film-processing, wax-resist, fingering on the oboe, lifts in the dance, may all be learnt, and so, legitimately, taught. So too with objective drawing – children demanding training should be given it and, as far as circumstances permit, encouraged to prosper and do well in it.

The danger and frequently the trouble with the teaching of techniques is that they can so easily become an end in themselves, and mastery or excellence pursued for its own sake and not as a means to the representation of experience. Techniques can be taught – and technical expertise examined, compared, ascribed or found wanting. Children whose impulses are engaged will learn to master almost anything (even that fearsome machine the piano). However, anything easily examined is pounced upon as potential educational fodder, and the teaching and examining of craft skills in the arts has long been an abuse of the kind of arts education we are concerned with in this book. Such impulse-void technical mastery produces empty form and denies the arts their exclusive role as the mediators of expressive action. *Techniques and knowledge are useful only in so far as they secure a closer approximation of form to impulse.* Anyone embarking upon the teaching of technique or of knowledge about a medium or art form must know exactly in what relation such a technique or such knowledge stands to the child's expressive impulse and precisely when that impulse has been engaged. It is not really a question of which comes first, the expressive impulse or the technical skill. Clearly it is absurd to insist that techniques are learned in isolation from the intrinsic drive to use them expressively (an argument that was once frequently advanced by teachers of the crafts). It is also unnecessary to begin expressive work each time with some kind of direct emotional stimulus, waiting until the need for a new technique arises before teaching it. This way of doing things often feels like punishment to the child, who is frustrated by his own ineptitude. It is obviously a matter for individual judgement in the here and now of particular situations. Frequently the learning of a skill can itself trigger the impulse to use it – it is a matter of 'two paces forward and one back' for most of the time, the impulsive drive lacking representational technique and that particular expressive action ending prematurely. A higher technical level is then sought on the strength of the motivation generated. In the general sum of things *technique must always attend impulse*, even if it is also the fate of the impulse to be blocked by technical incompetence. The greatest treason is to do the right thing for the wrong reason.

4. *Imaging and Imagination*

The images of art, like the images of dreams, are sensuous symbols imbued with subjective meaning. They are 'feeling forms' in the sense that they have significance only because they embody feeling. To interpret the meaning of a dream we have to discover the feeling charge, the emotional quality, of the image. It is often as difficult to penetrate the images of art as it is to comprehend the dreams of someone else because the images in both instances derive from the particularity of their creator's experience. There are, of course, a range of universal or archetypal images that everyone seems to use almost instinctively, and that we can all readily respond to: such universal images are particularly useful if your intention is to communicate with your audience, or to manipulate it. However, imaging is usually a very personal activity serving personal ends and we are constantly using our imaginations to bring outer and inner realities into meaningful conjunction. Subject and object meet and fuse in the intermediate world of the imagination.

The images we produce as a result of a creative or re-creative expressive act have significance for us only if they are capable of evoking and organizing feeling: if they actually recall the impulse of which they are the sensuous reciprocal. In Winnicott's words, if they 'reflect it back'. The capacity to do this arises from the common principles upon which sensuous forms and sensate schema are structured. These common principles effect the mobilization of energy in time and space: affective energy mobilized in subjective time and space, corresponding to physical energy mobilized in objective time and space. We use the same concepts and the same language to describe inner feeling states and outer aesthetic structures because they are exactly analogous. The basic principles of energy organization are *attraction* and *repulsion*. These principles are manifested in our structures of feeling and in our feeling forms; it is because they are common to both inner and outer worlds (and, incidentally, to the intermediate world of the imagination) that expressive action is effective as the means of resolving feeling problems. As I have said before, we compose structures in the world 'out there' that exactly reciprocate structures in the world within us, feeling structures that is, affective schema. Schema are patterns, configurations, figures. Through our acts of creative self-expression we seek to embody those inner patterns in figures formed from media. These figures are the images of art.

When attraction and repulsion are equal then we have a state of balance or *stasis*: feeling in equilibrium.

Fig. 5.1

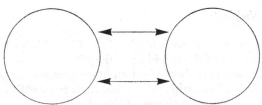

If we substitute the notion of *tendency* for that of stasis then we have structures representative of feeling imbalance (sensate disturbance):

Fig. 5.2

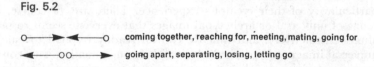

All our feelings are experienced in terms of the above basic percepts or of variants of them; likewise all aesthetic structures. The aesthetic concepts of harmony and discord, similitude and contrast, can be depicted in the same way – indeed they represent transitional schema, movements of feeling, inclinings towards and fleeings from. My point is that it is through expressive representation, through exploring and creating sensuous images, that we convert becoming into being, unknowing into knowing. So we grow in intelligent feeling and educate our 'aesthetic emotion'.

As arts teachers we must do all we can to keep our pupils' imaginations alive and their imaging rich and fruitful. This means constantly exercising their imaginative faculty through personal creative work and by introducing them to the imagery and the image-makers of art – to the 'realized forms' of painters, musicians, dramatists, and writers. But we must be very careful about the art we choose to offer children. The re-creative experience must be within their emotional and aesthetic grasp even if they do need our help in reaching for it. We should try to see that re-creative and creative work are closely linked. And we must see that learning about art takes place within the context of learning through art. Finally, we must always respect the distinction between public and private forms of expression and take care to organize our public performances and exhibitions with this distinction in mind. Failure to do so can prove as publically offensive as it can be privately damaging. Expressive images are potentially powerful medicine. Sharing our finished work with others, through performance and in other ways, is often a natural and spontaneous way of winding up an expressive/creative sequence. It allows celebration and evaluation. However, such sharing must neither be forced, nor, where the demand is legitimate (*it springs from the maker himself*) denied.

The Arts Subjects

It was never any part of my intention in writing this book to provide a detailed account of the teaching of the different arts subjects, still less to suggest how they should be taught or what the content of each syllabus might be. My main purpose has been to establish the expressive principle as the basic theme of the arts curriculum as a whole.

Some of my fellow contributors have interpreted this theme in terms of their own classroom practice, and several of them indicate very clearly how the theme can look when fleshed out as a specific piece of learning. My assessment of the problems confronting arts teachers is not that they have been short of material to teach – short of curriculum stuff. Rather that what has been lacking has been a conceptual principle that would allow co-ordinated and effective action in the realization of their declared ideals. However I do wish to draw attention to what I take to be the distinctive character of each discipline – more to provoke discussion than in the expectation of agreement – and to comment briefly upon what I would take to be possible barriers in the way of the expressive curriculum.

In Gattegno's *Towards a Visual Culture*[1] I came across his original and idiosyncratic definition of music. It struck me as arresting and challenging. I quote it in relation to music – and then use it as a 'formula' for analysing each of the other subjects. I found it an interesting exercise – this attempt to speak plainly and to reduce an elaborate experience to a set of relatively simple concepts. At times I felt that I got rather out of my depth but I recommend the game to anyone who fancies describing his own subject with near mathematical clarity.

Education through Music
This is the passage from Caleb Gattegno.

> The teacher of music is one who knows that the first instrument is in our throat and is directly accessible to the self. On this basis he can give his students access to the music each carries and from there lead them to the awareness of the world of sound both as it can be studied in acoustics and as musicians have made it look. To own music is something else than to know pieces or even how to play an instrument. It is rather, as an example, the awareness that one is a vibrating system capable of resonance, or organizing in different time sequences [expressive] sounds that one can produce through one's pneumatic or muscular actions upon other vibratory systems.

That perhaps does not sound very 'musical' but it is all there (or almost. He fails to mention the word 'expressive' and I have taken the liberty of inserting it). It gives us our general structure and establishes music education as an essentially creative and participatory process. I would want to add, just for emphasis, that in music, as in the other arts, we value process and know-how as well as products and knowledge about products. We are concerned with the making of subjective images using music as our medium – and, of course, with the creative response to realized musical forms. The 'particularity' of the music education in any school will emerge from the skills and predilections of the music staff, the material resources of the school, and the musical needs and abilities and tastes of the children.

[1] Gattegno, Caleb, *Towards a Visual Culture*, Outerbridge and Dienstfrey, 1969.

Any particularity will do (it would be pointless to be specific), provided the conceptual basis (the theme) of the curriculum is sound. There are, however, certain basic conditions and resources essential to education through music, such as space, silence, elementary sound sources and sound-reproductive apparatus and, on occasions, 'listeners'.

Education through Visual Art

The teacher of art is one who knows that the first instrument of visual depiction is the hand, that the first pictures are drawn and the first sculptures carved in 'significant' space. It is basically enactive – even dramatic – in character. Expressive gestures and gesticulation are at the root of visual representation – it is only a short step from ephemeral shapes in the air to more permanent and more sophisticated mark-making on receptive surfaces and modelling in responsive materials. (The enactive turned iconic.) On this basis the art teacher can give his students access to the powers of depiction each carries, and from there lead them to the awareness of the worlds of light and space both as they can be studied in physics and as artists have made them look. To own one's powers of depiction is something else than to know works of art or how to do perspective drawing. It is rather, as an example, the awareness that one is a 'light-receptor system' capable of seeing (interpreting visual information), and of organizing in different spatial dimensions expressive visual phenomena that one can produce through one's muscular actions.

This perhaps does not seem to have all that much to do with visual art but it is all there. It gives us our general structure. Again we would stress that we value process and know-how as well as products and knowledge about products. We are concerned with the making of subjective images using two-dimensional and three-dimensional art as our medium – and, of course, with the creative response to realized visual forms. The 'particularity' of the art education in any school will emerge from the skills and predilections of the art staff, the material resources of the school, and the depictive needs, abilities and tastes of the children. Any particularity will do (it would be pointless to be specific), provided the conceptual basis (the theme) of the curriculum is sound. There are, however, certain basic conditions and resources essential to education through art, such as space, light, shade, surfaces to work on, materials and tools to work with and light projective apparatus.

As with the Visual Arts, Gattegno's passage can be adapted to each artistic discipline in turn: I continue the exercise just for the hell of it.

Education through Drama

The teacher of drama is one who knows that we behave dramatically when we simulate action for another, and that this is a universal behavioural faculty innate in everyone. We are all actors. We all make dramatic use of ourselves to represent our experience to others: the dramatic instrument is ourself. Drama is enactment pure and simple. (Like dance, however, it also acquires a depictive character in performance.) On this basis the teacher can give his students access to the drama each carries within him (in their sense of themselves as actors mediating the drama that is their own lives). And from there he may lead them to the awareness of the world of human protagonism both as it can be studied sociologically, psychologically and historically, and as dramatists and actors have made it look. To own drama is something else than to know plays or even how to act in a play or direct a production. It is rather, as an example, the awareness that one is a mimetic system, capable of causing others to suspend disbelief, and projecting and entering simulations of actuality, of organizing oneself in different time-sequences and spatial configurations as a human being enacting for others. Drama implies 'performance', actual or imagined.

This perhaps does not seem to have all that much to do with drama but it is all there. It gives us our general structure. Again I would stress that we value process and know-how as well as products, and knowledge about products. We are concerned with the making of subjective images, using drama as our medium, and of course with the creative response to realized dramatic forms. The 'particularity' of the drama education in any school will emerge from the skills and predilections of the drama staff, the material resources of the school, and the dramatic needs, abilities and tastes of the children. Any particularity will do (it would be pointless to be specific), provided the conceptual basis (the theme) of the curriculum is sound. There are, however, certain basic conditions and resources essential to education through drama – enacting human beings, space, light, a surface to move on, silence, and, invariably, audiences.

Education through Dance
The teacher of dance is one who knows that a dancer feels the body moving, and that dancing is directly accessible to the self. It is essentially enactive, though in performance it is also depictive. On this basis he can give his students access to the dancing each carries and from there lead them on to awareness of the world of human movement as it can be studied in physiology, and as dancers have made it look. To own dance is something else than to know dances or even how to perform in a certain dance style. It is rather, as an example, the awareness that one is an articulated system capable of movement, of organizing in different time-sequences and spatial configurations expressive movements that one can produce through muscular actions in response to feeling impulse.

This gives us our general structure. Again I would stress that we value process and know-how as well as products and knowledge about products. We are concerned with the making of subjective images using dance as our medium, and, of course, with the creative response to realized dance forms. The 'particularity' of the dance education in any school will emerge from the skills and predilections of the dance staff, the material resources of the school, and the dance needs, abilities and tastes of the children. Any particularity will do, provided the conceptual basis of the curriculum is sound. There are, however, certain basic conditions and resources essential to education through dance – a moving human body (bodies), space to move and a surface to move on, light and silence.

Education through Creative English (The Art of Words)
The teacher of the art of words is one who knows that words are icons (sensuous forms) and not just discursive labels – that the word can be made flesh. On this basis he can give his students access to the 'figuring in speech', each carries, and from there lead them to the awareness of the world of words both as the study of language behaviour, and as poets and story-tellers have made words look. To own expressive language is something else than to know poems or novels or even how to write blank verse or how to organize a plot. It is rather, as an example, the awareness that one is 'a vibrating system capable of resonances' and a symboling system capable of 'figuring in speech'; of organizing in different time-sequences, spatial and temporal configurations, expressive words that one can call to mind, symbolically represent or utter through one's 'pneumatic and muscular actions'!

This gives us our general structure. Again I would stress that we value process and know-how as much as products and knowledge about products. We are concerned with the making of subjective images using spoken and written English as our medium – and of course, with the creative response to realized verbal forms. The 'particularity' of creative English in any school will emerge from the skills and predilections of the English staff, the material resources of the school, and the verbal needs, abilities and tastes of the children. Any particularity will do, provided the conceptual basis is sound. There are however certain basic conditions and resources essential to education through English – an instrument to write with, a surface to write on, space, light, and silence. Spoken and written words. (Eliot's 'shabby equipment').

The creative use of English merits a further comment. I certainly feel that enthusiasm for creative English has tended rather to out-strip understanding, and the general failure of English teachers to convert their academic subject into one perceived by the pupils as creative (see my Schools Council Working Paper) testifies, I believe, to a widespread failure in the teaching of the expressive use of words. Creative writing often amounts to little more than inviting children to write about themselves – it might be better called 'personal' writing.

The creative and expressive use of words means image-making in words – it means 'figuring in speech'. The old sciences of rhetoric and prosody attempted to deal with this side of language use – as the laws of grammar and logic governed the impressive use of language. We would not wish to go back to teaching the rule-directed use of words (whether for expressive or impressive purposes) any more than we would wish to see rule-direction governing the expressive use of other media. As with art, music, dance and drama the expressive use of words, written or spoken, must have impulse at its centre, and the first thing our creative writers, readers, talkers and listeners need to be able to do is to distinguish verbal forms that are impulse-centred from those that are merely empty forms, shams and fakes; to distinguish between passion and bombast, eloquence and salesmanship, charm and speciousness. Then we need to revive an interest in, and nurture an understanding of, the way the medium works – in its six modes – and of the concepts and craftsmanship involved in mastering the expressive use of words. We need to teach children to hear the sound of language and to test verbal rhythms on the ear. Language uses many of the structural devices we have discussed elsewhere in this book, creating feeling forms through simile and metaphor, allegory and parable, antithesis, anticlimax, chiasmus, hyperbole, oxymoron and so on. Language has its own forms, suggesting spatial and temporal relationships; above all it has flow, motion, rhythm. 'The best words in the best order' catches the unique aesthetic experience we seek through language – sense and sensibility fused. English teachers need to revive their concern with form: subject-reflexive form.

Present studies of English-language development, and of language in education, place too much emphasis upon the study of impressive public forms and too little on the expressive and creative ways we talk and write. The creative aspects of English, including the recreative response to literature, will continue in the doldrums until this whole field is opened up through study by the teacher and research by the scientist. For the moment, creative English goes the way of many other recent 'right' moves in education – launched upon a wave of totally proper enthusiasm but foundering for lack of the essential quality of understanding needed to power it. I feel we have to get expressive English right if we are to educate children's representational use of words.

*   *   *

The differences between the arts subjects are as important as their similarities because between them they offer a *range of expressive outlets*, each making demands and affording opportunities that are unique and quite specific. One may not substitute for another. They are distinguished not merely by the technical demands or sensuous character of the medium, but also by the nature of the imaging and expressive action that each demands. Enactive improvisation, for example, is more publicly demanding than iconic improvisation (acting is more public than drawing). Musical composition can be more private and more personal than, say, improvising a group dance. Some of the arts (notably writing and musical composition) have become very abstract; others (like clay modelling and dancing) remain very direct, sensuous, and immediate. The arts curriculum needs all five traditional subjects as outlets, and subject specialists need to be aware both of the links between their own subjects and the other creative arts, and of the uniqueness of each of them, when they are considering matching their pupils with creative opportunities appropriate to their temperaments and the needs of the moment. It must be obvious that there are enormous advantages to be had from an organization that allows full and free contact and movement between these essentially related elements of what has to be one curricular department: the Creative Arts department.

Designing the Arts Syllabus

When, as teachers, we settle down to think about what we shall be doing with the pupils we have taken on, our thinking will be influenced by several factors:

(i) an individual child's current level of expressive functioning;
(ii) the educational 'climate' and the resources available to support our teaching (i.e. personnel, buildings, materials, equipment, attitudes, relationships and so forth);
(iii) our estimate of the child's expressive potential;
(iv) our own, the school's, and society's sense of the extent to which development of that potential would be valuable.

Four factors – all absolutely critical to the way we elaborate and realize the curriculum as action: more particularly as teacher-pupil interaction. In the next chapter I examine this matter in detail. What I would do at this point is simply to suggest that the arts curriculum be built outward from an understanding of the child and an assessment of where, in expressive terms, he or she is at any given time. Such a view will have significance for curriculum action because it posits each child-teacher encounter as the basic organizational unit. That means 'thinking in individuals' and not in year groups, bands, sets, classes or whatever. This is of course not to say we can no longer usefully work in groups and with groups – indeed where group impulse is the essence of the work (as it frequently is in drama, dance and music for instance) it would clearly be nonsense not to do so. But there is an obvious difference between the decision to work in groups, taken specifically in relation to the nature of the medium to be worked, and similar decisions that have nothing to do with the medium, possibly nothing to do with the arts but are organizational arrangements of more general convenience, meeting quite different criteria. As things are, teachers of the arts are unlikely to be granted many concessions in this matter. However, I hope to be able to show that there is a good deal they can do nevertheless to correct present organizational follies.

'Thinking in individuals' also means that we have to abandon the idea of subject-based year goals – of a syllabus that places batik, lino cuts and introduction to colour in Year 1; 3D and silk screen printing in Year 2; plastics, pop art and Chinese calligraphy in Year 3; etc. We are really very unwise when we make decisions about curriculum content on the grounds either of some generalized notion of personal development (psychological and physiological) from year to year, or of the benefit of everyone's having a go at everything at some point in say the first three years. It seems to me we are certainly deluding ourselves if we are planning on the basis of fine developmental steps, negotiated more or less simultaneously by everyone in the class. We need, rather, a very broad set of categories within which to 'place' the children individually (e.g. pre-adolescent, adolescent and young adult) with some fairly clear notions about people's expressive behaviour and expressive needs in relation to these phases (remembering of course that there will be major differences between the sexes and much individual variation anyway). Such general categories might help us to establish the broad lines of our approach to teaching individual children; at least they will help us with our opening shots at initial engagement. And as for everyone having a go at everything, in the first place such a mechanized idea is bound to mean a lot of children having to work with materials and in ways that are at best unproductive and at worst deeply inhibiting, and in the second place it suggests that arts education is about skills, techniques and sampling as distinct from the deep absorption with possibly recurring feeling impulses in media that the individual finds evocative and appropriate, and in respect of which he is prepared to work hard to develop a high level of expertise.

Such a curriculum, built upon individual impulse, must evolve organically. The likelihood is that a detailed account of curriculum action could only be rendered in retrospect. Decisions would have to be taken largely in process, on the job. At the back of such a teacher's mind would be the considerations that we have been discussing: at the moment, when he pauses for reflection, he mostly hears only the examination chariot hurrying near. He would need an outline plan for each particular encounter with a pupil or group, a plan based on an assessment of where things were left last time and of the most likely line of development. However, this plan would have to be an extremely flexible one that would allow the teacher to take account of the unexpected – the current attitude or mood of the child or the group, a particular opportunity or problem that might arise. The syllabus would then take shape as 'case notes', compiled after the event. This way no two classes would ever be alike in form of work, though there would of course be an underlying conceptual similarity. Between the outline curriculum that I have proposed and the particularity of each classroom encounter would be an intermediate syllabus or list of specific goals under each of the four major headings we have been considering. Essentially we need an individual syllabus for each child – built in action and documented for future reference. Each arts department, however, needs an agreed underlying conception of the curriculum that will engage the expressive needs of the children. There is of course a price to pay for such spontaneity: the apparent difficulties of management and organization, to say nothing of the teacher's work load, become nightmarish to contemplate. In practice, however, they prove much less enervating than more traditional methods. I feel that operating along these lines would demand a reappraisal by all concerned of what would count as basic and absolutely essential requirements for their subject. We could not afford to be distracted by frills and fads and the sampler style of curriculum thinking to which the arts have been so much prey in recent years. For instance we might feel that people in an open space was about all we really needed for drama and people in a remote place all we really needed for music.

These are issues we shall consider again. For the moment I simply wish to advance some general principles. In practice we shall be concerned with the achievement of acceptable compromises between conflicting claims for time, attention, space and resources. But we need to establish the basic principles that will guide our thinking and help us arrive at informed decisions concerning the nature and management of the arts curriculum that we can defend on educational grounds:

1. The basic educational unit in the arts is the individual pupil-teacher encounter.
2. The long-term aim of the arts curriculum is to further the healthy emotional development of the child by encouraging creative self-expression.
3. Our specific objective is a child's mastery of the means of expressive representation: effectiveness as a maker and user of imaginative symbols.
4. The elements of the arts curriculum are these:
     (i) sensation and sensuous experience itself;
    (ii) understanding presentational and representational media;
   (iii) craft skills that allow the control of media relative to impulse;
   (iv) imaging (and use of realized forms).
5. The children we encounter will be passing through different developmental stages – affective, cognitive and psycho-motor. We need to understand these processes in general terms, be able

to 'place' individual children in respect of their own development and support the progressive realization of their potential – particularly their potential for a full and responsible emotional life.

The arts curriculum looks like this:

ig. 5.3

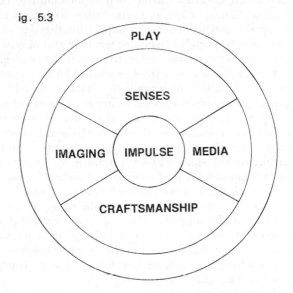

That is the essence of the arts curriculum whether we wish the arts to work separately or together. Sensation, media, craftsmanship and the transcendent power of imagery; impulsive activities protected by their essential playfulness. The above diagram includes all the elements essential to a curriculum in the arts. It matters not whether we see ourselves as members of a department or of a group of departments. It matters not whether we teach art or music or drama or whatever. If our aim is to enable children to use representational media expressively in the production of subjective symbols, then we shall need to give equal consideration to each of these elements.

We improvise: variations on the theme of personal creativity. We make broad distinctions between the expressive needs of pre-adolescents and adolescent pupils. We await the research results that will help us make the syllabus more child-based rather than subject-based. And we do not mean children's 'interests' – rather a conception of children's emotional and imaginative development. In Chapter 14 I offer a line of thought on syllabus making. But it needs another book.

The Creative Arts Department

We teach our pupils the process of creative self-expression using the different arts as educational media: hence our claim to education through (rather than in or for) the arts. Every arts teacher is first a teacher, using the arts to develop a pupil's intelligence of feeling: that means that arts specialists who are teachers and also musicians, painters, dancers, writers, recognize that their first allegiance as educationists is to the arts as a whole rather than to one particular art. *An arts teacher specializes in arts education.* That he should also be a practising musician, painter, dancer, writer is a significant qualification for the job – it is by no means the only, or even the most important one. His specialism is education. His skill is teaching. His relation with a pupil is not that of master craftsman to apprentice. He will certainly teach skills and set standards by his own example but the educational process is of overriding concern for him.

It is not only helpful, it is essential, that every arts teacher should grasp the creative process in art and should have at least a basic understanding of and feeling for each of the major artistic disciplines. His own expertise as an artist, specializing in one particular medium, will find its expression within this overarching idea: he is an *arts teacher* – no longer simply or merely a teacher of art, music, dance, drama or English.

With us the process is the product. Given agreement on this point, we find no irremovable bar to collaboration, and indeed wish to be regarded as a teaching team, bound together by a clear understanding of the purpose of arts education and our role as arts teachers. This does not mean that we must invariably work together on the same educational projects or in the same room. Of course there are many occasions when we need to and must be able to. What it does mean is that even when working very much as a single art specialist, we are aware that we belong to a teaching team devoted to making arts education a vital force in the lives of our pupils and the life of our school. We are conscious of and committed to our colleagues.

The arts department logically comprises only those teachers working in the following disciplines who subscribe to this conception of 'education through the arts'. (Those doing so will differ from school to school – the basis of the department will be this shared conception. Many other factors are relevant but only this one is absolutely essential.)

Visual Arts (2 and 3D work) and including film, photography and visual mass media

Drama

Music and Dance – including aural mass media

Creative English (The Art of Words) – including verbal mass media

In many schools Drama and Film are tied to English teaching, and Dance to P.E. In terms of the logic of the arts curriculum these arrangements are illogical.

The Creative Arts Teacher

I wrote earlier of the idea of the 'good enough' teacher. This is rather a clumsy phrase but it is not intended grudgingly or condescendingly. Winnicott uses it when he writes about mothering (and, by implication, fathering) and, when I first came upon his use of it, I found the phrase profoundly consoling! He was writing especially about the vital importance of the mother's role in fostering the child's capacity for play, and he suggested that we should drop all notions of absolute motherhood, of the quintessential or perfect mother, and seek out those fundamental qualities and capabilities which, if present in the mother, should guarantee that the mothering would be good enough to support the spontaneous development of the child, establishing a viable basis for personal stability and maturation. Winnicott also incidentally seemed to be suggesting that it really was not so very difficult to be 'good enough' for the purpose. Most mothers seemingly have a great deal going for them – and, presumably, most fathers too.

Rather than setting up a model for the teacher that would immediately rule most of us out, I prefer to uncover the bare bones in good-enough teaching – and then to accept that good-enough teachers come in all shapes and sizes, and are to be found amongst most if not actually all conditions of men and women: men and women who feel that they teach best when they are most themselves, most at home with themselves, who feel no disjunction between the person they feel themselves to be and the person they offer or present to their pupils. Maybe already this is a tall order – perhaps we have to qualify the idea by saying that such people, while perhaps reserving or holding something of themselves back, are still able to offer a personality capable of an honest relationship, and what is offered is felt by the pupil and the teacher himself to be true, real, authentic. I don't think we should expect arts teachers to be better than the next man; however, if they are to be good enough for their work, they must be authentic. Fakes and phoneys will not do. There must be neither low cunning nor high conning. You have to be prepared to let the kids into what you are doing – and sometimes into how you feel.

Picking about among the bare bones, we come up against this notion of authenticity. I think there is a further essential qualification. We cannot be expected to 'love' all the children we teach – we probably find children on the whole likeable (otherwise we must be mad or will soon become so) but we might reasonably find caring deeply for them all rather difficult. It does seem to me, however, that

the essential teacher (the good-enough teacher) cares passionately
for the child's potential knowing. It is hard for me to put clearly
what I mean into words. It has nothing to do with putting an arm
round a sad, or an attractive child. It has nothing to do with concern
for their dental health or home circumstances or particular
emotional problems – with their scholarly or aesthetic achievement as
such. It has to do with a sense of every child's potential for independence, for self-control, for the full realization of his or her powers, and
a recognition of the innate (perhaps thoroughly inhibited) *desire* to
learn. If teaching is a passion, then the passion arises in the meeting
of the pupil's desire to be and the teacher's desire that the child be
so. The good enough teacher loves the child enough to help the
child become freer: this is the teacher's devotion.

Authenticity and devotion then, in the sense that I have defined
them and for the purposes I have set out. Authenticity so that a truly
nurturant relationship may occur between pupil and teacher.
Devotion so that the child may become freer. Not free. Nobody is
ever free. But we can become freer, 'free enough'.

Now it goes without saying that some activities subsumed by the
term, teacher, may not demand either authenticity or devotion. I
will not bother to go into that, except to say we can teach children
about springtime as the sergeant major taught the 1914–18 soldier
how to 'ease springs' – pressure is all. But to be an arts teacher, *to set
out to help children express themselves creatively*, you must be authentic in
your relationship with them, and you must be devoted to their
wanting to become persons. Nothing less would be good enough –
and perhaps it is a bit of a tall order. I do not see a way round
it; I just take comfort in the fact that most of us have a lot going
for us.

Let us pursue this idea of being good enough for one's pupils a
little further. Perhaps we can be more precise about these bare
essentials. If we look at our models of the creative–expressive process
and of the arts curriculum we would have to say I suppose:

(i) The good-enough teacher knows the creative process at first
hand, so can speak with authority and understanding from
personal experience, and he will know when to speak and
when to be silent. (Many teachers have an intuitive grasp of
the process.)

(ii) The good-enough teacher keeps his own senses pretty sharp,
loves and understands his chosen medium, is a fairly skilful
(even though limited) craftsman, and leads a reasonably
healthy imaginative life. So he will be able to give good and
timely instruction and set a useful example.

But this may not be quite all. Our earliest consideration of the
pressures associated with the creative process would seem to suggest
that the teacher must be able to give the pupil dutch courage when

his spirit flags and his nerve fails. Must be able to 'cover' embarrassment and contain frustration. Must be able to 'hold' the pupil emotionally when the going is hard – not offering ways out so much as encouraging and rewarding perseverance and tenacity. It may simply mean being a good companion in the dark, lonely times when nothing will go right. You can't be good enough for any child for whom you are not prepared to do that. Someone else might do it instead – fortunately there are always the other kids to help out. We can turn to the group when our own resources fail us.

Play is such an important part of the creative process. I have already referred to the importance Winnicott attaches to the mother's role in fostering the child's spontaneous playing (and so laying the foundation of the whole of its cultural experience). He goes on to write about the relationship between client and therapist and makes the point that therapy occurs in the overlap between the play of the one and the play of the other. There can be no therapy without playing on both sides. This seems to me to apply also to arts education. Unless the teacher can play and until the pupil can play there can be no learning, no new knowing, no growing. So the teacher must be able to play – and play with the pupil. That is to say to enjoy doodling, formless functioning in the medium – dangling the line here and there until one of Klee's magic fish suddenly bites beneath the surface and the line takes us for a walk instead. We are hooked. The good-enough teacher is a playful child still – and knows the 'intimate' character of play, the rules of the game, and can be trusted as a playmate. Such a mate is still respected (children do not usually abuse adults who play with them provided they play properly) – here lies the basis for the partnership that I feel must in the end characterize the pupil-and-teacher relationship. Neither knows best. Each needs the other. They have to develop a true interdependence. Mutuality.

To recap: authenticity, devotion, playfulness, mutuality, knowing useful things, and setting a good example, these things more or less make you 'good enough'. Given these bare bones, evaluation becomes an acceptable kind of stock-taking between partners.

My list could go on and on but then it would not be the bare bones any more but rather some kind of idealization of the arts teacher. I think I have covered the real essentials. Given these resources, a reasonable job can be made of arts teaching; you do not *have* to be good at curriculum design and management, 'aware' of the other arts, expert at transactional analysis, communication theory and group dynamics. These skills might help, as would such personal traits as being lovable, wealthy, energetic, intelligent, attractive, sociable, reliable, clean, sexy, etc. But they matter less (thank God). I have always maintained that arts education is in the mess it is because arts teachers are not really confident about what they are doing. And I would not be writing all this if I did not still believe there were some truth in it. 'Knowing useful things' (like what creativity actually means), and being in a position to set a good example (not necessarily as a conventional social being but at least as an artist and craftsman) *are* important and I have said so. But where arts teachers have perhaps fallen down is in lacking the confidence to stand by the best in themselves and their work, and to assert that they really do know what is best for the burgeoning creative spirit.

Of course the harsh realities are a good deal harsher than I have been. The good enough teacher has to satisfy or modify the expectations of colleagues, head teachers, parents, school governors, union bosses, and society at small and at large. We all know too well what all that means – and since I am neither writing an encyclopaedia nor a survival manual I do not feel I need go into it. If you cannot meet those expectations, or bring about some reformation of them, you won't want to be in business long anyway. So you do what you can.

But all that has nothing, absolutely nothing to do with being 'good enough' to teach the arts to children. And the trouble is that many arts teachers have forfeited their claim to arts teaching because they have betrayed, somewhere along the line, the very qualities in themselves which they absolutely could not manage without. It is not that we did not have a lot going for us: it is what we have done with what we had. All those innocuous surrenders of the spirit; all those intimate and irredeemable capitulations.

6 The Creative Process in Arts Education

Painting is a bitter struggle, terrifying, pitiless, unseen: a duel between the artist and himself. The struggle goes on inside, hidden on the surface; if the artist tells, he is betraying himself!

LE CORBUSIER, *My Work*

Recap

To teach subject-reflexive action through the arts you need:

(a) to have a clear conceptual grasp of what you are doing and why you are doing it – and be able to speak and write about it for yourself and for others. (This might entail having to learn the basic 'language' needed to think and communicate with.)
(b) to participate appropriately (and so, effectively) in the pupil's expressive acts.

So far we have been concentrating for the most part on the questions 'what' and 'why': I now want to move on to a consideration of the question 'how', but still at the general conceptual level. We need a model of our participatory action as well as of the curriculum itself and it is to the devising of this model that we must now turn. We will take as our point of departure the description of the creative process that we discussed earlier, by which feeling becomes form. I suggested that we should conceive of that process as involving interaction between impulse and medium. Gradually a form emerges from such interaction that resolves the feeling impulse, and which may be used to reach it. Each subject-reflexive action in the medium would, hopefully, refine the representational form until the maker felt either that he had achieved a satisfactory reciprocal of the impulse, or that, for one reason or another, no further refinement were possible and the action should be stopped. I will repeat the diagram in stages:

1. The expressive impulse is aroused and the tension built up seeking a means or medium of expression. (We will go into how it is aroused later.)

Fig. 6.1

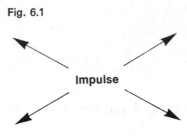

Impulse

2. The medium is presented and the energy of the impulse projected through it.

Fig. 6.2

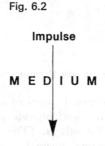

Impulse

M E D I U M

3. The medium resists the impulse and reciprocates it and we are aware of this reciprocal interaction as we test the suitability of the medium to our expressive purpose.

Fig. 6.3

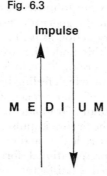

Impulse

M E D I U M

4. If we are to have any hope of achieving a satisfactory resolution we must be successful in 'centring' the impulse in the medium –

much as the potter centres the clay on the wheel in order to harness the energy of the centrifugal 'impulse'.

Fig. 6.4

Impulse

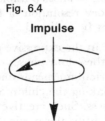

5. Once the impulse has been centred in the medium then the process of resolution really gets under way, and by a series of refinements the medium assumes a representational form that as nearly as possible reciprocates the impulse. *Provided the impulse has been properly centred in the first place, the only bars to a satisfactory resolution will be some inadequacy in the medium or problems arising from a lack of medium control on the maker's part.*

Fig. 6.5

Impulse

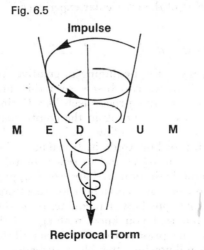

M   E   D   I   U   M

Reciprocal Form

If we accept that this, or something very like it, is what happens when we express ourselves creatively, when we create sensuous forms that constitute personal images, then this is the process at the heart of our expressive arts curriculum and, if we are to teach personal expression through the arts, this is the process in our pupils that we have to engage with and participate in as teachers. Looking at this process our programme of participation would seem to involve the following considerations:

   (i) seeing that the pupil is expressively motivated – has an expressive impulse;

(ii) selecting a suitable medium or suitable media;

(iii) helping the pupil centre the impulse in the medium;

(iv) cquipping the pupil, as far as possible, to control the medium so that a satisfactory resolution of the impulse in representational form might be achieved.

Curriculum management in the expressive arts means being able to participate effectively in these four phases of the creative process.

Managing the arts curriculum means understanding the creative process in the arts and making the children skilful and confident in the handling of that process. Such creative skills may be 'taught' if the teacher is able to identify the particular learning need of the moment. The creative process as I have outlined it involves a number of related events, and, as arts teachers we must be able to assist the pupil at each point: that is to say in achieving an adequate level of expressive motivation, in centring the impulse in an appropriate expressive medium, and in bringing the feeling 'problem' to a satisfactory resolution. Arts teachers must know when to concentrate on the senses, when on media, craftsmanship and imaging – especially how to ensure that feeling animates every action and remains at the heart of the curricular experience.

Emotion Recollected

What is beginning – the beginning of creative work in art or any other field? Perhaps we can best answer this question if we think what beginning a creative process feels like. Facing the empty page or the blank canvas – standing in the empty space or being silent amidst the silence. Simply feeling you have something to do and not knowing what it is or how to do it. If you are being asked simply to recall something you know and to repeat or rehearse, recreate it, there will be some hesitation perhaps, some apprehension lest your memory fail you or your capacities for repetition, rehearsal, and reproduction prove somehow inadequate. If, on the other hand, you know nothing but that you know nothing – if the form you seek exists nowhere, since prior to the creative act all that you have to go on is your own unknowing, the felt disturbance, the simple recognition that you have a problem but not being able to define it – how great is the apprehension, how much more virulent the inhibition.

We move blind into subject-reflexive action. The expressive impulse is blind. It seeks itself in the medium – its sensuous reciprocal that is – and it will not know itself until the reciprocal has been found. (It is the experience most of us have had at one time or another when we suddenly catch ourselves realizing what it was we wanted to say only when we have actually said it.) To make such a move – to commit our formless unknowing to the formless medium trusting in processes which we can at best only partially control and, hence, with no guarantee of landfall at the end of the journey – demands courage and faith. It is perhaps just as well that when courage and faith fail we have necessity to prick us on. We run the risk of finding ourselves no better off, no further forward. That we frequently embark in fear and trembling, and launch into the cloud of our own unknowing more in desperation than hope, only serves to emphasize the positive character of such action – creative because it means surrendering what we know for what we might know, what we are sure of for what we can only guess at, what we are for what we might become. Forming. Seeking new forms, new meanings. Creative self-expression makes great demands upon us simply by virtue of its essential creative character. The chances are that the moment of insight will come unexpectedly and by an obscure and tortuous route – such moments do not occur simply because you work hard, try hard, apply yourself. There is no justice about it!

The stress of creative self-expression is increased because the knowing sought is subject-knowing, self-knowledge – the resolution of emotional 'problems'. Expression always involves some element of self-exposure – and self-exposure when in the throes of creative exploration can be a very special form of torture. Most people will know the tension and perplexity that attend the kind of experience I am describing here. You do not have to have been trying to create a work of art to have felt it. When we transfer this experience from the privacy of the study, the studio or the home, to the secondary-school classroom it is not difficult to see the tensions in the task facing the teacher who is looking to begin creative self-expression.

Expressive impulse provides the essential drive of the arts curriculum – without the expressive impulse there can be no expressive action. The chances are that should you actually stimulate the 'real' emotions of the class in response to some environmental event, and then invite them to express them, the children will try to defuse the situation somehow. Perhaps by inhibiting their feelings or by faking their response, reaching for a hand-me-down solution, a cliché, as an alternative to responding 'for real'. The tension of the situation might be felt to be so great that only violent discharge or avoidance are possible. What we really need to arouse an expressive impulse is an act of reflection or recollection. We get the class to act upon *the recollection of a previous emotional experience* rather than to experience a real emotion in the here and now. The pressure of actual feeling usually rules out all possibility of reflection – or tends to do so. So we prefer to work with impulses as 'recalled feeling events' rather than as fresh disturbances – something that will further distinguish our work from that of the therapist. When we stimulate expressive action it will be a licensed or protected experience – marked off from reality and encompassed within the spirit of play. So we say to our pupils, 'Let's imagine what it would feel like to . . . let's remember what it felt like when. . . .' We will get them to draw upon 'emotion recollected in tranquillity' – and to accept a degree of allowed disturbance for the sake of the expressive work we wish to do together. Some teachers, as I have said already, prefer to duck the idea of working with feeling, but this is not the way. Those who see personal expression as the key goal of arts education will be very wary of overexciting children and will look for subtle (sometimes indirect) ways of stirring feelings that will serve as an expressive impulse.

Occasionally there may be special circumstances that justify the eliciting of a reactive response (tears, pandemonium, violence) but only when there seems no other way forward: when we sense the need to shift the 'block', whatever it may be, that lies across our path. But we are concerned with growth, with knowing, and that is achieved by creative rather than reactive means. I worked for some years on a summer drama school for American high-school students and I came eventually to accept that some 'reaction' was unavoidable at the outset of the course. No matter how mild the stimulus, for the first couple of sessions or so there were always shrieks and tears. I suppose it had to do with the long journey, and being away from home (many for the first time) and the generally 'high' feeling which was simply in the way of any other response. Once the reactive responses were out of the way the 'real' work could begin.

Some classes, individuals from time to time, may well need to blow their tops before any subtle and genuinely creative growth-point can be found. Or it might just be that the feeling element of the work has to be left to one side for the time being and 'recovered' through a more objective, technical, or severely practical approach so as to allow actual feeling (arousal) levels to drop. However these are exceptions to our rule, which is to evoke the shadows rather than the substance of the feeling world to prime the expressive act.

Beginning creative self-expression with a class, the teacher must beware of arousing emotional responses that are actually disquieting, and must be prepared to cover the strains of creativity itself: fear of failure, loss of face and personal disorientation. However there is no dodging the beginning, even though you approach it by the most subtle, most tortuous routes, and a teacher needs patience and confidence to help get things started. The process, once underway, has its own strains but we shall come to them later.

Apart from taking the obvious step of keeping felt tension, vulnerability and the sense of personal exposure within tolerable levels by deliberately regulating both the strength of the expressive stimulus and severity of the creative task, we simply *have* to 'think in individuals' here. We shall probably need to provide quite extensive cover or protection for the child during these highly sensitive moments, whenever they occur. This, I suspect, is again something we do instinctively. If we think of little children playing: most of us are aware how being stared at spoils their games, and how totally disturbing can be the attention of someone 'outside' the game. We

still feel the same way when our adult play is observed in this detached and uncommitted way.

Play is a special, 'licensed' form of activity (it belongs to Maslow's
B type activities) and is 'protected' from reality by a tacit understanding among players and non-players that it is a valid world
apart. All play, all games viewed in terms of the 'real' world, are
kinds of nonsense. They are only games. Mere foolishness. Folly. Yet
they are significant enough for all that, and we know (from Piaget
and others) something of the adaptive significance of play. Creative
self-expression is a similarly 'protected' area of experience; we feel
(or should feel) a natural reticence in the presence of another's
expressive actions. We are usually very considerate and tactful in our
comments on them, often feeling strongly impelled to support and
give encouragement. To be accepting and open. We know somehow
that we are in the presence of something fragile and that the maker is
very vulnerable in respect of what is in the making and what has
been made. The situation is infinitely more acute in the process – we
frequently avert our eyes from the expressive behaviour of others,
not just because their momentary loss of face, self-surrendered, is
somehow threatening to us (we no longer know quite where they are)
but because we do not want to put them off, spoil something for
them. The initial phases of the expressive process are highly sensitive
moments, and the least increase of disturbance or tension may be
sufficient to jeopardize the whole endeavour. Things are very different later on. When the impulse has been centred and we have the bit
between our teeth there is often no stopping us – but at the beginning
it is literally touch and go – 'Touch me and I let it go'. It is very
much up to the teacher to beware of this, and of course for the class as
a whole to be aware of the problem in themselves and for others.
Hopefully, if we are really 'thinking in individuals', we will not have
thirty people all beginning at the same time.

Beginning expressive work often means providing emotional
cover – even actual physical cover. Privacy. Not always in the same
degree for everyone but usually to some extent for most people. A
protective circle must be drawn about these first, tender steps
towards expressive form – such as we draw around ourselves and
around children playing. *I may actually have to begin the playing myself –
and to draw the pupil in to join me.* Cover, privacy, may not be enough.
These 'moments of beginning' may very well be experienced by
some children as very daunting, even depressing when nothing
appears to be going right. Again, we can probably all think of
children with the grumps, restless and disagreeable, immediately
prior to a period of deep engagement. It is as if they knew that they
were going to have to let themselves go but were resisting it to the
bitter end. It is also symptomatic of 'unknowing'. Then, in the
initial period of disorientation (when we let go of self, where are we
after all?), come the panic and the accusations – 'I told you I

couldn't do it!' or 'I still don't know what to do!' – and the demands
for instant rescue from all this insecurity and loss of face. Again, the
sensitive teacher will try to see that the child does not take on too
much, and will provide some structure as well as cover for as long as
this seems necessary. The child must be kept afloat long enough to
get the courage and conviction necessary to swim alone. For it is lone
swimming we are talking about, and when you first fall in, the water
is very cold. Lacking courage of their own they will certainly need to
draw upon ours. They will need our example and companionship.
We know this because we have felt it too.

The teacher is a match-maker (as in prize fighting), pitting the
child against himself (not against other children). This element of
self-contest seems another essential feature of creative action. In the
expressive curriculum the action is self-expressive and the prize at
the end of the contest is self-discovery. And new Being – or quality of
Being – in the world.

So much then for the general problems we are certain to encounter
from time to time whenever we ask children to risk themselves in
exploratory, creative situations – problems by no means experienced
only by teachers of the arts. It does not matter whether we are
introducing a new medium, teaching a new skill, trying to bring
about an appreciation of a new piece of music, a new picture or
poem: to the extent that we are demanding a restructuring of the
familiar in response to an encounter with the unfamiliar, we threaten
a child's equilibrium, and we can expect resistance and reaction.
When, in such circumstances, we also require representational action
of the child (in speech, writing, drawing, instrumental or physical
performance) we can expect such resistance and reaction to be the
more acute.

The Expressive Problem

With the arts, as we have seen, the creative process takes a particular
and discernible form. Our concern now will be to consider the
implications for the arts teacher of this process as *the central activity* of
pupils in the classroom. For that is what is being proposed. We are
suggesting that children in school should be makers of personal
symbols, that their art work should be impulse-directed and that our
task as their teachers is to make them masters of the self-expressive
process in their own right. Our expertise must lie in our grasp of that
process and our capacity to build the appropriate skills in our pupils
– some of which we have already discussed in some detail. Our hope
is that the pupils will become increasingly independent of us as their
understanding of their own creative process deepens and as they
master the instrumental skills that we and our colleagues have to pass
on to them.

Before discussing the teaching of this process I want just to make clear what I mean when I speak of it as 'the central activity of pupils in the classroom'. I mean simply that no matter what our concern might be at any one time – we might quite properly be engaged in activities that are neither directly emotional nor express-ive – we will always be looking for the right moment and the most favourable circumstances to set this central creative process going. A particular child's (or class's) interests, anxieties, lack of skills, may require us to make extensive and protracted excursions, may hold up the purely expressive work for long periods. No matter. Given an understanding of the overall purpose and direction of the arts curriculum as a whole, we will always be in a position to get our bearings, to orientate ourselves, take stock and realign or refocus the work as necessary. We know what our pupils need to be able to do if they are to master the process I have called the central activity of the arts curriculum. I am not, of course, saying that it should be the only activity. Still less do I wish to imply that the arts teacher has to begin each lesson by setting a sensate problem and then move, via holding forms, to a satisfactory resolution in time for the bell! We shall wish to change the emphasis of our work, in response to our sense of a pupil's or a class's needs, from lesson to lesson, week to week, month to month. The arts curriculum involves the acquisition of knowledge and skills of many kinds, and our task as curriculum managers will be to decide what is appropriate when. What I am saying is that the root skill we are concerned with is subject-reflexive action and that we shall always be evaluating our children's work from this point of view. Precisely when we decide to set the process going for a child will be a matter of personal judgement. It seems likely that the older a pupil becomes, the more demanding will the process be; younger children will probably engage in many more creative projects than older ones as a way of building the necessary skills and confidence.

When we speak of teaching the skills of subject-reflexive action what do we mean? And how are they to be learnt? Taking the second question first, the skills will largely be learnt in practice. Children will participate in the creative process itself, repeatedly giving form to feeling and building the necessary know-how in their bones. There is a strong element of intuition involved in the process itself anyway, and learning-by-doing will reinforce this deeper knowing. But we will also talk to them about the process, study its working in the lives of other (perhaps famous) image-makers, examine their own achieve-ments and difficulties conceptually. The head and the mind have their parts to play. Nevertheless mastery of the process of subject-reflexive action will come principally from acting subject-reflexively. As for the skills that have to be learned – they would seem to comprise:

  (i) being able to sense or evoke and respond to a feeling seeking form;
  (ii) being able to formulate that feeling as a problem to be worked through;

(iii) being able to keep the original impulse at the centre of the refining process from which the resolving image will, hopefully, emerge.

We have already said something about the arousing of the expressive impulse – we have looked at the idea of stimulating the expressive response and at some of the problems that sometimes attend such stimulation. We have also seen that the impulse may perfectly well be aroused indirectly, in consequence of work and experience that is not overtly emotional – in particular I have recommended the approach I call 'doodling with the medium'. But we must now look rather more closely at the skill of beginning expressive action that is subject-reflexive for it is not enough simply to arouse a feeling in a child, even if it is a 'feeling seeking form'. The child needs to grasp the imaginative character of the expressive problem he is working on if he is to be able to focus his attention, centre his consciousness upon it and hence to work effectively. He needs to be able to lay hold of the feeling material he is to work with and to find a way of working it. *He needs to comprehend the particular expressive task as an expressive problem: as an image to be realized.*

The ultimate aim of subject-reflexive action is the production of an image – a sensuous form. This sensuous form will have, if it is successful, the power of evoking or recalling the sensate impulse that gave rise to it – it will be able to do so because it 'embodies' that impulse. That is to say, there will be something about its sensuous structure that matches the affective structure of the impulse – it will be an outward and visible symbol of an inward, emotional state. The word *gestalt* is often used to convey this symbolizing power of the sensuous form – its emotional impact or meaning. A sensuous form can only have meaning if it really works as a whole – if it is, somehow, composite, integrated. The *gestalt* of a sensuous form is the emotional impact of its wholeness. In a sense we may say that the problem for the image-maker is to discover which particular sensuous form carries the *gestalt* that most nearly matches the way the expressive impulse feels.

The sensuous form evolves at the end of a problem-solving process – much as we would expect to find a solution emerging from an algebraic equation. We adopt the problem form of the algebraic equation in order to resolve a difficulty – to know the value of a quantity perhaps. *The importance of the 'problem form' is that it provides us with the means of resolving the 'difficulty'.* Until we can arrange the known and unknown elements in accordance with the logic of the particular problem form we have adopted (there is always a risk, of course, that we may have adopted an unsuitable problem form) we have no hope of resolving our difficulty.

Finding a sensuous form with the right *gestalt* is no more a hit or miss affair than resolving a mathematical problem. There is a logic about it, as we have seen already. The solution (sensuous form) emerges from the working out of the problem – in the case of the arts through material or symbolic media used expressively. First, however, the difficulty (the sensate disturbance) has to be set in a form that will permit its resolution – it will not, of course, guarantee it. The feeling seeking form must be expressed as an image. Once we have 'formulated the problem' as distinct from 'sensing the difficulty' we have a procedure for achieving a resolution.[1] 'While a pupil is only aware of the difficulty there can be no hope of a resolution; once the difficulty has been expressed in the form of an image he has a procedure to work with. Converting a feeling into a 'problem form' that will allow its resolution is an *imaginative act* (Coleridge called imagination the 'esemplastic' power: the forming faculty). Sensuous forms (images) are structured aesthetically. To create personal images or icons children need appropriate aesthetic formulae to work with. We select a formula as an hypothesis about the deep structure of the activated (because unassimilated) feeling schema. If the feeling form (icon) resolves the impulse (something we can only determine subjectively sensing our own composure) then our hypothesis was correct.

The problem forms of art are unique to art. The logic of problem-solving in the arts is peculiar to the arts, though we shall be aware of analogies with other representational forms, with mathematical procedures, for example. In the arts we are concerned with the logic of sensuous or qualitative experience; by 'logic' I mean the rules or principles which give sensuous experience its own special meaning. It is not the logic of mathematical or philosophical thought; it is, as we have seen, a logic derived from sensation itself. The arts 'mean' aesthetically: each sensuous form is made up of discrete sensuous elements ordered into a coherent configuration, an aesthetic whole. This ordering is achieved by means of one of a limited number of ordering or structural principles, principles unique to sensuous experience. We have already touched upon them earlier. The simplest forms are contrasts and semblances; we sense that one sensate element is related to another because it stands against or contradicts it, another pair or set of elements are related by the way they complement or resemble each other. It is the perception of contrast or semblance that binds them into a whole and that forms the basis of the form's *gestalt*. These two basic principles have been elaborated by Witkin (*The Intelligence of Feeling* pp. 178–79) to make up a total of eight categories: contrast, semblance, discord, harmony, polarity, identity, dialectic, synthesis. He suggests that the first four are characteristic of the sensate ordering of pre-adolescent children and the second four of mature or higher level ordering. These principles of aesthetic structuring are the problem forms of the arts. When we

[1] An important book on problem finding in the arts has appeared since this chapter was written. The reader is strongly recommended to look at *The Creative Vision* by Jacob W. Getzels and Mihaly Csikszentmihalyi, Wiley, 1976.

wish to translate feeling into form they provide us with the means o
ordering sensate experience – they are at once the logic inherent in
the structure of sensuous form and the logic of sensate experience
itself. Feeling and form share the same deep structures: these deep
structural principles give us our expressive formulae.

When we have aroused, or sensed within us, an expressive feeling
seeking form we have a sensate difficulty. Before we can actually
engage in subject-reflexive action we need to formulate this sensate
difficulty as an expressive problem: that is to say, we need to grasp the
sensate elements or material that comprise the difficulty, and adopt
one of the principles listed above as the means of imaging and
resolving the difficulty. It is very like making and testing an hypothesis. Our 'difficulty' arises out of our inability to sense the deep
structure of the sensate disturbance – it has one but we do not know
what it is. To find out, we need to project it through a medium: in
order to do so we must be able to get hold of it somehow, that is, to
formulate it as an expressive problem. We take the sensate elements
cool and warm or light and dark for instance, contrast them and project our sense of the cool/warm, light/dark contrast through a
medium that will 'image' it. So the sensate difficulty becomes a
sensate problem as the feeling of warm contrasted with cool, or of
light contrasted with dark, and we seek a resolution of that disturbance by working the problem form, i.e. by making a sensuous form
that embodies the formula in a particular image. Though we may all
be aware of these feelings and share them at a general level, they will
have a particular meaning for each of us individually. Our images,
our sensuous forms, will reflect our individuality, our unique experience, but their deep structure should evoke the same basic *gestalt*
in all of us.

Getting started means, therefore, having an hypothesis: more
precisely, having sensate material and an hypothesis concerning its
possible deep structure. As teachers we shall wish:

1. To give children repeated experience of handling such problems.
   This will mean our devising and setting expressive problems for
   the children to work.
2. To help children to turn their sensate difficulties into expressive
   problems for themselves. This is likely to be the more difficult
   task though we should recognize that on many occasions the
   formulation of the sensate problem may occur intuitively and
   quite spontaneously.

Discerning the sensate character of a feeling seeking form is not as
difficult as perhaps it sounds: it is a question of finding out *how a
feeling feels*. All feelings or moods evoke characteristic physical
sensations: emotionally we feel ourselves opened out or closing in,
moving towards or moving back and away. Sometimes both opposed
sensations at the same time. Then we are aware too of feelings that

leave a bitter-sweet taste, of pains in the neck, hearts in the mouth, of being on edge and so forth. These and such like are the sensate material of which sensate impulses are made. The moods – anguished, tranquil, troubled, blue – suggest deep structures that provide us with possible problem forms to use in the making of our sensuous wholes. If we decide to set problems for our children, we will formulate them much as Witkin suggests in Chapter 8 of *The Intelligence of Feeling.* If we decide to help the children to formulate their own, or to work with those the children are already engaged on, then it is this deep structure we shall need to be able to identify.

In Chapter 8 of this book John Woolner provides us with a striking example of a teacher intervening to formulate the expressive problem for the pupil. The project is discussed in more detail there, but it will be useful for us to consider briefly what took place. Whatever drew the girl to try and draw the conker shell in the first place must remain a matter of conjecture. What is manifestly clear is her preoccupation with the spikes. It is the spikiness of the spikes that she wants to represent. Her 'difficulty' at a technical level lies in the problem of three-dimensional representation – but the teacher grasped the *affective* difficulty underlying it and addressed himself to the depiction of spikiness that would allow her really to get to grips with her feelings. He suggested a two-dimensional approach that reduced the technical difficulties and allowed her to image the spikes as flashing blades ranged around a circular hub – we cannot tell at this stage whether in defence or attack although the ambiguity is assimilated in the 'final' image (Fig. 8.4). The flat blades are echoed in the flat triangular shapes between them: her holding form already presages the harmonious composure of the resolution she eventually achieves. The sensate difficulty has to do with the acceptance of suffering and aggression as two sides of the coin of personal survival: of being pricked and being 'prickly'. She formulates this problem for herself – prompted by the teacher's intervention – in her holding form (Fig. 8.2): her key image.

Setting an expressive problem means offering the child with an hypothesis concerning the deep inner structure of particular feelings seeking form. The expressive problem once formulated has to be expressed in terms of the experience of the image-maker. Mere conceptualization is not enough though: there has to be arousal – sensate disturbance has to be evoked to the point where the expressive drive cannot be denied (it may, of course, be resisted but that is another matter).

> The setting of the sensate problem is the evoking of a specific gestalt, a sensate ordering in the context of the pupil's experience.[1]

Essentially this means the teacher must see that the child is *actually experiencing the gestalt.* The child has to have a formula to work

[1] Witkin, *The Intelligence of Feeling,* p. 172.

to – one that will allow the organization of the *particular* experience into a personal image. To do so it will not necessarily be sufficient merely to expose a child to a series of pictures, or read a story or play a piece of music. Or take the class into a landscape or a churchyard. An expressive difficulty may not have been aroused by these encounters within the child at all. Embedding the *gestalt*, evoking 'sensate ordering' is a much more precise task for the teacher. It often demands the refashioning of a child's perceptions, since although some stimuli may immediately evoke the appropriate sensate ordering, it may on occasions prove more difficult to get the child to 'sense' the problem clearly. The problem form (the hypothesis) must be grasped if it is to be tested and resolved.

And if the teacher is to know that the problem he has selected or identified has been set in the particularity of the pupil, the pupil must formulate or represent his or her own sense of it – preferably in the medium that has been chosen as the means of representation. *The 'holding form' – to be discussed more fully in a moment – is at once a formulation of the sensate problem in that it represents its gestalt, and a blueprint for its final expressive resolution.* It is a problem form because it represents the impulse in the terms in which it will be resolved. The child's holding form will tell the teacher whether the problem has been set since, for all its 'particularity', its deep structure will have discernible general characteristics – if successful the structural characteristics of the sensate impulse itself.

Sometimes there will be no difficulty in getting a child to sense the sensate form of, say, a piece of music chosen as a model. The structural character of the music – its internal harmony or disonance, let us say – will be felt immediately and rendered (formulated) in a holding form that clearly demonstrates that the child has got hold of it, that the expressive problem has been set and can now be worked out. There will be scenes from plays, excerpts from films, pictures and poems which will be similarly evocative for some children – different ones for different children on different occasions. Their holding forms will tell us whether they are properly centred. As teachers, though, we shall need our own formulation of the problem if we are to assess the accuracy of theirs.

As I have said, there will also be times when the problem we wish to set may require very careful evoking in the child. It is all too easy to offer a stimulus to a child and assume that the problem that we have discerned will be immediately perceived by the child when in fact the child may either be unable to make such a perception at all, or only be able to do so after a good deal of effort by himself and the teacher. Very often a response to stimulus material is baulked by our being distracted by irrelevant elements or considerations that for one reason or another take our attention. We all know what it is to look at a painting or listen to a piece of music and just not be able to 'see' or 'hear' it. It is as if we were on the wrong wavelength altogether – off key, off beam, out of tune, out of touch. But perceptions sometimes correct themselves spontaneously, and we achieve the cognitive alignment necessary for engagement. And our perceptions can be helped – a good critic or a sensitive teacher can help us 'see'. Not the particularity of their own seeing but the basic *gestalt* or aesthetic structure at the heart of the organization of the piece. And we need to be cognitively aware if we are to tune in to the experience ourselves.

Helping children sense the deep structure of the stimulus material is the same as helping them respond to (appreciate) the realized forms of art. However, we must beware of allowing the full resolution of impulse through response to the realized form we have chosen as the stimulus (where the realized form is a work of art) if we wish the child to project that impulse for his own representational purpose. Of course not all stimulus material will be capable of allowing this full resolution of the impulse it evokes – but I have certainly known it happen. I once used Wordsworth's sonnet 'The world is too much with us . . .' to set an expressive problem: one of the group made a fine piece of sculpture that certainly carried the coiled power of the poem ('The winds that will be howling are upgathered now'). Another member of the group got totally involved in his response to the poem, however, and had no expressive energy left for image-making of his own since it had been resolved through the realized form itself.

I once spoke at a conference that was held in a beautiful eighteenth-century mansion in Yorkshire. The building had belonged to local gentry who used to top up their coffers by exploiting the natural resources of their lands – and the labour of the local people. I was making the point to my audience that the grounds of the house could well provide a stimulus for various kinds of 'expressive' as well as 'impressive' activities – art as well as environmental studies. One teacher said that his kids would not see anything especially beautiful about the grounds (I had not spoken of their 'beauty' actually – only of their emotional meaning). They would roam about, he said, running up and down the formal steps, leaping over the trimmed hedges, rolling down the banks, and demand a football. He also said that as far as he was concerned that was fair enough: he would as soon they enjoyed themselves and responded spontaneously as try to structure their learning too precisely. Many would be 'learning' something through play – they would all be getting useful exercise and expressing their *joie de vivre*. He was pulling my leg a bit – he thought I was getting too 'airy fairy'. I think he was being too imprecise.

He was certainly right in assuming that, let loose in those spacious surroundings with their terraced lawns, formal rose-beds, fountains, steps and gigantic trees, the children (he was thinking of primary-school children) would probably not immediately be impressed entirely in the same way I was. I was aware of the theatrical and ritualistic implications of the design, and of the way those implications made you feel, as onlooker and as actor or participant. Standing at the focal point of the paths and steps I sensed both my own smallness and the swelling within of pretensions to personal grandeur and power. It is a garden designed to be ceremoniously 'worn' as well as admired. From the top lawn you could just make out the coal mine in the valley and the rows of the back-to-back houses of the townsfolk.

If I wanted to use the setting of that place as a stimulus encounter for children I would have to get them to 'see' it first – to feel themselves within it as a *special* place. I would have to carry them beyond their perceptions of the place as a potential playground or football pitch to the point where they felt more of its symbolic meaning: their spontaneously vigorous responses would provide me with an appropriate start, but the demand for the football would be an irrelevance unless turned to my purpose.

Such a place is stock full of affective meaning – I do not pretend to have worked it all out here. I simply wish to make the point that the setting of the problem as I might formulate it would probably involve me in 'educating' the children's perceptions so that one sort of response (play) might be replaced by another set of responses *more appropriate* to the expressive task I wished them to engage in. They would somehow have to be made to 'feel' that setting as a total form having its own *gestalt*, before they would begin to respond appropriately to it, and so express their response to the feelings that such a place evoked in them. I might need other stimuli (music, paintings, photographs) to help to make my point, to 'set' the problem. Their holding forms (drawings, dramas, dances etc.) would then tell me whether I had managed to set the problem I had formulated for them or not.

As a teacher I must be able to formulate the problem a child is working on; whether I do so in advance, as it were, or, by identifying it in process, does not matter. I need my own formulation if I am to be able to help the child achieve his resolution – and know when he has done so. The child formulates his perception of the sensate problem in the holding form he makes; as a teacher I will probably formulate mine conceptually (and represent it in words). But there is no reason why my own formulation should not be non-verbal as well. Verbal and non-verbal representation can complement each other: words that help us in our formulations may not help children to 'see' in the way I have been speaking of. Setting the problem may therefore involve all the following:

(a) presenting it in one or more stimulus forms that reinforce each other;

(b) representing it non-verbally in a holding form of one's own (beware the child's imitative response here);

(c) representing it verbally: giving it a name. Talking about it.

Sensate stimuli supported by some discussion will be the normal pattern. The teacher is the go-between in this situation – and will need to be more explicit and less elusive than either the image-maker or the stimulus image. The teacher formulates the sensate problem in general terms – in terms of its generality. The child formulates the problem as a particular image in a particular medium.

With the expressive impulse aroused, the teacher and the pupil now select the medium to be worked, and, following Witkin, I would suggest that stimulus medium and representational medium should be different. That way the pupil's form making will not be influenced by the stimulus form being used to provide the structural model. The end of the process is the evaluation of the sensuous form (image) in terms of the expressive problem as formulated. The *gestalt* should be the same. If the problem was formulated as a contrast, then contrast will be the deep structure of the image: if the problem was formulated as a dialectic, then dialectic will be the deep structure of the image. The problem can be formulated in general terms for all pupils: it has to be set and resolved, however, in the particularity of each individual pupil's experience. The problem may be chosen by the teacher or simply stumbled upon by the pupil. In both cases the teacher is obliged to identify it in order to participate in the process of its resolution and evaluation. We work with individual responses guided by universal principles.

Other writers on the arts and on aesthetics have attached similar importance to some of the concepts Witkin offers, although I have not found anyone who has taken the idea as far as he has. Charles Henry in the 1920s, for instance, advanced a theory of aesthetics based on what he called 'simultaneous contrasts'. He suggested that feelings could only be known in relation to other feelings – in particular, in contrast with other feelings. Every expressive form implied its opposite, and the poise or equilibrium of art was achieved through this characteristic of the aesthetic response. Itten, the great Bauhaus teacher, develops an entire theory of the expressive use of colour based on the idea of the contrast: contrasts of hue, tone, timbre etc. A 'contrast', however, is not in itself a sensate problem since the *specific* sensate character of the problem is absent. I have known teachers, trying to follow *The Intelligence of Feeling*, base all their projects in art and drama on themes such as contrasts, harmonies and so forth. This is to miss the point Witkin is making. The formula is made up of two elements: the sensate element plus the structural element. So we speak of the warm-cool contrast or the bitter-sweet polarity. These are problem forms (formulae) that allow the working of an impulse through an expressive medium and the resolution of that impulse in an image or representational symbol.

Perhaps the following example may further illuminate this discussion of the problem form. I am indebted for it to one of the contributors to this book, Len Jenkinson. It was he who drew my attention to the problem form that Dylan Thomas uses in 'Fern Hill'.

In fact it is a form that Thomas repeatedly uses, and this should be reassuring to teachers who worry that their children are not working over a sufficiently wide range of experience. The problem that Thomas explores in this poem and repeatedly elsewhere is beautifully encapsulated in this verse:

> Nothing I cared in the lamb white days, that time would take me
> Up to the swallow thronged loft by the shadow of my hand,
> In the moon that is always rising,
> Nor that riding to sleep
> I should hear him fly with the high fields
> And wake to the farm forever fled from the childless land.
> Oh as I was young and easy in the mercy of his means,
> Time held me green and dying
> Though I sang in my chains like the sea.

The formula he is using is the 'green and dying' dialectic. Given that basic structure, the complex feelings evoked by childhood memories could be structured, organized and worked out. Joy and grief as one. The dialectic is the structural character of the original sensate schema – it is also the key to understanding the deep structure (*gestalt*) of the sensuous form itself (the poem). An expressive formula is made up of sensations plus structural principle, in this case the green and dying sensations plus the dialectic principle of organization. The poem embodies tragic feelings about childhood embodied in dialectical form: one supposes that Thomas arrived at his expressive formula intuitively. On many occasions our pupils will do the same, in which case our job will be to discern the formula they are working to. When they cannot formulate the expressive problem for themselves we must help them do so. We shall also wish to set them expressive problems that we have chosen in order either to extend their expressive range or to deepen their expressive awareness.

I shall conclude this discussion of the expressive problem with an illustration taken from my own recent work. On this occasion I had decided to choose the sensate theme myself, to suggest the problem form the group was to use. I was working with a group of about twenty arts teachers on the topic 'Linking the Arts in Education', and I wanted to show how work in the different arts could emerge from a common starting-point. So I planned a piece of curriculum around the feeling of inertia, of being trapped. In thinking about how I would set the group a problem relevant to my chosen theme I began to explore for myself the physical sensations of being trapped. I stretched out and felt dragged back. I reached up and was pulled down. My feet were stuck in the mud and glue – I was drained of energy as I struggled in vain to get through the morass. Images came to mind: the deadly weight of the albatross around the Ancient Mariner's neck, nets, spiders webs – in particular I found myself thinking of Claudius trying in vain to repent in *Hamlet*, and the inertia of Marlow's Faustus:

O, I'll leap up to Heaven! Who pulls me down?
(See, see where Christ's blood streams in the firmament!)

There is something of the same frustration and anguish in Wordsworth's sonnet 'The world is too much with us'. I wanted the group
to feel this frustration – the tension of the implacable trap (a relationship, an ideology, alienation, guilt) and to choose a problem form
that would allow its representation or embodiment in a medium.
While I was still working out my ideas I happened to go into the
'Creative Textiles' room; everywhere I saw threads and strands
under tension, stitches, nets, all manner of stretched patterns. In
particular I saw some stretched and torn polythene – the shapes of
rupture and tension were exactly what I wanted, as was the feel of
yielding and containing when I pressed my fingers into the sheeting.
Here was my own formulation of what I had in mind – I did not find
a conceptualization easy and the one I eventually settled on did not
please me. The sensation was of pushing against, of being dragged
back – of gluey imprisonment; the mood was anguish. The problem
form would probably be a polarization of the two feelings in a cycli-
cal or counterpoised form.

I began to devise a sequence of experiences that would set this
particular configuration of sensations in the consciousness of the
group. As we have seen, Witkin suggests that the problem is best
set in media other than the one actually to be used in the representational action. He also suggests that the problem may need
setting in several different ways. I entirely agree with both these
suggestions but, on the occasion I am describing, was perhaps
guilty of sensate 'overkill'! For a number of reasons I decided to try
several different ways of setting the problem I had chosen.

1. A drama game I call 'Cradles and Cages'. The idea is that each
   individual is first cradled and then caged by three or four others –
   they hold him and help him sense these two contrasted feelings. I
   then ask the 'subjects' to try to sense the pleasure of being caged
   and the horror of being cradled, and to respond accordingly.
2. I asked one of the group – a musician – to listen to a recording of a
   serene piece of organ music by Messiaen and, when he had sensed
   its quality, deliberately to resist and pull against it musically.
   This proved to be a very compelling experience for everyone – the
   pianist was actually sweating and trembling with the tension of
   the experience by the end of it. If I had wanted an image for
   Claudius, the Mariner or Faustus, he certainly had provided one!
3. Another drama game – 'Countdown'. Each member took up a
   'launching' position on the floor and prepared to rocket into
   orbit. I played a suitably energetic and dramatic record to
   accompany the countdown. With about five seconds to go to 'lift
   off' I declared a hitch and asked that the aroused tensions be
   held.

The frustration was considerable. After two or three repetitions of this experience – the climax unachieved – the feeling was well and truly established.

4. I contrasted this feeling with a record of Zulu chanting in the Zulu version of *Macbeth*. There is a marvellous rapport between the soloist and the chorus: the soloist acting as a springboard for the choral responses. Superb timing – total fulfilment.

5. I gave them the plastic sheeting to play with, inviting them to test its tensile quality, to feel its resistance and examine the stretch lines it made. This material, stretched across an overhead projector, produces remarkable visual patterns of tension. A dance/drama developed spontaneously.

6. Finally we took two speeches in Shakespeare's *Hamlet* – the prayer of Claudius already referred to and the speech of Claudius to Laertes in Act IV Scene vii lines 9–24. In particular I drew attention to the images – of arrows returning to the bow, of reasons that are both 'strong' and 'unsinewed', of stubborn knees that bow and hearts with 'strings of steel' becoming soft 'as sinews of the newborn babe'. I read the prayer speech giving full weight to the sense of defeated effort.

> My stronger guilt defeats my strong intent,
> And like a man to double business bound
> I stand in pause where I shall both begin,
> And both neglect.

I asked the group to find their own images for this feeling of double bind and to produce a form that involved the use of polarity or dialectic. This, over a period of a day's intense activity, they were well able to do. In several instances I was able to assist in the image-making process. We had a wide variety of responses – in different media and taking on the particularity of the experience of each individual maker – but all with the same deep structure at their centre. My original image of the stretched polythene was manifestly appropriate to each one. Though each form was a unique image, the deep underlying sensate structure was always the same.

Setting the problem means helping the student sense the sensate character of the feeling he is seeking to represent. It is rarely enough simply to expose him to an emotional stimulus – a picture, a piece of music, a landscape. You need to be sure he has responded *appropriately*, i.e. grasped the sensate character of the mood aroused by the stimulus material. This may mean – and often does – helping him to sense the deep sensate structure of that material. As we shall see later, this is also the teacher's task in acting as intermediary between the student and a work of art. Finding an appropriate problem form is vital if the student is to be able to proceed to the next phase of the expressive process, either to the making of a holding form or to the full appreciation of a realized form.

The Holding Form

Once the problem has been 'set', in the particularity of the pupil's experience, then the impulse may be given its first, albeit crude, expression in the medium. This first attempt at a representational equivalent should, to be really effective in providing a base for all that follows, encapsulate the structural essence of the impulse. It should 'hold' the expressive impulse both in the sense of containing it so that it is not lost sight of, or lost touch with, and in the sense of representing or capturing its essential structural character. It should all be there so that all that then needs doing is to refine it to the point where the image matches as exactly as possible the impulse that generated it. The difference between the teacher's problem form and the child's holding form is this: the problem form is a generality, it specifies in the most general way the underlying basis of the problem-solving process. When we speak of the warm–cool contrast or green and dying dialectic we are speaking of human emotional experi-ence at the most general level. We can all identify with these experi-ences. In our holding forms, however, we give expression to that general experience in *entirely personal terms* – terms that are particular to each one whose expressive form it is. We, looking on as an audi-ence, may sense the problem form being used. We may even be able to grasp and identify with the particular contrast or semblance someone has chosen to use as the means of working his impulse out (we might say 'of painting it out, or acting it out, or writing it out, or playing it out') and sense a movement of feeling within us that tallies closely with the way the maker's feelings are mov-ing. But, as we have already seen, this is a separate issue. The only thing that matters where the holding form is concerned is that it represent the author's own impulse as faithfully as may be, given that it is the first shot, the opening shot of the series, the ranging round. In terms of our spiral model we would expect to find that the holding form entirely encompassed the impulse, that the impulse ran straight and true through its centre.

The holding form is the first adequate representational act in the medium. It should not only hold the impulse, it should also be

Fig. 6.6

Impulse

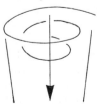

characteristic of its maker – it should answer to the image-making propensity of a singular sensibility. With the making of the holding form we move from the general to the particular: particular choice of medium, of technique, of symbolic material. The holding form, if it truly catches the flavour of the initial impulse, will serve as a point of reference for the remainder of the expressive process. All that follows is implied within the holding form, it is held there awaiting full expression. If the holding form is right then we can keep impulse at the centre of the remainder of the action, unless, as sometimes happens, the holding form actually resolves the impulse (as very often with Constable's water-colour sketches, for instance) in which case all work beyond that point becomes more and more mechanical and inflated: force of mind in the absence of force of feeling.

I shall be giving some examples in a moment of centring expressive acts in the medium. I hope, however, that the basic idea is now clear enough. As with the problem form, the holding form may also emerge swiftly and spontaneously. It may be stumbled upon by chance as it were, or encountered accidentally. It may prove stubbornly reticent on one occasion and so swift and true on another that the holding form itself resolves the impulse, the final image springs complete in the imagination of the maker. However, it is also fair to say that the holding form may have to be worked for, so it is important that one knows what one is trying to do. It may not always emerge in response to our efforts, but it should nevertheless be attempted. The arts teacher will certainly wish to see his pupils making holding forms as their first assay at a representational image, and elsewhere in this book you will find instances of teachers doing just that: helping children find their own holding forms as the opening stage of self-expressive work.

When a moment ago I referred to Dylan Thomas's poem 'Fern Hill' I suggested that it was possible to discern the basic structure (the problem form) that he used as his way of working his impulse through the medium of words. The 'green and dying' dialectic is an experience we are all likely to be familiar with. However few if any of us will know the place, Fern Hill, and none of us will know it as Thomas did. It will not have the same subjective meaning for us as it had for him. If we chose that particular problem form we would have to represent it in terms of our own experience – for instance we might not place that problem in the world of childhood reminiscence at all. He chose to do so because that was where the experience was centred for him. Fern Hill held the key to those poignant disturbing feelings. His memories of Fern Hill provided him with the images through which his feeling could be given form and in terms of which it could achieve the striking resolution of that last verse. The poem provides all we need, and it is obvious enough why he chose to explore these particular feelings in terms of that particular image.

The holding form is a basic sketch or outline of the feeling

character of the impulse. Such a form 'holds' the impulse and guides
its eventual resolution. Of such a form we say, 'Yes, that's how it is.
That's how it feels.' We can then proceed to its refinement. What
then remains is the final phase of the process as the impulse is
resolved in representational form.

Getting back to our question, 'How, precisely may the teacher
help?' we can see perhaps that what the teacher first needs is the
sensitivity and intelligence to assist the child in setting the feeling
problem in sensate terms (as one of formal, aesthetic structuring),
and then to discern, from discussion with the child and his own
response to the child's work, whether an adequate holding form
has been found. When a group impulse (mood) is involved, as is
sometimes the case in the performing arts, a group holding form
is required.

Resolution

If we think again of the model of the expressive spiral then, once the
impulse has been centred in the medium, there should be no major
bar to its achieving ultimate resolution in form. Such, at least
theoretically, seems a reasonable proposition. Given the process of
reciprocal refinement, we should end up with a satisfactory sensuous
form – satisfactory in the double sense that the form resolves the
difficulty (settles the disturbance) and permits the recollection of the
impulse that originated it. It is a matter of the probe homing on to its
target, achieving sensuous form through 'a series of approximations
to a resolution' (to use Witkin's phrase).

Fig. 6.7

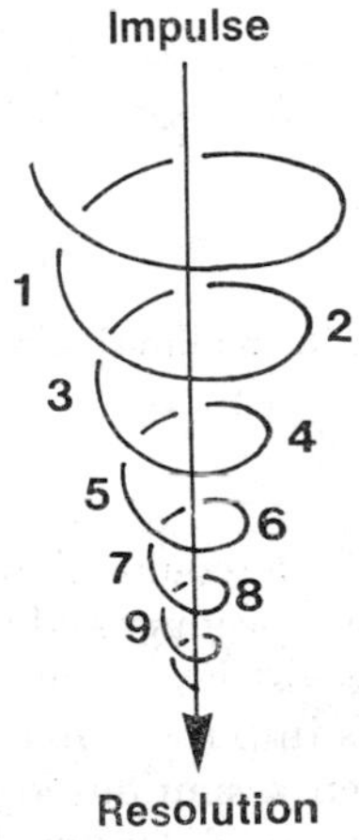

Impulse

Resolution

In this diagram I have suggested some nine approximations between
the holding form (the first loop about the impulse) and the final

form. In practice of course it would probably be quite impossible to discover specific and separate stages in the refinement of form in quite this way. In practice the number of 'shots' needed to achieve a satisfactory resolution of a feeling impulse will vary enormously, from a moment of blinding insight to a lifetime's work. However, it might be reasonable to suppose that, where prolonged delay in achieving at least an acceptable degree of resolution occurs that cannot either be attributed to some deficiency of the medium or in one's capacity to control it, such delay may point to a failure earlier in the process, that is to say, to insufficient impulsive energy, or the failure to centre the impulse in the medium. The latter is probably the more likely of the two. If the medium and impulse are not properly aligned, the mismatch will work havoc with the enterprise (as with uncentred clay upon the potter's wheel). We lose the impulse as the centre of the expressive act and the source of the form's expressive meaning. Without the impulse at the heart of the process we must inevitably fail to achieve its resolution. If any form does emerge beyond the point at which contact with the impulse was lost then that form will be empty and meaningless. (Unfortunately a good deal of expressive work is pushed beyond this critical point – with the result that no one, least of all the maker, knows what to do with or make of the result.)

Fig. 6.8

Impulse

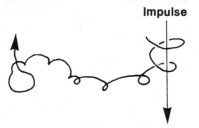

Failure to centre impulse in medium: loss of impulsive direction and 'collapse' of form

The result may be simply a confused mess. More usually some attempt is made to salvage a product and we end up with a fake. For example the pupil, having lost his impulse, may seek to realign the fated form to the teacher's impulse. That way no one is in control. We then have a form given a spurious logic by being made to conform to some idea, rule or model, 'externally' determined, in which case we would at best have a fine 'imitation' or something merely technically expert.

Fig. 6.9

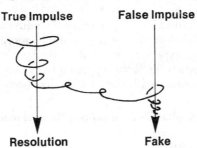

Distinguishing 'true' from 'false' resolutions can be an extremely difficult task for all concerned, especially when the maker lacks the confidence to speak of his own experience on his own behalf. The teacher's dilemma is to discriminate between public and private values – a topic we've raised earlier.

The medium itself provides the other major difficulty that might arise in this final phase of the process. As I have already suggested, the maker might simply lack the experience and expertise to control the medium and exploit its full potential. Teachers are usually very alert to this problem and often find themselves offering technical help and advice at this time so that the child becomes better equipped to 'say what he wants to say'. On the other hand the medium itself might baulk the expressive probe, by being in one way or another unsuited to the specific character of the expressive act. In both cases we shall end up with more or less of a 'near miss' in terms of the resolution of the impulse. There usually comes a time with most of us when one simply has to call it a day and say, 'Well, that's

Fig. 6.10

'Near miss'—failure of ultimate resolution because of some deficiency of the medium or inadequacy in medium control

something like it though I don't think it is exactly what I meant.'
The work stops.

Needless to say, this kind of a 'near miss' – with the impulse centred
but ultimately unresolved – is an infinitely more satisfactory outcome to a piece of expressive work than the spurious kind of resolution that occurs when the form is pressed to a completion beyond the
point at which contact with the impulse has been lost.

Summary
These then are the phases of the process the arts teacher must provide
for:
1. Stimulus encounter
2. Felt disturbance (positive or negative mood)
3. Models of expressive formulae (deep structure)
4. Projection of impulse through medium
5. Making a holding form (centring)
6. Reciprocation and refinement
7. Resolution of expressive problem in feeling form (icon)
8. Felt consummation (self-actualization)
9. Sharing (evaluation and communication)
He has a key role at every point along the way.

Illustrative Case Studies

In conclusion, I should now cite one or two examples from my own
experience as a way of illuminating the kind of teacher participation
I am talking about. Each example will I hope make clear the distinction between (a) the setting of the problem and (b) the lifting off
of the expressive act through the establishing of the holding form.

Study 1
I once worked one-to-one with an experienced adult pianist who was
a lecturer at Oslo University. Though he understood some English,
I knew no Norwegian so we did not talk much. He had agreed to
participate in an experimental 'demonstration' before the rest of the
members of a course I was leading – some 150 'arts' teachers. I had
never undertaken such a thing before, though I have several times since.

I explained that I was hoping we might find a holding form that
would interest and perhaps surprise him. We began with no particular feeling apart from the tension generated by the situation itself.
His experience meant we would have no technical problems (so my
own lack of musicianship would not be a hindrance); it also meant
that he was able quite quickly to master some of the pressures of the
situation. He was used to improvising and performing. He was not,
however, at all prepared for the way I was going to work.

I first asked him simply to doodle on the keyboard – to get the
feel of the piano. He began some runs and chords and then gradually
settled into a number of different melodic and rhythmical patterns.

I observed him closely, leaning on the piano, watching his hands, his face, his body. It was some time before he felt relaxed enough to doodle freely – he kept sliding into familiar forms and clichéd resolutions. But he was beginning to respond to the piano now, so I began 'pushing him' about the keyboard – asking him to vary mood, pace, tempo. Breaking up the patterns and helping him to discover his options. All the while the intensity of his involvement was growing. His body began to move in sympathy with his playing – he was not just listening to the piano, he was beginning to 'move' with it. We had been working for perhaps fifteen minutes.

I immediately placed a rather indistinct black and white photograph on the music stand of the piano. I had been hoping for a melodic line – what actually emerged were a string of 'broken', 'offbeat' rhythmical shapes. He kept playing – trying one and then another rhythmical shape – as he bent over the keys and scrutinized the picture. He moved back, half closing his eyes, then bent forward again to examine the picture more closely. He did not take his eyes off the picture but gradually the rhythmical pulse deepened and strengthened. On and on he went, pounding away at the keys, his feet working the pedals. Suddenly, I sensed he had found his holding form. He was grooved and had begun grooving. (Afterwards he told me that what had interested him in the photograph had been the light and dark contrasts rather than the images or content.) I felt at once that he had no further need of me and indeed so it proved to be. He led a jam session lasting a further thirty minutes or more, involving most of his audience either as extempore musicians or dancers. We discussed the experience with the course on the following day and he was able to discern the three phases I have referred to.

Discussion:
(a) The impulse had been evoked by the real but controlled tensions within the actual situation focused with the help of the picture.
(b) The problem was later formulated as a dialectic: light-dark.
(c) The particular holding form was the rhythmical 'shape' that became the basis of the improvised jam session.
(d) The spontaneous jam session was the sensuous form that resolved the feeling problem.

Study 2
An exercise in writing, based upon the sound, and muscular, sensuous feel of 'words'. Having played with the feel of speaking (by exaggerating mouth, tongue and lip movements, emphasizing hissing, gutteral and liquid sounds, using any words that come to mind, the group (teachers on an in-service course) was asked to find an object, and then write something based on the object but using words with a strong emphasis on their sensuous properties when spoken. I chose to work on a broken tile, actually collected by

someone else. First of all I tried to produce nonsense words that would somehow relate to the feeling evoked in me by the tile. I wrote:

Ga-dig gjarrack mate adzorapik bastamack cerne daxe fostack grekard

The next stage was to transfer some of this feeling to 'real' words and formal rhythms. A series of verses (lines) emerged. I was then able to work away at the images and the words with a sure sense of the relationship between them. It was not until the poem was almost finished that I realized the nature of the actual emotional experience I was writing about. Here is the poem:

> Down graded by the rack – crazed, split and
> Broken breasted, the drag of bone
> Upon bone, dusty and grit toothed, I saw
> The air that shivers, shafted and dark.
> Jelly-eyed monster on a slippery slope
> But blood stuck and sucking a bitter sigh
> While the sculptor strokes my thigh abstractedly
> Not noticing how the flesh moves yet. The gulls
> That swing and drift to cast a curling shadow
> I feel their wings press upon my mouth with stern admonishment.

Discussion:
(a) The experience began with play in word sound and the act of utterance.
(b) The impulse was evoked by speaking to/for the tile.
(c) The problem was formulated (though I did not do it conceptually) by the tile. (Like Hopkins' sonnet 'Thou are indeed just, Lord', it is about impotence.) I found feelings within me that stirred in response to the tile (stimulus form).
(d) The nonsense words as felt utterance became the holding form and the touchstone I referred to whenever an image, a word or a line was in question.
(e) Though it stops short of resolution 'the poem' seems to me the nearest I have ever got to making a sensuous form with words. I was genuinely surprised by the 'subject' when I eventually discerned the source of the actual feeling problem that the act of expression had revealed to me. I still do not know *what* it means: I know *that* it means.

Study 3
Hermione was coming to a series of regular weekly sessions that I ran for teachers. The tramp figure which she eventually produced in the course of an evening at home represented the culmination of several weeks 'incubation'. One of our first exercises involved browsing through colour magazines to cull material for a 'dream' image. The dream image was distinguished from a 'detective' puzzle: the organization of the former having an emotional logic and of the latter a conceptual logic. Hermione's dream image was a disturbing

one – a series of half recognizable images arranged around a picture of a man with a camera. There were disembodied fingers here and there. She had not planned it – it had formed itself as she played with the medium. She confessed to feeling rather frightened by what she had made.

Some weeks later I set up the exercise with words which I have just described. Hermione found an old broom-head lying in a tangle of grass. She brought it back to the studio and began to try to draw it, using green and brown wax crayons. The drawing was very 'flat' and, although quite vigorous, did not please her at all. During discussion she said she felt the same disturbance as she had touched in the dream collage – but she could not find any way to realize or embody it. A friend who knew her interests and skills suggested she might do something with fabrics, designing a costume for instance (something she loved to do and did very well). The effect of the suggestion was instantaneous. She said, simply, 'Yes', but on being pressed, confessed to seeing immediately the image she needed. She went home and in a period of complete absorption completed a little tramp figure. She was completely satisfied with it and said that it embodied the feeling triggered during the collage exercise and 're-cognized' in the broom-head.

Discussion:

(a) Again impulse was initially triggered by an object: the broom-head, rotting amidst the springing grass.

(b) She had albeit unknowingly identified the deep structure as harmonious, the essential elements of which were human and material decay (and by implication regeneration), the poignancy of the life cycle (the opposite of Thomas's 'green and dying'), and had begun to work towards a holding form in the dream collage. However she had not found one and spent a rather disturbed evening unable to proceed towards a resolution of the impulse she had triggered.

(c) The crayoning was another attempt to find – as she later declared – a holding form for the same impulse. The aimless walk had produced the broom-head: the problem lay in its transformation, in creating a symbolic counterpart for it rather than in simply depicting it. The battered old broom-head with its vigorous, sprouting bristles entwined with grass, was a dream image, like the collage. It had to be transformed into a personal icon.

(d) The suggestion from the friend produced an immediate solution in her imagination. She 'saw' her tramp at once – a vigorous 'green' old man's body in a tattered morning coat and high dress hat, his beautiful waistcoat of leaves and the soft green ruff of moss, presaging death, already evincing the return of the body to dust: hovering somehow, like Beckett's tramps, in existential no-man's-land. His feet bare and green, bony, spurting from the ragged ends of his trousers. There was no need for a holding form since the form sprang to mind complete. There was no way this impulse could be lost. She went home and was totally absorbed in the realization of the figure, noticing with mild surprise how by chance she seemed to have to hand just the materials she needed. But images have a way of sucking necessary things into themselves once the energy is organized as a vortex of expressive consciousness.

Study 4

When is a 'holding form' not a holding form? The answer is 'When it's a losing form – a releasing form'. I was working with another group of teachers on the holding form idea and, having talked about it for a while, suggested they might like to take the word 'Power' and see whether they could not produce a holding form for their own feeling response to that word. I was rather astonished at the intense commitment and considerable productivity of the group as a whole; a number of apparently quite effective forms were produced, if the people concerned were to be believed. Eric was not so pleased however. He had found what I had had to say fairly irritating anyway and, given the key word 'Power', had gone to work with some energy on a largish piece of clay. The 'form' he finally ended up with was certainly a somewhat tortured one – the clay bore the marks of having been pretty thoroughly mauled about. When questioned about it Eric said he had enjoyed working the clay – indeed he had got rather happily carried away pounding and scoring, twisting and gouging. He had enjoyed himself. But looking at it now he was disappointed – it was worthless; it meant nothing.

At the time I was not able to make any very helpful comment. I rather wondered whether he just had it in for me and was standing out against the general good feeling. However, on consideration, I recognized that what he had produced was a releasing form rather than a holding form – that is to say a form that bore the marks of what he had felt, that testified to his empassioned actions, but did not in any sense act as a reciprocal to impulse. His expression had been reactive – he had simply used the clay to release tension, not to effect an image. He had not been interested to 'watch' what was happening, nor to allow the clay to answer him back through his hands. He had abused it, bruised it. His action had not been representational.

That is how it seemed to me when I had had time to reflect upon it. The act had all the marks of reactive expression, and the clay contained nothing, represented nothing. Was truly formless and so unsatisfying in itself. The man was spent, but he was not held. Having had to listen to me he had needed to respond reactively before anything more constructive could occur. We were still some way from creative self-expression. My key word had perhaps been ill-chosen for him: or maybe he would have fared better if we had formulated a sensate problem, not merely evoked a feeling.

Study 5

Lilli is a Danish movement teacher. She was in her late thirties when she came to work with me for a year as a private student. Lilli had been quite seriously unwell and, with permission from her school, had decided to take a year off to allow herself to make a full recovery, and to refresh herself both personally and professionally. She had to make a number of financial sacrifices in order to come and, having done so, was determined to throw herself heart and soul into this new venture. It meant in the first place that she had to master spoken and written English.

We used to meet regularly for discussions about arts education and she joined a number of my classes, keeping herself pretty much to herself initially, but gradually daring more and offering more. I was anxious that she should do some expressive work of her own and soon discovered that she was – and had been for most of her life – a diary addict. She wrote detailed notes at the end of every day, and found great pleasure and reward in doing so. She told me she had been writing poems for some time and had recently 'produced' a collection of poems which she had shown privately to some close friends. The responses of her selected readers had been rather mixed and she felt unsure about the actual quality of the poems. She also said she was interested in drawing but had no confidence in that medium – she had a sister of considerable talent, married to a successful professional painter, and the family naturally looked to them to set the standard. Lilli felt her own work to come well below what constituted acceptable 'art'. However she did the odd doodle and I was surprised to find after some months, that she was doing tiny ink drawings of hills and trees. She was living in a rather isolated village and, through her journal writing, had become very involved in the local countryside – she had her favourite walks, views, skylines and trees. The trees seemed to attract her especially, and she developed a kind of game of her own in which certain trees were given particular 'personalities'. Not just personalities as trees, but the trees came to stand for significant people in her life. She said she would 'talk' to them playfully as she passed and think and write about them in her room in the evenings. She made symbols of them.

The first drawings I saw were pinned up in her room – they measured perhaps two inches square. The subject was a clump of pine trees on a hill top some miles from the village. The ridge ran across the horizon for about five miles and these pines stood out stark and strange against the sky. She had climbed the hill to see them at close hand one Sunday and taken some photographs. What was singular about the clump – apart from its prominence on an

otherwise clear horizon – was the broken and shattered forms of most
of the individual trees. I expressed pleasure and interest in the
drawings but offered no special or particular advice. The drawings
however gradually proliferated, at the same time growing bigger.
From the very tentative and restrained initial figures there began to
develop forms that would carry much more information, and information of an increasingly subtle and complex kind. Then with a
suddenness and passion that was simply staggering Lilli began to
produce large and detailed drawings of trees, literally by the dozen.
She was completely obsessed by her subject and overjoyed at her
capacity to express herself in this medium. She did little else for
weeks, making forays into the countryside (including a car journey
to Wales) for fresh material, making sketches from nature and then
working them up on her return. The drawings may have lacked
technical finesse (she battled away at technical problems all the
time) since she was totally untutored, but there could be no denying
their power, nor their significance for her.

Her trees were for a time the delight and centre of her life. One
felt that here were years and years of stored up energy, finding
creative release through a naturally endowed though untutored
talent. The flood of work was, as I have said, astonishing. Eventually
the time came for the return home and to teaching again – in fact to
many of the frustrations that had contributed to her illness. The
circumstances, she found, had not changed, but she felt that she to
some extent had. My news of her now is that she is at least coping
with her problems and making headway with her personal plans;
the latest 'trees' however no longer seem to have quite the old conviction about them and show no real development since she left for
home. I say this without any implied judgement about either the
'personal' value of that expressive outburst in the long term (whether
or not the experience was 'therapeutic') or about the apparent
failure to move on, expressively that is, to something else or something more. This is simply what happened, at a particular time and
in particular circumstances.

  Discussion:
(a) Lilli's sensate problem form was complex and 'dramatic' –
    essentially the dialectic between strong, beautiful, living forms
    and their doomed splitting and breaking; between a feeling for
    the titanic and the sublime on the one hand, and suffering and
    ultimate weakness on the other. My own feeling is that the trees,
    at their best, achieved a tragic equilibrium.
(b) This tragic sense might have taken any form – she chose a visual
    medium and the tree became the holding or organizing image
    for her. However they were also powerfully dramatic and kin-
    aesthetic in feel.
(c) She was never to my knowledge entirely satisfied with the

results she achieved, so we must pronounce the final versions as 'near misses', since she would do so. They represent an act of considerable personal courage, however, and one could confidently say of the work that it left her feeling very much more herself. Left her with knowing in her bones and a real basis for self-confidence: trust in oneself.

(d) She rejected her habitual media – the body and the written word – for one which somehow seemed to be more suitable and intuitively right. Perhaps she simply felt that this medium was the appropriate one for representing her feelings about people. Such was her choice when that particular expressive moment came.

Study 6

In the study that follows I show how failure to formulate a sensate problem properly made the solving of the problem impossible: mere stimulus was not enough. Perception of the problem form was also necessary and came fortuitously in the process of the image-making itself.

I was working with a group of drama teachers on an in-service course and, having done some preliminary talking, suggested some exercises that might provide material for further discussion. My theme was the nature or character of the dramatic medium and we spent some time doodling and playing. I eventually asked the group to create a dramatic image for themselves – through improvisation – based upon the Seven Deadly Sins. We had a quick quiz to make sure we knew what they were (and came up with about sixteen) and then set about 'growing' a character. People worked for the most part on their own, but you could not but be aware of those around you. Some spontaneous relationships sprang into being. It was the sudden occurrence of such a relationship that proved to be the critical moment for me. I do not always 'join in' my own sessions but on this occasion I did.

I had decided to be Envy and was soon gliding along behind other people, or padding swiftly here and there, pursuing particular individuals and watching them out of the corner of my eye. All this seemed fair enough and I certainly felt I was making some headway, locating the feeling of being envious (envious being). But I was floundering for an image until my eyes suddenly caught those of Gluttony – for that is who she undoubtedly was. She was standing in a doorway watching me in considerable apprehension. For a moment I was not sure what she was up to. I had noticed her some minutes earlier apparently making off with a dish of biscuits (the housekeeper had laid 'tea' for the course in the hall). Her sense of guilt was what arrested and attracted my attention. It was like a nasty–attractive smell in the air. Our eyes met and in that instant we became partners: carrion and vulture. How I loathed her. How she feared me. My perception of myself changed at once, and I could 'see' myself, objectively as it were. I was suddenly wearing a neat but slightly faded dark grey suit, shirt, (soiled) collar and sober tie, grubby underwear, Church Warden black shoes. I folded the newspaper I was carrying into half, then half and half again until it was a sturdy baton. I beat my thighs with it hard and walked briskly but lithely to and fro. (None of this was thought out. It just happened.) My quarry hid from me – darting into corners and doorways, down passages. For long periods I missed her altogether – a pain grew in my left arm and I developed the habit of massaging the hard knot with my right hand. Then I noticed, on one of my inspectorial visits to the hall, that the entire tea table had been cleared!

My God, I was incensed! I knew exactly what to expect. There, sure enough, on the floor of the passage leading to the cloakrooms were the plates of biscuits and cakes, all hidden under papers. I gave voice to my indignation, speaking aloud to myself, certain she was somewhere within earshot, and with great speed and officiousness restored the plates to the table. My quarry hid and watched me with tears in her eyes.

Afterwards we spoke together briefly about what had happened. She told me of the 'transformation' that had come over me as we first caught each other's eyes. She said my eyes were terrible and her fear had been almost unbearable. For me Envy had acquired real meaning, as Gluttony had for her.

Discussion:
(a) Although I had a fairly specific stimulus (image word Envy) I had not been able to *formulate* my sensate problem so I drifted expressively from cliché to cliché. I could not feel the *gestalt*.
(b) Until I met Gluttony. In wanting to destroy Gluttony I became aware of my own murderous appetite – and my need to placate a ravening hurt. Her way was to come forward – mine to hold back. We rocked in eternal, insatiable counter-poise, perfectly attuned to torment ourselves by touching our pain precisely. My sensate problem could now be felt. I had my holding form in the knot in my arm. I went on to build my human volcano with rapid strokes. Between us we also had a holding form for a piece of drama: standing opposed in mutual accusa-tion: her running like water, my getting knotted.

7 The Use of Realized Form

In *The Intelligence of Feeling* Witkin cites the use of realized form as one of the four principal aims of arts education to emerge from discussions with arts teachers. He used this term to cover all those activities that centred upon 'educating' pupils' responses to works of art – to the feeling forms of others. This whole area of the arts curriculum has been a somewhat controversial one for some time. On the one hand teachers have been anxious not to foist their own tastes upon the young and yet, on the other, they have rightly felt bound to introduce their pupils to the works of art that are their cultural heritage. Several teachers have expressed with almost missionary zeal to me their commitment to this idea. 'If we don't show them these marvellous things then they may miss them altogether and their chance be utterly lost.' And yet these same teachers very often admit to a sense of futility as their best intentions seem to fall so far short of realization. The children do not see what the teachers are getting at. They seem bored, untouched, inaccessible. They cannot, or will not, see or hear or understand. The teachers cast about for an explanation in the 'class' barrier or the 'intelligence' gap or the 'generation' gap. Of course not all their efforts are frustrated, but all the same it is often very difficult to get the secondary-school pupil to see what you are driving at when you show him a painting by Turner, or read him a poem by Blake or play him a piece of Mozart. And it is hard to see why this should be so, despite the obvious difficulties. In desperation some teachers turn to contemporary pop, to teenage culture itself, only to find that their pupils are not interested in acquiring discriminated responses or making critical appraisals. The pop scene is their scene and we are somehow trespassers, and we make ourselves rather ridiculous into the bargain when they sense we do not really respond with any conviction to their music, their scene.

Earlier in this book, in the section on 'Imaging', I spoke of the need to help children to make the images of others into personal forms which they can use to evoke and resolve feelings of their own. This is not as easy as we might wish it to be and yet it is important we succeed, and I feel sure, given an understanding of what is involved, that we can. The arts represent a vast compendium of symbols which we can all use to order feeling, and those who have experienced the power of art to make them whole will care passionately that this world be opened up for their pupils. The question is, how?

We have already discussed the use of realized forms to evoke an expressive impulse – to set a sensate problem for a pupil to work on – and there are a number of examples given in this book of realized forms being used in this way. But it may be one thing for us to see the sensate structure at the heart of a poem or a picture; it is another to set the problem in the consciousness of the pupil – for the pupil to see or feel it too. In which case we have a very special job to do, one essentially the same as that allotted by John Dewey to criticism: 'The function of criticism is the re-education of perception of works of art; it is an auxiliary process, a difficult process, of learning to see and hear.' This re-education (or simply education) of perception is, as we have already stressed, an essential aspect of the arts teacher's work. Helping someone else to see, however, is no simple task – it means finding a common language that will enable you to draw the other to meet you where you are. Once again we are at the edge of a thorny old question: that of the 'particularity' as against the 'generality of an experience. I am not saying that it is the critic's (or the teacher's) job to make the other see the 'particularity' of what he sees, it is rather to evoke the underlying sensate structure that allows identity of perception at the level of generality. The successful critic/teacher will be able

(a) to perceive the general aesthetic/affective structure of the 'image' (realized form);
(b) to evoke that structure in the consciousness of the other.

To be able to reveal the deep structure, the critic needs to be more explicit, more conceptual than the artist was, and yet not merely conceptual, for really good criticism works much as poetry does, and is itself something of an expressive equivalent of the original. The role of the intermediary is clearly of the utmost importance – it is also a very demanding one. Demanding of extreme sensitivity to the responses of the other as well as to the qualities of the subject itself, so as not to go beyond the priming of the response system he is seeking to activate.

Criticism is fraught with dangers. Striking the right balance between the evocative and the discursive is very difficult – and all kinds of 'conceptual' traps lurk. It is so easy to pre-empt the authentic and particular response you are trying to arouse. It is also easy to get distracted by other matters, historical, cultural, moral etc. Dewey says, continuing the passage already quoted: 'The conception that its business is to appraise, to judge in the legal and moral sense, arrests the perception of those who are influenced by the criticism that assumes this task.' The critic/teacher seeks to educate rather than to arrest perception. Our job is to *intercede for the image*. Critical dissection need not be lethal, but it can easily become so.

I think of the process of recreative perception as essentially similar to the process of expressive forming. Both are projective. Both involve the resolution of impulse in feeling form. The act of responding to a work of art has often been described as creative, and I think we can see what this means if we think of our model of subject-reflexive action. Impulse is again the essential starting point, only this time it seeks the structure of a pre-existent form. If our act is recreative rather than representational we have to discern the basic structure within the form we are probing – which is, in a sense, the reciprocal of that first movement of consciousness in the medium, the making of a holding form. The recreative probe needs to be 'held' very much in the same way as the representational probe had to be. The critic/teacher's task is to see that the sensate problem is 'set', and that the recreative probe is similarly held or centred. Given the *gestalt*, we can probe the form with our sensing and build up its full particularity for us, to the point where we know our feeling, and the form resolves the impulse it evoked within us.

It is a genuinely *recreative* process: from impulse to form. But this time we probe a form that already exists and allow it to take on full particularity for us as we do so. Provided our formulation of the *gestalt* was accurate, and we remain centred in the form during the probing process, we should achieve full resolution in the end. We might not get properly centred to start with, and we always run the risk of losing control in the process, especially if we become distracted by irrelevant information and lose the vital homing signal. The process of recreation is, like the process of creation, essentially *subject-reflexive*. It is impulse (rather than rule) directed. Once the problem has been set and a *gestalt* (holding form) found for the recreative probe, then the process of resolution goes forward by means of a series of approximations. The teacher must and can participate in the recreative process.

I feel that this appreciation of the response to realized form should give the teacher an altogether greater chance of 'educating perception' than has perhaps been possible through more traditional approaches. I hope the readers of this book will become as enthusiastic about 'art appreciation' as I now feel. Certainly I find myself adopting a whole variety of new techniques in helping students to respond to literature, for instance. In winding up this rather brief excursion into the critical field I shall once again cite one or two examples by way of illustration.

Here is something I found amongst the CEE work of an Indian girl in a London comprehensive. She had been on a school visit to the Tate Gallery and bought several postcard offprints: it had been suggested to her that she might use them as the basis for creative writing – stories essentially. The paintings she chose were:

'Nevermore', Gauguin
'The Sick Child', Edward Munch
'Swinging London', Richard Hamilton
'The Golden Age', Benjamin West
'The Married Couple', George Grotz

It seemed to me that her comments showed in several cases that she was clearly responding to the central feeling idea of each painting. There was also some indication, I feel, that she had grasped something of the 'morphology of feeling' – Susanne Langer's point that the basic feeling structure can equally well carry happy as sad feeling content. In some instances both, paradoxically, at the same time. She was not tempted to play the art criticism game, nor to run off into her own fantasies. Sometimes she adopted the reflective (or calculating) mode but always, one feels, to come back to the picture, seeking deeper affective meaning. The teacher's comments seemed less secure than hers, as if he were not very sure of the real nature (the subject-reflexive character) of the recreative act. His response was merely supportive where it might also have been instructive.

> These paintings were chosen at random not only because I liked them but because to me they suggested several different stories, and because they could be described quite clearly. Even though the feeling I get is always the same, one of sorrow, dismay and darkness, the story is always different, it can either have a sad or a happy ending.

> The two paintings express no feeling of encouragement but seemed to be isolated from everything and everybody and wondering why we ever do things and what is the point.

> Although 'Nevermore' is supposed to be an abstract, I see it otherwise. It reminds me of a book called *The L-shaped room*.

> The kind, gentle, loving mother standing in desperation by the bedside of her sick child. Full of grief, hoping that her child may soon recover, while the child comforts her not knowing what is to happen.

The teacher singled out the following paragraphs for comment and endorsement (marginal tick).

> It is not often a parent will express his true feelings towards his child, perhaps because they could be later taken for granted. For example, my dad, although being hard and strict, will occasionally show his feelings for us. He will sometimes call me for instance into his room and in his consideration ask how I am progressing at school or what sort of a day I have had. And it is after I have talked to him that I realize that it is not that he does not love or care for us, only that he does not know how to show it. And

I feel that his hardness and strictness towards us has proved to be for our benefit. (Tick.)

Nevertheless the problem of parents not taking enough interest in their child is something which cannot be overcome unless parents begin to feel a certain responsibility towards their child, especially the mother. She is the one who should spend time with the child and give it love, kindness and understanding, even after marriage. (Teacher: 'Very good' + tick.)

She wrote a poem about the Grotz picture – this is the last verse:

> There is no future for us
> We have nothing left.
> Our children, married and gone
> Not knowing how we felt
> You are old and so am I.

(Teacher: 'Good – I like this painting and this poem.')

The girl seems to have grasped the tragic contradictions inherent in these pictures and to have sensed the character of the particular and similar impulse they each evoked in her. I feel she was well on the way to a full response, and absolutely ripe for informed participation from the teacher.

I have recently been looking at a painting by Rousseau with a group of teachers on an in-service course. The painting is his 'Carnival Evening'. We studied it on a number of occasions and for a period of several hours all told. Only at the end of that period did we actually look for and discover the title the painter had given it. I had 'prepared' the group for the idea of the recreative response by 'leading them' (something of a euphemism I suspect) into Britten's setting of the John Donne sonnet 'Oh my black soule' and Blake's poem 'Sunflower!' This time I simply stuck the picture to the blackboard and invited them to respond to it in any way they wished. I did not suggest a formulation of the sensate problem – though the implication was that they should seek it for themselves. I hesitate to describe the painting but perhaps I should just give a hint as to its 'content' – readers are strongly advised to get to know it for themselves. The painting shows two small black and white 'pierrot' figures (man and woman) in a 'natural' setting. They stand facing the viewer on a narrow strip of very dark green grass. Behind them a screen of tall trees is sharply silhouetted against a luminous pale sky. There is a heavy bank of white clouds cutting the picture horizontally more or less in two – they are tinged on the underside with pink. High up in the picture a full moon hangs motionless among tiny pin pricks of stars – and there are three strange little clouds hovering more or less midway between the moon and the couple. The three clouds, the moon and the man and woman have an odd two-dimensional 'cut out' quality about them that contrasts strongly with the three-dimensional feel of the vast spaces opened up behind the pair. Part of the tree 'screen' is formed by a large dark summer house to the left of centre. It too has a gauze-like character, with the bright sky pricking through. Despite its many 'realistic' elements the picture nevertheless conveys a disturbing sense of unreality: it borders on the surreal while remaining somehow very real. (It is a marvel!)

Responses varied: one of the group immediately set to work on a collage, another began writing a story, someone else went off for a walk. Several people considered a sound interpretation and, the following week, one of the group turned up with a collection of photographs and in a state of some excitement began to compose a series of images on the floor that caught something of the picture's flavour. But the teacher in question – a painter – complained that his painterly training made it almost impossible for him to see it naïvely. When in due course we got down to discussing the *gestalt*, someone suggested the contrast between day and night and the unsettling tricks that unreal lighting played on one's perceptions. No one seriously objected to my formulation – it sounds horrible but these formulations tend to – 'Dawn: the coming and going identity.' It seemed to contain all the elements, pointing to the intersection of there and then in the here and now that contained what had been and what would be. That I had named the picture 'Dawn' when it was supposedly 'Evening' was not to get the essential structure wrong: time and space are in a similar state of tension and fluidity either way. The 'screens' seemed to be somehow the essential image in the whole piece, as significant for what they masked as for what they revealed. With this formulation it was then possible to go deeper into the particularity of the image. I certainly feel that picture is now very much 'mine', and can easily recall the blank unseeing character of my initial probing. It was the dawning perception of the picture's sublime paradox that finally allowed access to my fully awakened sensibility. Here is a poem written by one of the group; Gweneth:

> Two-faced dawn with your swinging gate
> Where further in is further out,
> Moving to is moving from
> and light is only night made late.
> Shadow the fingers of the sun
> And let me know when day is done.
>
> Breaking down with your clarity
> Hiding traces of the dark
> Sharpening light on drifting mist
> Probing cover without pity.
> Gently with my dragon-fly –
> So it may live when you will die.

We concluded our final session on the picture in some disarray having disagreed over my suggestion that, although there could be many different 'right' responses to a work of art, there are some that are actually incorrect or inappropriate. For instance to be unable to 'see' the picture because it reminds you of the sadness of Pagliaci or because you know a lot about Rousseau's life is to have allowed 'inappropriate' factors to interfere with perception. As J. H. Gribble points out in his paper 'Pandora's box: The Affective Domain of Educational Objectives'[1] it is not enough to ask if a child 'responds emotionally to a work of art' as distinct from merely conceptually. To know whether a child has responded properly or adequately, we need to know that the child responds 'with the appropriate emotion'. The implication is – and I think most of what has been said in this book so far would support it – that we can identify expressive problems, set and resolve them. If we can, then there may be those that miss the point, not merely in mistaking concept for percept but in mis-reading the essential *gestalt* itself. Gribble goes on to make the point about the education of perception in these terms:

> In the analysis of a child's affective response to a work of art, for example, it is crucial to get at the way the child sees the work. The only way we can get him to feel differently about it is to get him to see it differently.

The use of realized form means getting children to feel differently about books and pictures and music by getting them to 'see' them differently. This makes great demands on the teacher as intercessor – as one who can reveal the affective character of a work of art and heighten perceptions. If the pupil is to 'see' a painting at all it has to be 'set' in the particularity of his own experience. Once seen it may be felt. Once felt it may be used.

[1] Taylor, P. H. and Tye, K. A. (eds.), *Curriculum, School and Society*, NFER, 1975.

PART TWO

Practical Matters

8 Creating a Personal Symbol

John Woolner

Introduction

John Woolner describes a deceptively simple-seeming piece of work. I feel he supplies a clear example of exactly the kind of teacher-pupil encountering we have been discussing. His contribution shows how, given a conceptual framework to inform his own perception of that encounter, a teacher may give full rein to his intuitive responses to a pupil's needs. In this case he seems to me to have been entirely right in his identification of the sensate problem, manifest in Lindscy's first piece of work. He did not formulate it as the 'soft/sharp contrast' but saw that she was interested in depicting the spikes of the conker shell and was having difficulty in doing so. That she was also 'aware' of the softness within the shell seems to me to be borne out when she actually turns the design inside out as it were (Fig. 8.4) to resolve the impulse in a total form. The teacher's grasp of the 'affective tendency' of the initial image allows the making of the holding form (Fig. 8.2). As Mr Woolner himself says, the work was probably carried beyond the point of resolution in the final piece (Fig. 8.5). Since I first saw this series of photographs and heard the author's account of the project it has stood for me as a fine example of the movement from sensate problem, through holding form to resolution.

M.R.

In the account which follows I shall describe an attempt to work in the way Witkin writes of, i.e. 'from within the expressive act'.

In our work in art the traditional stimulus is provided by studies made from observation, and in the exercise I set the group in which Lindsey was working, I was concerned to explore the nature of the expressive act made in the actual presence of observed objects. I wanted to investigate the degree to which the nature and character of the object being studied influences the development of subjective response. Previous observations seemed to suggest that the presence of the actual object often hinders a response of that kind, and that this aspect of our work needed closer investigation. It seems likely that a lack of understanding of the nature of 'drawing', a sense of obligation to make things look 'real' and a lack of technical skill, are contributing factors. It is possible too that the mode of encounter, limited as it is in visual studies mainly to the visual sensory stimulus, might be a factor, and this is a line of inquiry which I hope to pursue to much greater depth in the future.

We perceive with feeling. Perception is coloured by subjectivity. This was the valuable lesson that Lindsey's work taught me. (Lindsey is fifteen.)

I set up a very orthodox exercise in which the members of the group were asked to choose and study one natural form, selected from a number provided. I placed great emphasis on concentrated looking, and made some remarks about pushing the quality of concentration to the point where a new level of perception would be attained.

In this kind of situation a triangular encounter is built up between the object, the response of the child in terms of his perception and feeling, and the response of the teacher who is a trained artist with all that involves in terms of his own perception and vision of the object.

The five illustrations of Lindsey's work which follow seem to me to demonstrate very graphically the cycle of expressive activity deriving from observed studies. They are numbered in chronological sequence but should not necessarily be read in a linear sequential way. Each one is an attempt at a resolution of a problem, and should be read as that, perhaps, rather than as a developmental sequence; each successive stage does not necessarily build on the previous one.

Lindsey chose to work from a horse chestnut on the basis, to use her own words, that she wanted 'something interesting'. Her decision to use the horse chestnut is quite interesting, too, because it seems to suggest that, subconsciously perhaps, she was seeking an object (for reasons which appear later) which could be assimilated into a feeling form already existing, possibly partly obscured, in her consciousness, and which could be accommodated to that form. In a special sense the feeling for the characteristic quality of the horse chestnut was already present in her mind before she chose to work from it.

Two technical problems emerged for her (Fig. 8.1): one was to create the textural quality of the green skin of the shell, and the second was how to create the illusion of spikes coming out of its surface. She worked very laboriously for a long time and was obviously struggling. At the end I decided to show her a schematic

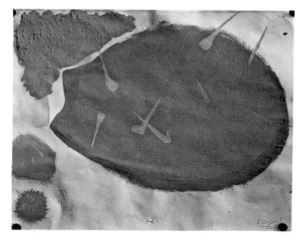

Fig. 8.1

Fig. 8.2

Fig. 8.3

Fig. 8.4

resolution for the problem of the spikes. What I tried to give her was a 'schema', that is to say a convention for looking, an aid to perception, which is more than a formula for how to draw something. At that point I became involved within her expressive act. She then produced the schematic form shown in Fig. 8.2, and the interesting point here is that she alone made the decision to use metallic foil for the spikes. The reference to sharp blades is obvious, it is becoming symbolic. The subjective response is beginning to develop, it is an object of pain.

Lindsey then expressed dissatisfaction at her inability to give the illusion of three-dimensional form to the spikes, and again I gave her a 'schema'. This time it concerned the use of light and shadow to give the illusion of depth, and I made a quick pencil sketch to show her what was involved. Fig. 8.3 shows how she used this demonstration in a painting. We have moved away from the 'appearance' of the conker and are operating in the world of symbolic language.

The symbolic form is now developed further in the next piece of work, carried out at home. This contains a most interesting development. Now the blades are turned inwards (Fig. 8.4). The previous forms have been objects of pain, existing externally as symbols of feeling, but this image is one of pure feeling, epitomizing internal anguish, a most profound expression of the feeling of pain, a truly expressive feeling form without reference to objects outside itself. It is a pure feeling form.

At this stage I made a mistake. Up to that point I had merely shown her codes of practice, technical methods to overcome representational problems. Now I had a vision of something she might

Fig. 8.5

make as an end result, deriving from my own knowledge of 'Art', from looking perhaps at twentieth-century sculpture in the galleries, a vision quite outside Lindsey's experience, of course. I suggested that she should make the form in three dimensions to fit within a box. She co-operated and built a form within a polythene bag which is surrounded by 'blades' (Fig. 8.5). Significantly, however, this last piece of work was abandoned before completion.

Some time later I discovered that Lindsey has a deep personal experience of pain stemming from early childhood, and it is apparent that the memory of the experience is still very much with her. I would argue that the feeling form which she created was to reconcile the experience of pain with the sense of her own unity. Her sense of totality, when it came to the discovery of the essence of her being, needed to include this element of pain. Symbolically she was attempting to reconcile the two.

I think that it is necessary for me to add that all my work is not subjected to such intensive examination, but whilst I would accept that there could be different interpretations of the symbolism in Lindsey's work, one thing is clear, the absorbing interest which she showed in her studies does mean that something important and meaningful at a personal level was happening.

9 Art–A Way of Knowing

Len Jenkinson

Introduction

Len Jenkinson provides an example of school work that exemplifies some of the major ideas to be found in Part 1. He presents children's work in the context of his own thinking about the curriculum, and I feel they stand, for all his own reservations about them, as fine examples of curriculum making in the visual arts. Mr Jenkinson describes a project that attempts to bring out the special meaning of creative work in the arts – he contrasts what he gets the children to do with their activities in the more strictly academic area of the curriculum. In order for the children to switch into the appropriate way of working in the arts he develops a sustained and elaborate programme of what we might call 'cognitive acclimatization': he only introduces the stimulus for the creative work when he feels the children are cognitively ready. The children's responses to the stimuli he uses provide clear evidence of his success, and throw up a number of very interesting ideas that call for closer study.

M.R.

Education is today directed toward intellectual specialization; the education of the emotions is neglected. Thinking is trained; feeling is left untrained.[1]

SIGFRIED GIEDION

The major part of my contribution here is a description of some work done by my fourth-year pupils in their art lessons and lunch-times over a period of some five weeks. The actual description of the stages of the work and the pupils' responses should itself shed light on the conceptual framework within which I operate, and for this reason,

[1] Giedion, Sigfried, 'Space, Time and Architecture. The growth of a new tradition', *The Charles Eliot Norton Lectures for 1938–1939*, Oxford University Press, 1971 p. 878.

with the exception of a brief introduction, I have restricted theoretical considerations almost entirely to those arising directly out of the procedures adopted.

The practical work is, however, very closely linked with theory in this project, and the description I offer has given rise to many opportunities to quote at length from various sources – this I hope I have resisted. Rather than do this, I have chosen simply to direct the reader who wishes to explore the theoretical background to what is presented here to the following sources: (a) *Philosophy in a New Key*[1] and *Feeling and Form*[2] both by Susanne K. Langer (those chapters of these volumes concerned with the significance of music are particularly relevant); (b) *The Philosophy of Symbolic Forms*[3] by Ernst Cassirer (particularly Volume 3: *The Phenomenology of Knowledge*, concerning 'Expression'); (c) *The Intelligence of Feeling*[4] by Robert W. Witkin (particularly 'Resolution – from within the Expressive Act', and within this chapter the section headed 'The Setting of the Sensate Problem'); (d) *Arts and the Adolescent*, Schools Council Working Paper 54[5] by Malcolm Ross.

The relationship of the material listed above to my day-to-day experience in the art room needs clarification. I hope the description of this small project may go some way to affording that clarification. I may say at the outset that I find the theoretical material extremely valuable in that it reinforces what I have come to know on an intuitive level, and that some understanding of the creative process enables me to structure the content of art lessons in a more effective way.

Since the description of the project is my main concern I will be fairly brief in introducing it and setting it within the context of my general teaching aims.

I regard art as a basic way of *knowing*.

I regard art as an expressive activity; when the pupils 'do' art they are creating forms expressive of *feeling*.

I have begun recently, wherever possible in my teaching, to present the pupils with an emotional stimulus for art work. Since they are all individuals, their work and their responses to the stimulus vary. As the art teacher I can, however, enter into their creative process without (to borrow some of the words of Robert Witkin) trespassing on their particularity, because I understand the 'generality' of the problem they are dealing with – I understand the *structure* of the problem posed by the stimulus, i.e., the structure of the 'feeling' it creates. The nature of the creative process is such that it is only when words are used or forms are created that the feeling is realized. Drawing, for example, can begin with the desire to express

---

[1] Harvard University Press, 1969.   [2] Routledge & Kegan Paul, 1953.
[3] Yale University Press, 1965.   [4] Heinemann Educational Books, 1974.
[5] Evans/Methuen Educational, 1975.

a feeling, but the marks which are made in turn shape that feeling – a reciprocal activity or cycle is set up. We must all of us have had this experience with language – it is only when we find the word that we hold, and thus in a sense 'behold', the feeling. This is why I describe art as a way of knowing, and why I regard art as having a primary function in the education of the adolescent.

During the course of the project I shall describe, some of the pupils seemed to begin to grasp the broader implications of what they were doing; the fact that this was a way of knowing, that it was educationally valid, seemed to surprise and delight some of them.

This leads me to define the role of my art teaching in relation to the rest of the school curriculum. I hope the following passage may be useful in describing the way of knowing I am seeking to facilitate, and how this may differ from the concerns of the rest of the curriculum.

> So-called 'common sense' does not carry this literal formulation of its ideas of things, persons, etc., very far in the way of elaboration. Common-sense knowledge is prompt, categorical and inexact. A mind that is very sensitive to forms as such and is aware of them beyond the common-sense requirements for recognition, memory, and classification of things, is apt to use its images metaphorically, to exploit their possible significance for the conception of remote or intangible ideas. That is to say, if our interest in 'Gestalten' goes beyond their common-sense meaning it is apt to run us into their dynamic, mythic, or artistic meanings. To some people this happens very easily; in savage society, at least in certain stages of development it seems to be actually the rule, so that secondary imports of forms – plastic, verbal or behavioural forms – often eclipse what Coleridge called 'primary imagination' of them. Since data and experience, in other words, are essentially *meaningful structures,* their primary, secondary, or even more recondite meanings may become crossed in our impression of them to the detriment of one value or another.[1]

I see my art teaching as being concerned with Langer's 'Secondary imports of forms', their 'dynamic, mythic, or artistic meanings'. From my limited knowledge of the rest of the curriculum (I encounter virtually no discussion of 'aims' among my non-art colleagues) I would characterize the work which takes place elsewhere among non-arts subjects (and even, sadly, among other arts subjects) as being concerned with Langer's '. . . common-sense requirements for recognition, memory and classification of things'. Obviously this is a generalization; it is important to realize that I am describing the possible, scarcely articulated, aims of the rest of the curriculum – the pupils, in the nature of things, will use the curriculum at all levels.

Many of the other school subjects are concerned with 'abstract' knowledge. The symbolism they are grounded in is largely discursive

---

[1] Langer, Susanne K., *Philosophy in a New Key* (Oxford University Press, 1951), from the Chapter 'The Fabric of Meaning'.

and of a 'linear' character – they differ from art in this respect. A distinction is often made between art and the other subjects in this way; people say, in art we are concerned with the subjective response, elsewhere they are concerned with the objective world; the arts are about affective development, the rest about cognitive development. But we can look at it in a slightly different way. I would prefer to say that in art we are dealing with a different sort of *meaning*.

It is very difficult to convince people of the importance of artistic meaning in education, and of the importance of art as a way of knowing. It is perhaps interesting to reflect that the most obvious area in which people pass beyond 'common-sense' knowledge and the rational is that of personal relationships – the choice of friends and partners is often arrived at through the exercise of the way of knowing that I am trying to describe – perhaps this may be a useful analogy.

The arts do not provide an alternative way of knowing. To borrow a phrase from Witkin again, the child must find himself in the world, as well as finding the world in himself; the two are equally important. For all but the artistic genius, a balance between the two is desirable.

What is not generally realized is that there are structures in the world of aesthetic experience. In exploring the world of artistic import we are not moving into chaos – I quote Langer again:

> ... Moreover, the same symbols, qualities, lines, rhythms – may occur in innumerable presentations; they are abstractable and combinatory. It is quite natural, therefore, that philosophers who have recognized the symbolical character of so-called 'sense-data', especially in their highly developed uses in science and art, often speak of a 'language of the senses', a language of musical tones, of colours and so forth.[1]

I have tried to explore something of this 'language' in the project which follows.

The Project

> All the senses have feeling at their base, and this creates so intimate, powerful and ineffable a bond between the most diverse sensations that through it the strangest phenomena arise ... Among creatures of sensibility, who gain sensation through many different senses at once, this grouping of ideas is inevitable, for what are all our senses other than mere modalities of one positive power of the psyche ... With great pains we learn to separate them for practical purposes, yet at a certain depth they always operate together.[2]

HERDER

[1] ibid.
[2] Von Herder, J. G., quoted by Ernst Cassirer in *The Philosophy of Symbolic Forms*, Vol. III, *The Phenomenology of Knowledge*, Yale University Press, 1965, p. 32.

I have written about this project now it is finished; I did not plan it on paper before I began, although I knew roughly what I intended to do. I am indebted to a friend for providing me with what was to become the major stimulus for this work. I was lent a gramophone record which carried a track featuring a solo on electric guitar. I listened to this music many times at home and soon began to realize that it was really something special. At that stage I had no notion of using it in my teaching. When I did think of doing this I was eager to give the pupils the opportunity of hearing the music but seriously doubted if they would 'hear' what I was hearing – in other words I thought it was a stimulus which was too far away from the pupils' experience to be effective. The record was called *Alone Together* by Dave Mason, and the particular track was called 'Look at You, Look at Me'. I had not heard of the artist until I was lent the record. It is quite an old record and now, sadly, deleted.[1] After trying the record at school it quickly became apparent that the pupils liked it – they expressed an interest in it and inquired about it. I therefore decided to present it among a choice of two other starting points for work.[2]

Stimulus 1:

'Baubles, Bangles and Beads' sung by Dionne Warwick. From the L.P. *The Greates Hits of Dionne Warwick* (Hallmark SHM789. Track 6 side 1).
'People Make the World Go Round' sung by The Stylistics. From the L.P. *The Best of the Stylistics* (Avco 9109 003. Track 5 Side 2).
A reproduction of the painting 'Broadway Boogie-Woogie' by Piet Mondrian 1943.

Stimulus 3:

'My Baby, My Baby, My Own' sung by Diana Ross. From the L.P. *Touch Me in the Morning* by Diana Ross (Tamla Motown ST ML 11239B Track 1 Side 1).
Sheets of photographs of empty desolate streets.

(I would like to record at this stage that I feel no embarrassment at having drawn on what is described as 'popular music'. I regard much of the musical material from this source as having considerable artistic merit and interest, particularly in the relationship of form to feeling – to those feelings evinced by contemporary life.)

I wanted to ensure that the work was to be about the feeling generated by the music in the individual pupil, and not about the music itself; I have initiated work in the past where pupils have tried to find a visual form for a piece of music. In technical language this latter type of work is concerned with 'denotation', i.e., the

[1] Now re-released (ABC Records, ABCL 5191).

[2] Because of the limited space available to me, and for the sake of clarity, I have chosen to disregard these two other starting points and the work done as a result of them. In the event the pupils who chose to work from these starting points were in the minority. I list these starting points here for the interest of the reader, who will also find an illustration (Fig. 9.22) on p. 157 of a painting done as a result of 'stimulus 1'. (The numbers stimulus 1 and 3 refer to the order of presentation – the guitar music formed part of stimulus 2.)

relationship of the symbol to what it represents. This is a type of 'projection', whereas what I was to be concerned with here was 'connotation', i.e., the relationship of the symbol to what, for want of a better word, I shall call the 'conceptualization' of the individual pupil.

The fact that the pupils were to work with visual images, although presented with an auditory stimulus, itself helped to distance the stimulus from their expressive act and reinforced the idea that their concern was to be with the content of the experience rather than the form. As a further aid to this, I cast about for a piece of writing which had the same 'feeling' as the music, i.e. a piece of writing with regard to which my response demonstrated the same structural characteristics as I recognized on hearing the music. What I am describing here is what Cassirer called 'Expressive perception'. I found it almost impossible to find anything which meant the same as the music (music is more powerful in evoking an emotional response than other forms since its form is more nearly analogous to that of our feelings), however I made do with quite a lengthy passage from the book, *The Cruel Sea*, a key paragraph of which I include here:

> At one point during the night the thin crescent moon came through the ragged clouds and illuminated for a moment the desperate scene below. It shone on a waste of water, growing choppy with the biting wind; it shone on the silhouettes of men hunched together on rafts, and the shadows of men clinging to them, and the blurred outlines of men in the outer ring, where the corpses wallowed and heaved, and the red lights burned and burned aimlessly on the breasts of those who, hours before, had switched them on in hope and confidence. For a few moments the moon put this cold sheen upon the face of the water, and upon the foreheads of the men whose heads were still upright, and then it withdrew, veiling itself abruptly, as if in pity and amazement, it had seen enough and knew that men in this extremity deserved only the decent mercy of darkness.[1]

The passage also includes descriptions of men dying in the water and men surviving and being kept alive as long as possible by others, yet the passage as a whole is such that the type of detailed description given here is less compelling than the general feeling induced by the character of the prose style; were this not the case some of the descriptive detail would have become obtrusive.

Having chosen the stimulus forms I thought appropriate, and that I understood at a structural level, I could not, however, present them to the pupils straight away and expect them to begin work. If I had done this I feel sure that nearly all of them would have been unequal to the task – they would have 'got stuck'. What was needed, I decided, were some exercises which encouraged the type of thinking –

[1] Monsarrat, Nicholas, *The Cruel Sea*, Penguin Books, 1956, p. 294.

the type of knowing – that was necessary. Above all I needed to hint at the idea of feeling transcending different forms – I needed to help them – to hint at an expressive language.

Fig. 9.1

Accordingly, I adopted the following procedure (I shall first describe the stages of the project and illustrate them with the work of one pupil – Bonnie, aged 14 years 11 months):

1. I demonstrated how it was possible to make a variety of textures with a paint brush. I then read aloud adjectives, each of which had to be represented by a square of texture of uniform size. The list of adjectives was carefully composed to include, among visual qualities, those qualities apprehended by the other senses.

Thus, as well as words such as 'glittering', there were words such as 'sad' and 'quiet'. The list was as follows:

1. Soft/hard
2. Smooth/rough
3. Scratchy
4. Light/heavy
5. Quiet/noisy
6. Calm/troubled
7. Far away
8. Sad
9. Wrong/right
10. Strong/weak
11. Warm/cold
12. Glittering

Immediately after painting each square (or mark) it was labelled and all opposites were bracketed together. Some pupils found it difficult to restrict themselves to the square format, but I think it was important and simpler that the problem was dealt with using one variable only. There is tremendous scope in the use of dry, scratchy, or watery paint in various patterns (Fig. 9.1 shows Bonnie's exercise).

2. The next exercise was to put the words into categories or groups, each of which was to have the same sort of 'feeling', and a heading was to be found for each group. Bonnie had some difficulty with her lists (the same word appears in more than one list and there is one list without a heading), nevertheless, the exercise worked for her – the lists constitute reasonably coherent groups:

Misty-dreaming	*Cross or Depressing*
Soft	Rough
Calm	Scratchy
Far-away	Noisy
Quiet	Troubled
Smooth	Wrong

Dense	————————
Hard	
Heavy	Glittering
Noisy	Right
Cold	Light
Wrong	
Strong	

Obviously the composition of these lists varied within certain limits; the choice of headings became a very personal matter and the positioning of the words 'right' and 'wrong' was interesting.

3. The next exercise consisted of transferring the headings on to a new piece of paper and listening to recordings of discrete sounds, taped from a John Cage record. After some practice at painting sounds (on the back of the paper), now using different shapes as well as different textures, although still only one colour, the pupils were asked to listen for sounds which seemed to fit under the headings and to paint them there. (Fig. 9.2 shows Bonnie's exercise.)

The pupils were now beginning to handle the same qualities in words, marks and sounds, and I felt fairly confident about presenting

Fig. 9.2

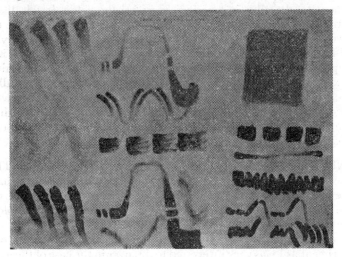

them with the realized form I had chosen for the stimulus. I made it clear that it was the feeling of both parts of the stimulus *together* which we were dealing with.

4. I now actually presented the starting point. In the case of the music I played the record twice and insisted on concentration and 'eyes closed listening'. I also offered advice about not letting the attention wander and 'following the thread of the music'. I felt hampered in presenting the music by the lack of a proper sound system; throughout the project the records were played in mono on an ancient 'Dansette' machine and they are now considerably the worse for wear. If more than one pupil adjusted his position in his chair the subsequent creaking all but drowned out the subtleties of the music. I was, however, satisfied that the presentation of the stimulus had been successful. I still held back from starting the pupils on drawing and painting; instead I asked them a very short series of the same questions about the starting point, to which I required one-word answers, for example: 'Night or Day?', 'Bright or Dull?', 'Quick or Slow?' These lists were to be seen as notes towards a painting and could include any other thoughts the individual pupil might have. Bonnie's list was as follows:

Complicated	Lack of hope
Muddled up	Night time
Bright and dull colours	Lonely
Abstract (maybe)	Strangers

5. After this I presented them with the stimulus again, and asked them to describe in writing, very briefly, what it felt like. I stressed that this was to be what they really thought and they were not to let anyone see what they were writing. All the activities I have described so far took place in silence; this I tried to insist upon. The last activity, the writing, was the first genuinely expressive part of the work. I had some reservations about allowing the expressive impulse to be realized in words, but I knew this would be easier, and felt it would afford a check when the drawing started in that the pupils could assess their drawing by comparing it with what they had written.

What they wrote helped to stabilize or *hold* the feeling. These pieces of writing were thus the first 'holding forms' the pupils made; since they subsequently made a drawing as a holding form, they were to have the advantage of having two 'equivalent' holding forms.

I also regarded this writing part of the project as something of an experiment as I was very interested to discover in the case of the guitar music just how the qualities it possessed would be described, and to what extent the same response would be evoked in different pupils (more on this point later). Bonnie's writing was as follows: (Where grammatical errors appear in the pupils' writing I have left them uncorrected.)

> The music and the passage both give the feeling of struggling. The music gives the feeling of trouble, people in need of help, hope, faith. The passage gives the feeling as well. They both were in a way sad as well as hopeful. The music gives the feeling of not knowing (whether as in the book, the people will come back). The matter is life or death.

6. At this stage the pupils finally began drawing. Using the same piece of paper which bore their writing, the pupils tried to make a fairly quick drawing – a 'holding form' which expressed the feeling. The drawing could be 'realistic' or 'abstract' (in the event very few pupils tried to do 'realistic' work, and of these all subsequently abandoned their attempt in favour of 'abstract' work). Chalks and crayons were used for these drawings. (Fig. 9.3 shows Bonnie's drawing; she did not need to complete it before starting her painting.)

Often several attempts were made at the drawing but they were all fairly quick; no drawing was worked on for any great length of time – drawings were improved upon by doing a better one, i.e. one which more nearly approached the feeling. It was easy to see the reciprocal activity, referred to earlier, taking place. The forms created – the resistance offered by the media to the expressive impulse – beginning to effect and shape the expressive impulse itself, the subjective response.

As in previous work of this type which I have initiated, it was fascinating to see the emergence of a specific category of forms, and this among groups of children with no access to each other's work (in work of this type it is obviously unwise to display drawings and paintings until a later stage). The written work also demonstrated that there was a great deal of agreement about the feeling – the pupils had grasped the 'structure' of the problem, although each regarded it through his or her particularity. This is all the more fascinating when we recall that the guitar music has no words to offer a lead.[1]

Fig. 9.3

The forms which began to predominate in the drawings can perhaps best be described as groups of shapes half-way between a wave and a curl. The waves obviously came from *The Cruel Sea* but they merged very nicely with the repeated curl which was a very accurate visual equivalent for the guitar sound. Suns, moons, and teardrops also began to appear, and forms which seemed to grow or struggle upwards. Some of the pupils began to use forms which they were recalling from biology lessons. It has occurred to me that forms cannot come from nowhere.

7. Once these forms began to emerge in the drawings I was able to intervene and offer some technical help in making them better, for example, in the case of those pupils who had arrived at what I called the 'curly-whirly' shapes. I showed them how to use the side of a piece of chalk to get more effective curves and the

[1] See written extracts on guitar music, p. 157.

illusion of three dimensions into twists and curves. This was obviously a most crucial stage of the work and I had to be very careful not to influence the way the thing was going, and to restrict my intervention to that which helped the pupils towards what they seemed to be after, rather than setting them on a new track of my own.

8. When the pupils were ready they embarked on their final painting. I gave them all black paper because I thought that was most suitable and would help them, like the background when your eyes are closed – more empty than white; as it turned out many of the paintings had the background colour changed. The painting was to be a resolution – most of the pupils now had several drawings growing in refinement. Most of them drew on the paper in chalk first and nearly all used rough paper for experimenting with colour mixing and so forth. (Fig. 9.4 shows Bonnie's final painting; for her first drawing, see Fig. 9.3.)

Where a pupil asked for help to achieve a particular affect, for example, one colour fading into another, I tried to show how to achieve this. The music was played many times during each of the art lessons and the visual material and book were to hand throughout.

I shall now go on to give further examples of the pupils' work. In these examples I shall present what the pupil wrote first and follow this with his or her drawings and painting, and my comments where appropriate.

Dean, 14 yrs 11 mths (Figs 9.5 and 9.6).

The music and the book have a lot in common. The book starts sad and uninteresting, it then flashes into a feeling of hope and gradually bears this feeling into the listener. It ends with a half hope, half despair, but before the end it is just a full source of power.

    (a) Complicated, it is muddled, but as the hope comes over it is orderly.
    (b) Drab and fighting a losing battle with a hope to win.
    (c) I can't think of anything to describe my painting of this except the sea in a bad mood.
    (d) The dawn is breaking on a cloudy day.
    (e) The rolling hillocks of the country.

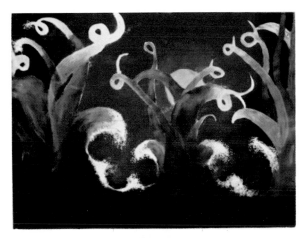

Fig. 9.4

There are countless examples in musicological literature and among the utterances of great musicians, that bear witness to the central importance of living form, the semblance of spontaneous movement, in music . . . one is forcibly reminded of the insistent note of vitalism, the universal agreement on the organic quality of all space composition, that runs through the comments of the masters of visual art . . . and it would be hard indeed not to entertain at least the hypothesis that all art works, no matter in what special domain, are 'organic' in the same sense. (Langer, S. K., *Feeling and Form*, Routledge and Kegan Paul, 1953, p. 130.)

Fig. 9.8

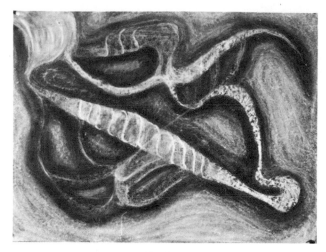

Fig. 9.11

Fig. 9.19

Fig. 9.5

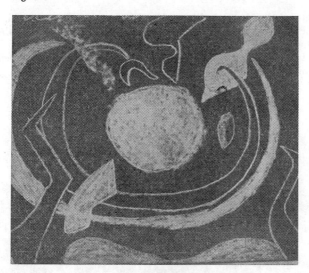

Fig. 9.6

Dean wrote a title on the back of his painting 'The Tempest'.

Beverley, 14 yrs 9 mths (Figs. 9.7 and 9.8)

> Something that is not reality, sad and far away from the world, a partition between peace and war. On the verge of death, and on the other hand the start of life.
>
> Sad, dreaming, gathering confidence, crying, shouting, repeating, searching.

Fig. 9.7

Paul, 14 yrs 11 mths (Figs. 9.9, 9.10 and 9.11)

This music is heroic in that it depicts a success after a struggle.

Paul asked for help with blending the colours but the problem of painting what he wanted was too great so I gave him a box of oil pastels.

Fig. 9.9

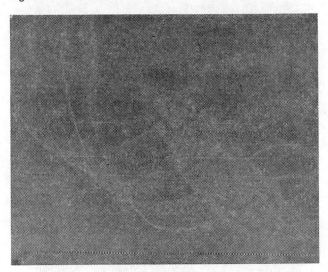

Fig. 9.10

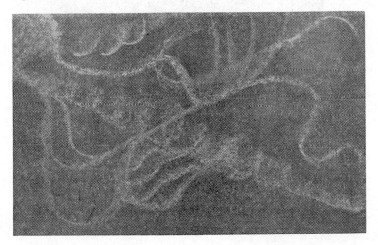

Caroline, 15 yrs (Figs. 9.12, 9.13 and 9.14)

The music seems to be enveloping and quite lively but I don't like it. It seems to be a lonely person trying to make friends.

Fig. 9.12

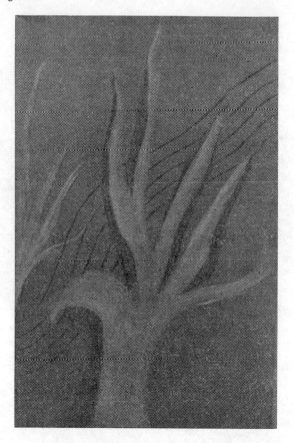

Fig. 9.13

Fig. 9.14

The image betokens a stronger response than is evident in the writing.

Sue, 15 yrs 5 mths (Fig. 9.15 and 9.16)

.... seems to have a note of happiness in it but it is cold, it somehow chills you. The playing goes on and makes it cold.

Fig. 9.15

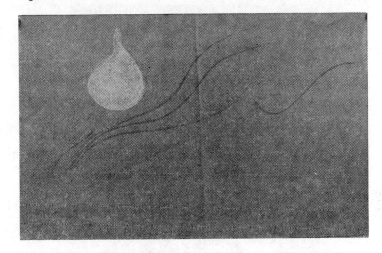

Fig. 9.16

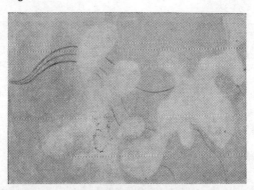

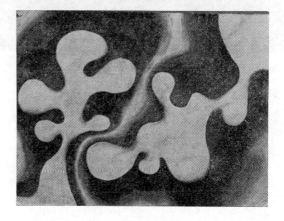

Sue asked for advice about how to paint 'the background' of her painting.

Bridget, 15 years (Figs. 9.17, 9.18 and 9.19)

The first part is sad and gradually leads up to something marvellous.

Fig. 9.17

Fig. 9.18

Kaye, 15 yrs 3 mths (Figs. 9.20 and 9.21)

It makes you feel very sad and depressed. It makes you feel lonely and unwanted; it has a far away feeling; it is distant. It makes you think of all the people less fortunate than yourself and the people who have not got as much as we have. It also makes you feel of death. It has a big powerful way of putting all this over.

Fig. 9.20

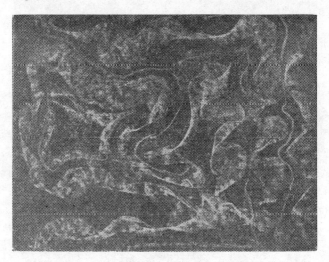

Fig. 9.21

I think it is fair to say that Kaye is among those who normally find some difficulty with art. She benefited from exercises using the side of the chalk.

Sarah, 14 yrs 6 mths (Fig. 9.22)

Fig. 9.22

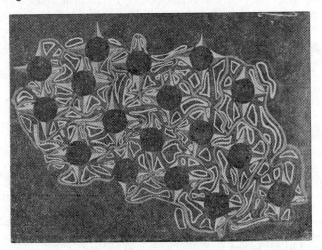

This piece of work was done from one of the other starting points and is obviously of a different character (see footnote p. 139).

Written Extracts on Guitar Music

As I have mentioned, I was extremely curious to discover as much as I could about the response to the music, and as the project progressed and I saw what was happening, I decided to play the music to some third-year pupils and get them to write about it. Space does not permit me to offer any sort of analysis of this written material, but I would ask the reader to look for points of similarity in the different extracts, and also to note that in many cases seemingly opposed feelings seem to be existing simultaneously (we may recall Bonnie's 'sad as well as hopeful').[1] Here I quote Langer again:

> It is a peculiar fact that some musical forms seem to bear a sad and a happy interpretation equally well. At first sight this looks paradoxical, but it really has perfectly good reasons which do not invalidate the notion of emotional significance . . . For what music can actually convey is only

[1] See Witkin, R. W., *The Intelligence of Feeling* on 'Dialectics' and especially p. 174.

the *morphology* of feeling, and it is quite plausible that some sad and some happy emotions may have a very similar morphology. This insight has led some philosophical musicologists to suppose that music conveys general *forms of feeling* related to specific ones as algebraic expressions are related to arithmetic . . . If it reveals the rationals of feeling, the rhythm and pattern of their rise and decline, and intertwining in our minds, then it is a force in our mental life, our awareness and understanding, and not only in our affective experience.[1]

It seems to me that if it really is true that music reflects only the morphology of feeling then it is an ideal stimulus for our purposes, since in reflecting only 'general forms of feeling' it presents the pupil with what Witkin has called a 'sensate problem'[2] without intruding on the level of his or her 'particularity'.

I have chosen a cross-section of girls' writing. At third-year level the boys were less successful at expressing their feelings.

D., 13 yrs 5 mths

It was a relaxing feeling which made me think happy thoughts. It was an organized sound and smooth. A happy yet a sad feeling was caused. . . .

G., 14 yrs 1 mth

The guitar solo gave me the feeling that life was relaxed whilst it was complicated and muddled. When the bits were repeating themselves it was like someone in life had done something wrong and was trying to get it right by doing it again, and in the end they succeeded. After that it seemed to get louder as if they were triumphant at their eventual success . . .

J., 13 yrs 8 mths

Although it was trying to reach something it couldn't but it kept trying, working up energy and then rushing for it, but getting caught in the hustle and bustle.

S., 13 yrs 11 mths

This piece seemed organized as every piece that is faster comes just where it's needed. It seems a quite sad record as though a person is missing a friend. It seems just as though it has been squashed a bit, but only slightly. It sounds like it was a piece of country music. It seemed a slow relaxing record except in a few places where it quickened its pace. It felt smooth with a few bumps in it . . .

A., 14 yrs 5 mths

The music made me think of a round shape which is being squashed and deflated like a football with a puncture.

[1] Langer, S. K., *Philosophy in a New Key*, Harvard University Press, 1969, p. 238. Cf. Langer, S. K., *Feeling and Form*, Routledge and Kegan Paul, 1953, p. 126.

[2] 'Once it has been evoked directly the elements of sweet sorrowing are sensate experience. They constitute a sensate problem, transcending the particular forms through which it was evoked.' R. W. Witkin, *The Intelligence of Feeling*, p. 172.

R., 13 yrs 10 mths

This particular record had strong emotional feeling as well as being organized. Sometimes it sounded quite strong and pulling. It sounded like a friend crying for help, or somebody crying out because they are trapped, hungry and cold. Somehow I felt completely opposite to what I have just said. Sometimes it was like a warm tropical beach with nothing but you and the sun and sky, it's the sort of music you could sink into but I felt I couldn't very well.

V., 13 yrs 9 mths

My feelings about the record are as if someone was lost. He is staggering around looking hopelessly about him. Everything is strange. After a while of searching his hopes are lifted and he becomes quite happy for a short while, then all his happiness drains away as he realizes he has been wrong. He sinks, down and down, like somebody in a whirlpool. All the feelings go round and round faster until the picture is of a glorious muddle which no one can solve. There seems a certain amount of liveliness in the music but most of it is covered with chaos. There is power behind the music making the muddle seem as if it was forcibly made.

C., 13 yrs 10 mths

In the music I felt a great sense of power and emotional feeling being put across by the guitarist. It felt to me like a piece of music played when an aircraft is taking off or a rocket or anything of that nature. It felt like a really surging sound that made me feel engrossed in the music. It really was my kind of music. I felt that I could listen to it again and again it had such a great feeling of emotion, and if it was combined with a slow motion picture of a bird in flight or a machine it would, I feel, give an even greater feeling of tremendous power, emotion, and a feeling of being smarter than the whole human race.

S., 13 yrs 9 mths

This piece of music makes you feel as if you were coming home from a war, or from prison, and there was nobody to greet you, so it makes you feel a little sad, but it livens up at the end as if they put on a great party for you or something like that. It first makes you feel dull but coming towards the end it makes you feel happier. . . .

I find the references in these extracts to a change in the music e.g. '. . . but it livens up at the end . . .' rather puzzling since there is no marked change in the actual music. This is perhaps a rationalization, at the level of writing,[1] of the dialectic the music apparently conveys.

What becomes evident after a consideration of the whole of the work done from this stimulus (something which has not been possible within the scope of this contribution) is that both the third-year

---

[1] The sequential nature of writing – discursive symbolism – is ill-suited to the expression of the simultaneous existence of opposed feelings. This is possible with the presentational symbolism of painting, but it is the special task of music.

children writing and the fourth-year pupils in their paintings are all
dealing with one group of problems, one content, but they deal with
this each in his or her own particular way. Thus, in the writing, one
child may write of coming home from a war but then finding no one
to greet her, and another of a feeling of being hungry and cold and
yet at the same time of being on a tropical beach.

When I speak of art as 'A way of knowing' I am describing a way
of knowing which occurs for the child at an intimately personal level,
and yet a way of knowing to which the teacher may have access
through an understanding of the structural characteristics of the
sensate problem – the problem form. It may well be that this understanding can only be fully achieved through empirical work of the
type I have been describing where the music, for example, when I
first encountered it, created as much of a sensate problem for me as
it was to do for the pupils. This problem, if we can regard a sensate
problem in this sense, has now been solved – structured and thus
assimilated, and both the pupils and myself have grown as a result.
We have come to know something in a truly existential sense.

10 A Secondary School Art Course
Its origins, purposes, elements, and practice

David John Farnell

Introduction

David Farnell was associated with the 'Arts and the Adolescent' project almost from the outset. I first met him during the initial feasibility study (1967) and saw to it that he was appointed to the consultative committee once the project got under way. As a head of department, he has been able to translate his new thinking into organizational as well as curricular action. In his piece he tells how his personal philosophy as an art teacher developed and then shows what effect that philosophy came to have upon the art teaching in his school. It seems to me that the story he tells could equally well be told by a teacher of drama or music or English, given the same openness to ideas and the same imagination in applying them to the circumstances of one's actual situation. Mr Farnell's contribution is especially welcome because he presents many of the ideas that he found attractive in *The Intelligence of Feeling* in eminently understandable language.

M.R.

Origins and Purpose of the Course

To evaluate the true effectiveness of the secondary-school curriculum is by no means the relatively simple task of giving a grade to a sixteen-year-old's visible school produce. If the curriculum is to be considered as a medium of education, its effect can be evaluated only in the context of the life that succeeds it. A handy analogy might be to consider the process of secondary education as a journey to a new life, and the curriculum, the mode of travel. While it may be important to travel in style and to make a flamboyant landing, to reach the correct destination is of greater importance. The experience I will relate concerns the formation of clearer beliefs about destination and the design of a vehicle that I hope can make the trip.

The important change from negative to positive feelings about teaching occurred in me when I found myself the art teacher in a Cambridgeshire Village College after a spell in a 'thrashing school'. I could hardly believe the disparity between two experiences of what was ostensibly the same job of work. The Village College I joined stood for human dignity and the significance of the lives it served. Joining a Village College some few years after the death of their originator, Henry Morris, I became aware of the genius of this man only slowly and with annoying lack of definition. It seemed a natural step to use the opportunity of a sabbatical year to make inquiries about him. Two quotations well illustrate threads in his thinking. The first, from a lecture given in 1925, offers a perspective to examinations, curriculum, and 'schooling' generally:

> It is the intrinsic worth of the life that the ADULT leads, the working philosophy by which he lives, the politics of the community he serves in his maturity, the amount of efficient action he contributes to the community, that should be the main concern of education.

The second pertains more specifically to the subject of this book. Henry Morris used this as an introduction to an arts course for teachers in 1948:

> We can do a great deal in all places of education to nourish a taste for the Arts, but unfortunately the approach there is too often didactic, the miracle is reversed, the wine of art is turned into the water of discourse. The truth is that a desire and love for the Arts can only really be got by practising them continually. The emphasis should be on the need for the constant experience of the Arts, in school and particularly out of it, *as a normal part of living, and as necessary as food and air.*

Many people from time to time recognize their own standpoint in the words of another. A conviction acquires some kind of validation for having received expression. I began to see education's endproduct as the man, not the sixteen-year-old. This is not necessarily to treat children in school as adults, but to think of them as adults-to-be. The idea has far-reaching implications. And where arts teaching in particular is concerned, I strengthened my conviction that arts education has greater significance than its lowly curricular status suggested. How that significance could be satisfactorily described I was far from sure.

In those balmy pre-CSE days, the secondary-modern art teacher was often alone in the world, but king of his castle. The disadvantages of this state of affairs have received more publicity than the advantages, but advantages there were – and freedom was one of them.

Flights of fancy, crazes, band-wagons, all could be indulged with comparative impunity. The searches and wanderings of this period left me convinced that teachers were able to dominate apparent constraints to a marked degree. If only we knew the ideal order, we could very likely make it the actual one. From these freedoms came the conviction that art teaching was not to be a set of filters designed to separate the dross from the gold, but was to be more a form of introduction to a state of being. And that state of being is everyone's right. I grew to believe, too, that the curriculum is a change agent – not directly of society, but a changer of children, concurrent with their natural development.

Imagine my pleasure to find the Schools Council engaged on a project entitled 'Arts and the Adolescent', and my excitement to be involved with it in a practical way almost from its inception. Watching the project develop, glimpsing the workings of the mind of Robert Witkin, struggling myself with the questions thrown into sharp relief by Malcolm Ross's findings concerning the parlous state of the arts in schools, I found myself in a state of readiness for Witkin's *Intelligence of Feeling*. I must stress that it was not, however, immediately grasped hold of as the great panacea, but that it was dissected and subjected to long and painstaking scrutiny, and then hugged to the heart as an agent of optimism.

The major revelation of its first partial unveiling at a memorable conference at Dartington in 1972 was the statement *that the capacity to respond feelingly was directly related to the capacity to be motivated; that, in fact, the latter was dependent on the former. To the extent that the feeling intelligence is developed, to that extent is the subject able to be motivated.* Other implications have since commended themselves to me, but the first thrilling impact was the shock discovery that by no means could the arts ever again be considered controversial as a viable aspect of the curriculum, but that instead the arts are to be recognized and acknowledged as the only area of the curriculum whose essential nature involves the capacity to respond and act feelingly. This capacity is at the core of the capacity to be motivated. And the capacity to be motivated is at the heart of all free action. The arts, therefore, were transformed from handy trimming of the main curriculum, with certain Culture perks, to essential ingredient. No amount of departmental responsibility, or even allowances, could ever do for the status of the art teacher what that realization does for him. Such was the core of my understanding of Witkin.

The development of this feeling intelligence through an arts education had reverberations in the worlds of job satisfaction, mental health, cultural life involvement, zest, independence, and freedom. Its implications embraced power and politics, social change, mob hysteria and, directly, the impact of social change on the school.

Elements of the Course

Knowing clearly now the nature of the subject, namely the whole population, captive at its most impressionable institutionalized stage – adolescence; and having a reasonably clear notion of the man one wished the adolescents to be father to; and having observed that the arts curriculum area alone had at its core the *intelligence of feeling*, two new objectives presented themselves. The first was to utilize a working analysis of the actions that constitute a feeling response and the exercise of the faculty that caused development of the feeling intelligence; and the second, to organize for the children a five-year school art experience that would help to cause the desired changes.

The analysis I recognized was Witkin's, simplistically expressed thus:

Having the sensate experience;
Recognizing it as an opportunity for expressive action;
Owning a specific sensate problem;
Making a holding form;
Working in a subject-reflexive way through an expressive medium;
Realization;
Checking the finished work for its power to evoke and re-evoke the sensate experience that caused it.

Two more factors were to be isolated and then consciously built in to the five-year plan. The first occurred originally as a state of affairs to be put up with grudgingly, but it developed into a positive design element. Though the phenomenon has been variously expressed and felt intuitively, Eric Hoyle illustrated it clearly in a lecture given to Cambridgeshire teachers on 27 September 1973. He suggested that there is manifested in education a sociological drift best described as from 'closed' to 'open'. A few of the 'dimensions of change' he isolated are:

in curriculum: mono-disciplinary to multi-disciplinary studies;
in pedagogy: didactic teaching to discovery learning;
in organization: rigid to flexible structures;
in groupings: homogeneous to heterogeneous;
in pupil choice: low to high degree of choice;
in evaluation: single mode to multiple mode;
in control: positional to personal;
in professional relationships: isolation to integration;
in relationships with community: low to high involvement;
even in architecture: closed to open plan.

There is a process of change going on and it has made, is making, and will continue to make an impact on schools. Teachers must not try a Canute act. Instead we must make a plus out of an apparent minus.

These thoughts suggested a style of engagement with children that did not depend on the teacher's power as an authority figure, that gave the children a positive role in their own education, that counterbalanced somehow the children's new independence, and that caused changes in the consciousness of children that had a permanence independent of examinations, teacher's gaze, children's chosen occupations, or any other extrinsic pressure.

The second matter concerned the method of dealing with the actual making processes. One thing seemed clear: that both rule-directed and rule-abandoned activities were doomed to rejection. The swing to rule-directed activity seemed to cause work that was stilted and lacking in life. The swing to rule-abandoned work caused work that was ill-formed and without common viability. Neither was acceptable. Witkin's 'formula' commended itself strongly. The requirements are that the feeling-idea and the control of the medium (be it sound, visual form, movement or words) be brought into harmonic balance; that there be oscillations between the two; and that the oscillations be short and rapid rather than far apart and infrequent. The language is partly analytical, partly metaphorical, but its essence seems to emerge. The practical manifestations of this factor as a principle of teaching-studio action will, I hope, be evident shortly. The new awareness for me was that this approach to the presentation of learning activities was probably that elusive one, naturally practised by those people to whom we gave the name 'born teachers'. The 'born teacher' brought into harmonic balance the feeling elements of his teaching material with its knowing elements. The effect was a lasting affection for and facility in that teacher's subject. Perhaps it might be possible to make more commonly accessible those skills hitherto regretfully considered intangible.

I was now in a position to design a five-year course for my department with the following informing beliefs:

> that the school's end-product is the man not the sixteen-year-old or his produce;
> that the Arts have the vital curriculum role I have stated;
> that creative expressive actions could be described by a kind of formula;
> that the style of engagement with children had to cause them a positive role and should utilize sociological core tendencies;
> and that the teacher's imaginative engagement with the children within their expressive actions should at all times bring into alignment the feeling-idea and the control of the medium.

I have perhaps laboured the influences and guiding principles that informed my subsequent actions, but for a special reason: that it should be clear that the taking into the consciousness of beliefs is

the crucial step in course design. To work from a teaching kit without
personal commitments to the beliefs that caused it is seldom satisfactory.

Framework for Action

I devised a plan. It was tailored to my situation. The school had
grown gradually but considerably. From being the one and only art
teacher with occasional part-time help, working in one all-purpose
studio, I found myself in a block of three specialist studios and with
an assistant. The improvements were vast though far from ideal. I
was, however, able to recruit a sympathetic, intelligent and skilful
assistant. My aim now was to plan the course that utilized all the
resources fully and that satisfied its stated function.

I was able to organize the department to receive thirty to forty
children at a time with two teachers and three studios – a highly
favourable situation. All the children were to be taught by both
teachers in all three studios according to natural gravitational pulls.
The five-year course was to be seen as a whole, and its planned effect
was to cause the capacities I have already described by whatever
means the teachers considered appropriate with guidance from a
purposive general framework. The overarching aim was to cause the
development in the participants of their intelligence of feeling and
the particular cultured state of being, experienced as a whole-being
involvement in the expressive/creative life experience.

(You will have noticed that I do not take the fatalistic view that the
curriculum is powerless and that the children will be what they will
be in spite of what the schools subject them to. I do, however, agree
that school is not the only educating agent at work on the children,
nor the most influential. Families, homes and the growing-up
environment must take that role. Nevertheless, I subscribe to the
view of adolescence that suggests it is a time of turmoil and its
experiences can reinforce or weaken characteristics half-formed in
the early years. I see little point in the school other than as a centre
of vocational training and child-minding, unless the school's
intention is to play a part in the whole-being development of the
person. While I agree, therefore, that the changes incurred by
exposure to a particular curriculum may only be slight reinforce-
ments or minor erosions, they may be the crucial ones. For this
reason I talk unashamedly of the curriculum causing changes.)

I have stated the overall function of the course. To that end there
were specific objectives for the whole five years and for the individual
years. To those ends there were to be activities. As far as the children
were concerned, the pattern took this form:

activities $\longrightarrow$ year and course objectives $\longrightarrow$ overarching aim.

As far as the course design and the teachers were concerned, the pattern was reversed:

overarching aim (all pervasive) ⟶ course and year objectives (milestones) ⟶ activities.

One other element was considered: starting point. Starting point was at the beginning of the children's chain.

I have already expressed my interpretation of the overarching aims. It was hopefully assumed that the reaching of the objectives would support those aims. The objectives, firstly of the whole course, then of each year of the course, follow.

The whole course has to effect shifts in the children's attitude, skills, understanding and drive. They are to own the shift in their awareness that visual expression used to be a play activity but has become work. (In other words, it is not just a pastime, therapeutic exercise, release, escape, but has an element of disciplined problem resolution.) They are to move from a position of limited to broad 'vocabulary'. (In other words, they acquire all the skill and technical facilities they can accommodate.) They are to accept the shift from a low scope concept of visually expressive possibilities to a realization of wide scope. (In other words, they learn to recognize all sensate experiences as opportunities and raw materials for expression.) And, finally, the children are to move from a state of dependence on a variety of external circumstances and situations to a state of dependence on themselves.

To these ends, each year has its own special concerns. These concerns are by no means confined to one year. They are constant concerns and they overlap, but are given special emphasis at certain times. Succeeding year concerns do not replace those preceding, but are in addition to them. Clearly, the basic concerns describe only the flavour of a year's work, which also includes skills, procedures, activities and conversations according to the children's needs and interests as well as the teacher's whims and crazes. They are as follows.

In their first year, the children are to be caused to feel a high level of personal involvement with the activities and functions of the studios. The feeling they experience should be very positive. The children choose from the activities available.

In the second year, it is planned to cause a broadening of awareness of the scope of art activities and the studios. Children are introduced to activities, ideas and materials beyond those previously chosen.

In the third year the children's representation crisis is tackled by whatever methods the teachers can draw on. All activities are employed to strengthen seeing and recreating skills.

The fourth year is the year in which gaps in technical and technological skill are tackled.

The main concern in the fifth year is to hand the children over to themselves with regard to motive, starting-point, raw material, skills, and use of resources. The teachers' aim is gradually to withdraw from the role of motivator and to become consultants and advisors.

Such are the bases of the special year concerns. Diagrammatically this can be represented thus:

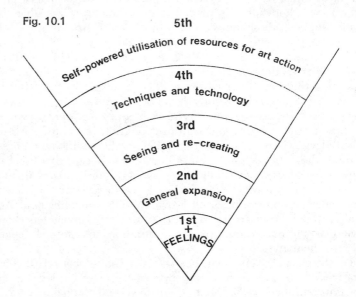

Fig. 10.1

5th
Self-powered utilisation of resources for art action
4th
Techniques and technology
3rd
Seeing and re-creating
2nd
General expansion
1st
+
FEELINGS

You will see that the work has a purposive framework that is unobtrusive to the children. It is possible within this framework to use whatever art activity a child may choose as a teaching opportunity within that framework, according to the child's stage in the journey. Even if a child were only copying a cartoon, there would be an opportunity to teach better seeing, perhaps pencil skills, some colour theory, a deeper feeling response, and more. Copying cartoons would greatly reduce his scope in other aspects of his development, but it nevertheless would provide a teaching opportunity, and it does have the one big advantage of having been drawn by the child from his own cultural bank. It is very important to acknowledge children's cultural position and draw them gently along, rather than to stand alone beckoning from afar. The single principle of utilizing the children's cultural standpoint can transform the nature of the teacher's engagement with them.

It would have been wonderful to organize a situation (as other contributors to this book may have done) in which the children owned a sensate problem and then chose the expressive medium most appropriate to that problem's needs – sound, movement, visual form or words. My plan had to confine the children on the whole to visual form. Central to the scheme is the principle of the children having a positive role. It has recently become necessary to curtail further this role in the area of choice of medium. However, choice is still a major principle, and any curtailment of freedom in this respect is sincerely regretted.

I have touched on three of the four strands in the organization of the course: the five-year and year objectives; the principle of encouraging the children to experience cultural reality in the studio; and the principle of the children's role being a positive one. The fourth strand is the principle already mentioned, that of consciously bringing into harmonic relationship at all times the feeling-idea and the control of the medium. Earlier I referred to medium as the expressive medium (paint, clay, words, sound . . .). I now use the word to mean not only the actual vehicle for the idea, but also the associated equipment and procedures, such as the sinks, the teachers, the studio geography, and any other part of the process, however humble. Two rules suggested themselves, rules of safety and economy. This way, most procedural matters could be established as matters of safety and economy rather than of behaviour. The traditional authority pattern was carefully being adjusted. A set of procedures was developed that would help create good studio practices and that did not rely on constant instructions. For instance, the children learn to locate their work, find a work space, and get on. Storage and recording systems are precise and managed by the child himself. I shall describe shortly how all arrangements within the studios are designed to give the teachers maximum time to engage directly with individual children.

Before I describe the scene of the plan in action, there remains the question of starting point. I will give this matter some emphasis for it not only elucidates ways of setting the ball rolling, but illuminates the teachers' roles at all points. Clearly the teacher is concerned with safety, economy and work habits. The approach I have adopted does a great deal to defuse the teachers' obsession with control, behaviour and conventional work-rates – not by condoning chaos but by causing a good work situation other than by conventional teacher presence. I will explain more fully later how this can operate.

You will remember that the operational definition of a creative expressive act that I recognized for the purpose of designing this course is:

> having the sensate experience;
> recognizing the sensate experience as an opportunity for expression;
> formulating it into and owning it as a sensate problem;
> sealing it in a holding form;

working through successive approximations of the whole towards successful realization in an expressive medium;

and checking the realized form for the power it has to evoke, and re-evoke the sensate experience that caused it.

How pleasing it is to find people from whom creative work flows and who therefore have no need for such a formula, but how frequently one has to work with people who claim to have no outlet for their creative energies or, worse, who claim to have no use for creative expression. All these groups of people and the shades, moods, and extremes around them, enter our studios and first of all require nudging into action.

In practical terms, a piece of work in visual media has three elements: an idea, a material and a method. The three elements are interrelated in a special way. Clearly the material and the method are frequently entwined – but not always. But before all three elements can work together harmoniously they have to adjust to each other. The idea speaks to the material, the material to the idea and so on.

This can be represented diagrammatically thus:

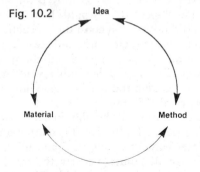

Fig. 10.2

Generally, the starting point can be located anywhere on the edge of this circle. Children may be offered a general idea, a material, or a method or a combination of these. The student then has a positive role. Having accepted an external starting point, he has contracted to make an aspect of it his own and to supply for himself the missing ingredients. For example, supposing he were offered the general idea of family (in whatever style of presentation the teacher thought right), the child's first job would be to make the subject his own (by way of sensate experience). He then closes in on an aspect of family he feels as an opportunity for expressive action (he isolates a sensate problem). This may perhaps be based on his experience of, say, the bond between a father and son, or anything he cares. His next task is to move round the circle, choosing the material and method he feels belong to his idea. The circle is completed. The three elements adjust to each other and then he is ready for the first gross approximation (or holding form) and he moves inside the circle.

The teacher moves imaginatively into the creative process of the child in whatever ways suggest themselves to him. The child may have chosen to model in clay. His first rough approximation may suggest to him that he must take recourse to observation to improve his seeing skill. His handling of the clay may convince him a certain technique should be used; the technique may call him to practise and perhaps explore the material. Such departures must sustain the oscillations between the idea and the expressive medium, or the link will break. The requirement for these departures is that they remain integral with their purpose, namely to cause the clay, the modelling and the aspect of family more successfully to become one. The process so far can be diagrammatically represented thus:

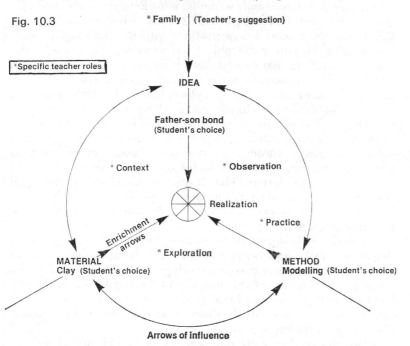

Fig. 10.3

Arrows of influence

Context appears in the diagram because at this stage the teacher may be able to expose the child to a context of realizations enriching to his notion of the general idea and contributing to his vision of the possible.

Realization occurs when successive approximations have moved from a gross to a refined state. The elements have worked together influencing and counterbalancing each other. The oscillations in consciousness among the elements have been rapid, short and frequent. The offspring of the union has its umbilical cord

broken and it stands alone. I shall consider the resulting art object
shortly.

As far as the studio process is concerned, a set procedure now
follows under the general headings of Evaluation and Development.
The procedure has the scope to be exploited at varying levels
according to the needs of the children. Evaluation might start as a
subjective response to the work expressed in such terms as, 'Can I
take it home now?' and can grow into a searching discussion. At
first, however, a very successful guide to the effectiveness of the
opening months of the course is the degree of affection the child feels
both for the activities and the produce. This could well be a far more
efficient teacher's measure than the teacher's opinion of the resulting
art objects.

Evaluation, therefore, at this point refers firstly to the child's
affection for his actions and, secondly, to feelings about the work. (It
is not to be confused with the teacher's evaluation of the curriculum.)
It is hoped the teacher's conversations with the child will be concerned with the power the object has to evoke and re-evoke the
sensate experiences that caused it. At a trivial level, the clay rabbit
may excite in its maker the feeling of furry warmth that caused him
to make the clay rabbit in the first place. Better still, it may rouse the
same childhood sensation in the teacher. It's a start! As the years go
by, the stimuli of sensate problems may well be sensate experiences
of infinitely greater subtlety, depth and importance. The pattern,
sensate experience through to realization and thereby back to
sensate experience, remains a useful operational description of a
creative expressive action. The threads of many such patterns all
going on at the same time can in some people become entwined and
entangled to such an extent that the whole experience of life can be
identified as a sensate experience, crystallizing constantly into sensate
problems, being encapsulated as holding forms in sketches, phrases,
shapes and titles, and being worked through expressive media in
bursts of minutes or weeks concurrently, according to the pull of the
moment. It is because of this tangling of the threads in an already
'art-educated' person that he sometimes will not accept that there
can be a formula that aids the description of this mysterious process
of creative expression so natural to him.

Before the reader reads on, perhaps he would submit to two
exercises. Firstly, if he himself is engaged in making what is normally
called art, I would like him to compare the processes I have described
with his own experiences of making. Secondly, I would ask him to
compare the processes with those revealed by the works, lives and
writings of great artists of the past. It is possible the reader will find
within his own experience and in his perception of the Masters,
illustrations of the 'formula' in action. The exercises might also
illuminate a link between sincere but naïve arts expressions of
children and the widest arena of all art.

Development is simply illustrated. A new circle is constructed to overlap the old one. The new made-object goes on the edge of the new circle. This object itself may take over the role of Idea. The same material may be on the circle, but a new method may be supplied. Or perhaps the same method and material may be used, but they may have suggested an entirely different Idea. Diagrammatically, Development may be represented thus:

Fig. 10.4

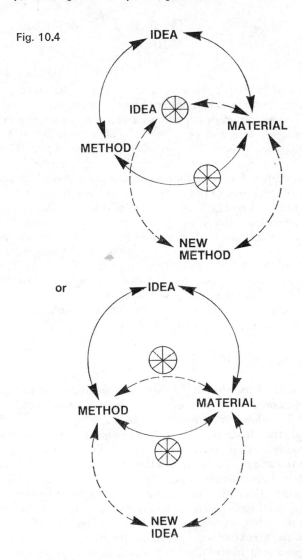

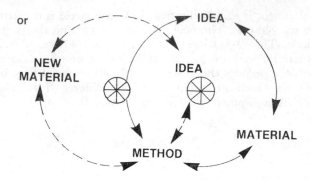

As you can envisage, the links are sometimes tenuous, at other times strong. Sometimes subsequent areas of activity have links only through the vagaries of subconscious association, at other times they form a series of variations on a theme – idea, material, or method theme. The whole process is recorded by the children in a diary. The diary has very many uses: technical notes, sketches, research, reminders. Its first function, though, is to make a record, at the very least of the experiences of the work session, at best of mind and heart processes that go into choosing, making and moving on.

When the children follow this procedure of moving their objectives along, and when they accept intellectually the responsibilities involved, the teacher has only a supporting role to play with respect to new stimuli for the new objectives. Sometimes it is all he can do to keep pace with what is going on. It is denigrating to suggest children bring nothing with them in the way of raw material for expression. Accepting these responsibilities, children often humble their teachers by the rich diversity of their objectives.

Studio Action

I have described the thinking behind the theories and the theories themselves; now let us take a glance at the studios at work.

On the first day back after a school holiday, but well into the school year, the children come to the studios, temporarily unaccustomed to school-based activity. First-year children, however, usually require at this stage only the instruction, 'Go.' They know where their work and the materials are kept. They know the activities that bring them pleasure. They quickly make a start. The teacher may wish to know what each has chosen to do before work starts, or he may go round to see what work each child has started on. As the basic concern of the first year is the nature of the pupils' involvement, this will be uppermost in the teacher's mind, though he will not waste opportunities to strengthen studio procedures, to deepen the child's engagement with his subject, to enlarge his working vocabulary and to widen his repertoire of skills. Some points the teacher may wish to make may be to the whole group, some to sections and some to individuals.

The first second-year session of the term might well open with discussion of experience as raw material for expressive action. The children might be refreshed about the repertoire of activities open to them. Their roles as learners would be emphasized. The teacher would be on the lookout for opportunities to extend the children's appreciation of the scope of the activity and of the studios.

The first third-year session of the term could well open with a non-visual presentation of a theme – like the idea of friendship. The children would be encouraged to focus on an aspect of the topic they recognize as theirs alone, to consider the problem visually and then to start to make. The opening ventures may be overtures to subsequent forays. The approach of the child at this stage, and the uses to which he puts the resources at his disposal, are most important. His seeing skills will be to the fore of the teacher's mind.

The first fourth-year session of the new term might be marked by technical instruction, say, in a particular animation technique. The session could start like this:

Some of you have probably been waiting to get here to get on with what-ever you have on your minds. You – make a start. Others of you may like to get back into the rhythm of visual work by working from something you see and making it your own. Someone else may like nudging into action by a suggestion of a topic area from me. If so, come and see me. Finally, for those who need it, I am going to spend some time on anima-tion techniques. Those interested, gather round.

The first session with the fifth year will be very much like that with the first year. The children take the initiative. The teachers are just part of the available resources. It is the nature of the teachers' engagement with individual children and of children's engagement with their experiences that cause maturation to be positive and strengthening. This initiative starts with the children taking on the responsibility for setting their own objectives. It incorporates the positive desire to feed off all the available resources in the context of children's new awareness of the vision of the possible.

Mid-term sessions with all the years have common strands. Firstly, there should be no dependence on the teacher for the initial action. Whether the teacher is there at the very beginning of the session or not, he should be able, ten minutes into the session, to observe a studio full of busy people. The children have collected their half-completed work, have found a work area, have set out their stalls, have tuned in to the stimuli that caused the work in the first place and are busy and frowning over their work.

At this point in the proceedings there is much for the teacher to do, some of it traditional, some of it enthralling. First the traditional tasks: the teacher must cause the studios to be used safely; the teacher must cause the studio materials to be used economically; and the teacher must cause a working atmosphere, conducive to good learning and making. (This will involve actual postures, locations, workmanlike organization, noise levels, opportunity to concentrate, opportunity to confer.) These three aspects of the teaching require sensitive teacher skills but are only supportive to the main part of the work.

For short stretches of time the teacher may stop all activity in the studio and go into some matter with all the children. At other times he may say, 'Carry on with what you are doing but lend an ear to what I am going to say.' Again at other times it may be appropriate for the teacher to work with a group of three or four children. 'John is having trouble making his buildings look right. Anyone else having the same problem, come round here.' The teaching style is mainly conversational, though sometimes bare telling or bare demonstration. Some, too, is coaching of motor skills.

All this important work takes place mainly outside the individual child's circle. Evaluation and development too take place outside the circle, though usually between the teacher and the individual child. Another important outside-the-circle role for the teacher is in the realm of the original sensate experience. The teacher may feel it important not only to cause the experience to be recognized as an opportunity for action, but may have to cause the experience itself. It is an ongoing job of the teacher to cause the capacity to respond feelingly to an experience to be enlarged. But from the moment a sensate problem has been identified and accepted, and up to the moment the chord between the maker and his work is cut, there is the important work for the teacher within the circle of the individual child. The precise nature of this action is informed by the general flavours of the total course.

The studio action described is also informed by two very practical principles: that the children have the greatest possible involvement in their own learning circumstances; and that the teacher be freed as much as possible from the problems of organization, management and control, to teach. The purpose of the teaching however is not just to create ideal teaching circumstances as an end in themselves, it is so that in good teaching circumstances, learning can and will take place.

Reflections

It is very difficult for me to be dispassionate in attempting to evaluate the experience of my last three years teaching art. My first observations are of some of the system's inherent problems. And the first one is that 'system' now is a barely useful word in teaching, for no situation seems to remain stable long enough for procedures to fix themselves firmly into a system.

The phenomenon of the self-powered nature of the work is at once very desirable but also tempting and misleading. It can not only lure the teacher away from the real engagement; it makes the actual teaching process difficult to discern. It renders teaching notes redundant, their place being filled ideally by a combination of the overall plan and the children's diaries; it makes casual help impotent; and it reduces teaching-practice students and tutors to apoplexy. One's colleagues become convinced that art teaching has nothing to it.

It is difficult to accept that it is the invisible effects of the teaching that are the most important, and they may be impossible to read in the visible produce. It takes astute and trusting head teachers, colleagues and local advisors to spot them.

Because children's experiences in the art department sometimes contrast sharply with their experiences of the school subjects they associate with examinations, it can take time for the children to learn efficient strategies. That so many in fact do so, remains a great strengthener to our convictions.

One final major disadvantage of the system is the bare fact of its distance from the main stream even of art teaching. There are times when the lures of safe class teaching become very insistent. When doubts invade, it is less easy to re-state your solitary allegiance to a basically private faith, than it would be to seek the strength in fellowship of an identifiable body, however small. Perhaps this problem will diminish.

When the studios are working at their best, no doubts sneak in. The studios are most hospitable places to be in. The children rush in to get on with their work. Their objectives are owned and set by them. The teacher, far from being the source of conflict, is the easer of the conflict between the child and his objective. The authority-obedience structure is virtually replaced by a need-satisfaction structure with all accompanying advantages. The studio has a professional atmosphere, without the commercial motive. The studio aura is to a large extent independent of the teacher's personality as focus, centrepiece, showman, policeman, judge, goad or guard. The teacher may teach.

Apart from supporting an atmosphere in the studios conducive to personal fulfilment through expressive media, the system allows for great variety of subject matter, treatment, style and media within one work area. As a result, the studios can be full of surprises for the teacher. Many of the topics tackled would never have been suggested by teachers.

There are modifications still to be made – some grudgingly, some of necessity. The diaries are seriously under-exploited. Not enough attention is paid to deliberate enrichment of sensate experience. Continuity of contact over time between the arts experience and the child is, however, essential, and when timetables and external factors cause the exposure to be fragmented beyond recognition, this system of teaching may as well be put into cold storage and be replaced by 'short courses'.

In my opinion, the system of art teaching I describe has already produced evidence to suggest that it has the power to fulfil its aims at least in degree. The evidence is that the young adults who leave us at sixteen after partial and imperfect exposure to the system are showing some of the characteristics we value. Some of them have taken into their consciousness the mechanisms for valuing creative expression; they accept and own a procedure for recognizing and exercising opportunities for creative expression; they become tuned to experience. They accept the responsibility for action and are willingly disciplined to its duties. Where expression is concerned, they develop confidence and self-esteem independent of examination grades. They become equipped to explore a response to experience through an expressive medium, and support their actions with words.

At a visible level, the children acquire all the usual skills according to their abilities and interests, and accept the 'pain factor' for the sake of their objectives. They have a vested interest in the efficiency of their learning. They develop a strongly positive attitude to studio activities and form strong association with the studio area. They work in the proud confidence that sincere offerings are acceptable. The work bears little resemblance to their teachers' work and reveals few teaching patterns. Final exhibitions have perhaps more culled images and teenage themes than formerly. The work significantly lacks 'flashiness' and is more clearly identifiable with the age of its maker. The surprises occur not only in the subject, treatment and style, but also in the depth of feeling response to experience revealed not only by the work, but in conversation and diary notes. The diaries have taught us that comparatively insignificant-looking work can sometimes be the only visible manifestation of most remarkable head and heart processes. But the work chiefly speaks for itself.

The system I have operated has not facilitated the production of instant window-dressing material. It has instead taken some of the pressure off the visual produce and made it little more than the natural manifestations of a desirable developmental shift within the person. Happily, those manifestations do seem to have a life of their own though they are significant only of a stage. They are usually more than adequate to the task of picking up in passing those certificates so commonly coveted. It always seems incongruous, though, when CSE and GCE times come round each year, to feel the teachers and the taught judged on the grades awarded to a room full of pictures. Those visible items may be scant evidence of the man's capacity to enter fully into a cultural experience of existence in his maturity, scant evidence of the success or failure of this vital aspect of the school curriculum.

11 An Expressive Arts Department

Anne Cole

Introduction

I first visited *Anne Cole* at her school to lead a day's in-service course for her Expressive Arts Department. I arrived a day early and had a chance to look around and get acquainted with the team and its work. To say I was impressed would be altogether to understate the impact of that first encounter. I was struck by the department's sense of direction and mutuality: the teachers were clearly devoted to each other, to their work as artists and to the children they were working with. And as far as I could judge the children reciprocated wholeheartedly. There was a general atmosphere of commitment, good humour and give-and-take among the staff that seemed to be completely infectious: I felt the decision to integrate the arts in this school was totally vindicated by the response of the pupils – from many of whom one could easily envisage disparagement and rejection in different circumstances.

I did not at the time feel the team's curriculum was quite what I was looking for, but, having said that, I must also add that there was evidence of more serious curriculum thinking among this group of arts teachers than I had seen anywhere else. Limited space in this book has meant that Mrs Cole has been able to do scant justice to the actual projects that the team and the children work on, but the organizational issues of working the way she does are well presented and the benefits in terms of team morale and team effectiveness within the school as a whole are manifest.

M.R.

Setting

The school, which opened in September 1968 with only first-year pupils, is a ten-form entry comprehensive school which has been designated an Educational Priority School. It is situated on a housing estate designed primarily as part of a large city's post-war resettlement effort.

Being in at the beginning of a new school which had a phased growth gave teachers a rare chance to collaborate and to bring to a developing community a wide range of experience, talent, ideas, scholarship and interests. With the small nucleus staff, all committed to the idea of collaborative learning as the best response to the situation as they saw it, a *unique* opportunity was offered to develop new techniques, to ensure not only cognitive growth but also (and here the emerging expressive arts department could come into its own) affective development.

The expressive arts department has now been an active force for eight years. Since the school's inception in 1968 it has tried to find ways of bringing art, dance, drama and music together to form a collective curriculum administered as a single department. As the school was firmly committed to the belief that the curriculum as a whole had to be relevant to the needs of all children, their interests and experience had to be taken firmly into account. Children's emotional needs do not divide neatly into subject divisions, and so it was felt that neither the content nor the modes of operation, associated with traditional arts teaching in secondary schools, were appropriate. The new curriculum evolved as the result of a great deal of discussion, constant reappraisal and alternate experiences of success and failure. From the beginning the staff were aware there would be problems raised by their commitment to integration, and a good deal of heart-searching took place before they felt that it was both educationally sound and practically possible for them to move into an integrated/collaborative framework.

Although the expressive arts department came into being in response to the beliefs of the foundation arts staff, teachers have since been appointed who have felt able to work within the established collaborative situation. Since collaboration/integration entails a measure of insecurity as new ways of working are developed, supportive structures are necessary for both staff and pupils. In this connection the staff readily acknowledge that nothing could have been developed let alone sustained without the constant help, encouragement and belief in the department of the head teacher.

Role of the Arts in the Curriculum

As this was a new school, the whole staff was able to take a fresh look at curriculum objectives and consider what they believed to be relevant to children growing up in the second half of the twentieth century. Some considerations led to the formation of broad objectives: to place an emphasis on collaboration rather than competition, on learning by discovery and enquiry rather than by instruction dominated by the teacher, and on the belief that pupils and staff need to be valued, and be seen to be valued, as individuals. Therefore the emphasis throughout the expressive arts department became collaborative between staff and between staff and pupils, in which both success and failure were shared.

The expressive arts area is one of six major areas of curriculum organization. The team of staff is headed by a co-ordinator whose responsibility is to lead them in translating the stated objectives of the school and of the department into curriculum content and a particular organizational pattern. However the concept of a large department such as this which brings 'arts teachers' together cannot function constructively except on a basis of mutual conviction. This has to be held by all the staff concerned, and has to be subject to constant scrutiny and reappraisal in the light of the needs of the pupils, of growing developments within the school and the induction of new staff.

Recognition that the arts have a great deal in common was not in itself the basis for the establishment of the department; there was also fundamental agreement on certain common beliefs:

1. That all the arts are media through which men express their experience – for the most part in a non-verbal way. (But we regard the experience that we give the pupils as being a possible break-through to verbal language as well.)
2. That in expressing themselves pupils are involved in the process of communication as well. It is recognized that often their modes of expression are only clear to themselves as the creators, and that there are circumstances when this is enough. But it is equally evident that care has to be taken to encourage the pupils to try to communicate their experience to others. It is felt that the principal value of the expressive arts lies in that unique satisfaction of having created something for oneself.
3. That the arts can involve a process of self-discovery.
4. That an idea or impulse may be equally well expressed in more than one medium.
5. That specialists in different art forms share language and concepts which enable them to communicate about essentially non-verbal ideas.
6. That children need to acquire technical skills in order to express themselves effectively.
7. That all art is concerned with form, with the shaping of materials.

In conclusion, if these beliefs are valid, there would seem to be a strong case for bringing the arts subjects together in the curriculum in a way that allows them to feed each other and to gain strength from the common ground that they share. The common beliefs of the department entail a redefinition of the role of the arts in the curriculum.

What of children? The very nature of the philosophy of the school forced staff to ask the simple but endlessly complicated and persistent question, 'Of what use are the arts to our particular children?' 'Particular' because it is essential when planning curriculum to avoid adopting ideas wholesale from other sources whose circumstances may be totally different from those that exist in your own case. All the members of the team felt instinctively that the arts had something of real value to offer to the development of children, but in most cases they were not able at first to be very specific.

To move on now to indicate how conviction has been translated into practice. From the start it was affirmed that the syllabus is the expression of the beliefs of the department, and as such had to be flexible, although flexible within an overall structure. Constant reappraisal has therefore been the catalyst for growth as the syllabus evolved. The practice of developing a curriculum and the methods of interacting with children can be observed in four distinctive ways:

1. Workshop activities between members of the staff to help to focus on a point of departure for the children, and to open up possible sources of stimulation and lines of inquiry in the arts.
2. 'Lead lessons' in which staff work together to present ideas and material that hopefully provide starting points for the pupils in all the arts.
3. Development of the ideas initiated in the lead lessons by teachers working within their own specialism with pupils.
4. A final 'sharing' with all teachers and pupils concerned, showing work developed in all fields from the lead lesson.

Lead lessons and sharings – the beginning and the end of all the project work–form the overtly collaborative framework that allows teachers and pupils to focus on the ideas explored in each topic. The arts are presented in this dynamic way as being actively related and complementary to each other. Lead lessons are normally held in the theatre at the start of each project and provide the initial stimulus to the pupils on the theme that they will explore in the following weeks. Through providing an exciting, stimulating experience it is hoped to provoke interest and discussion, which will lead to personal, individual or group creative work. However, the prerequisite of lead lessons for the teaching team is time – time for discussion, organization and careful preparation.

Sharings are the 'coming together' at the end of a project so that pupils and staff can share the work that they have been doing in each area. An atmosphere has therefore to be engendered which will encourage pupils to participate and thereby share their experiences with others. By the time a sharing is over most pupils have actively taken part in music, dance or drama, whilst pupils who have been concentrating on visual art talk about their art work which is displayed around them. Nothing, however, can be achieved unless a trusting and friendly atmosphere has been created. Pupils have to learn to listen and watch with sensitivity. They have to become sympathetic to others talking to them about their work, to those actually making music or taking part in drama or dance. As it can be very demanding and daunting to work in front of one's peers, pupils have to be encouraged to have an empathy with those out front so that a warmth is generated which allows participants to feel secure. One of the ways to do this is by staff joining in alongside the children whenever possible.

For the first two years a syllabus has been devised which allows the teaching team to work together in a collaborative manner. It must, however, be realized that an approach such as this, which emphasizes exploration and a wide range of expressive opportunities for the children, has within it a potential danger. Each of the four main arts areas has a language of its own and demands skills unique to its own discipline, and the children need to reach appropriate levels of competence if they are to express themselves adequately. Therefore, even though teaching tends either to follow broad themes designed to stimulate the pupil's imagination, or concentrates on concepts related to the character of the different media themselves, staff tend to start from the skills that the pupils have and work outwards from them towards the acquisition of specialist skills and understandings.

First Year
The first-year work begins with a three-week introductory course. The pupils are introduced to the staff, and the way the department works is explained fairly simply to them. They are then shown examples of work produced by pupils in the previous year. The emphasis in the first weeks is on fun and on relaxing tensions. The aim is to give the pupils some confidence in expressing themselves, in responding to their own physical and sensory experiences, and in beginning to take some risks in expressing their responses. Staff do all they can at this early stage to develop both the pupils' confidence and their sense of purpose.

After the initial induction a project entitled 'Natural and Mechanical Forms' begins. The pupils consider the human body as a machine and come to an appreciation of the way the body works by imagining it restructured. Emphasis is placed on textures and the pupils are helped to recreate the experience of texture graphically, using words, sounds and movement, at times on their own and at others in a combined way. They are also invited to bring along unusual and strange objects which can be responded to imaginatively and expressively.

The next topic is called 'Structure' and here structures with which the pupils are already familiar are examined, and all the different expressive media available are used. For example, the structures in which the pupils live, the structures of society such as home, family and school. Then the structure of life such as birth, childhood, adolescence and so forth. Most of the structures will be very familiar to the pupils but a few are tackled of which at present they only have second-hand knowledge.

The next topic is called 'Integration'. Having experienced the uniqueness of each discipline, staff now wish the pupils to come to terms individually with the philosophy of the expressive arts department. Staff try to get each pupil to do some kind of expressive work that naturally involves the use of more than one medium.

The final major topic of the year is an imaginative one, using such titles as 'Journeys to the Centre of the World', 'Dreams', 'Magic', 'Myths' and so forth, in the hope that the pupils will now have sufficient confidence in handling media to be able to realize a truly imaginative idea in expressive form.

Second Year

Broadly speaking, the approach that is taken is very similar in the second year. Again lead lessons and sharings are emphasized, and it is expected that during the development stages of each project the pupils will go on learning skills and acquiring greater expertise in the handling of media for their expressive purposes. The following topics have recently been used as a means of organizing the second year curriculum:

1. Basic materials
2. Mass media and television
3. Games
4. Relationships
5. Imagination

Third Year

In the first two years staff have been concerned with introducing pupils to, and allowing them to explore, a wide variety of media in the belief that at this stage it is the process that pupils go through rather than the end product that is important. Staff have been concerned with stimulating and educating the pupils' senses, encouraging pupils to look and become aware of what is around them, and encouraging pupils to use their responses as creatively as possible. Staff have also tried to help pupils become aware of the relationships existing between the different arts. By the third year our pupils have become used to exploring the creative possibilities of both their experiences and objects. They have acquired a basic foundation on to which third-year work can now be built.

If growth has been allowed for in the first two years, third-year pupils should be becoming sensitive both to their own expressive needs and to the need for further skills and technical expertise. Unless this particular need is gratified, their future attempts to express themselves are likely to be frustrated and eventually stifled. It is therefore considered that it is now very important to concentrate on giving pupils a thorough working knowledge of the opportunities available within the expressive arts area. This is essential to future development in the fourth and fifth years when a more sophisticated approach could not be adequately realized without the pupils first establishing this secure technical base.

Fourth and Fifth Years

Fourth- and fifth-year work in expressive arts comes under two headings:

1. Examination courses

Whether the arts ought or ought not to be examined is arguable but over the years art and music have become 'legitimatized'. We offer examination courses in these subjects at both CSE and GCE levels. We also provide dance, drama and photography Mode III CSE examination courses for those pupils who wish to follow them. It is interesting that a very high percentage of pupils follow arts examination courses, and yearly the numbers increase. Perhaps if we ask ourselves why, we might even be led to believe that their popularity is partly due to the experiences that the pupils have had within the expressive arts lessons in their earlier school days. It is not necessary to throw away beliefs just because examination courses are offered in the arts subjects. Instead the philosophy of the expressive arts area is brought to them.

2. Expressive Arts

Work in the first three years has prepared the pupils to work in both a skilful and expressive way in each of the arts subjects. In the fourth and fifth years pupils are therefore offered a wide variety of projects from which it is hoped that they will gain both satisfaction and enjoyment. By now pupils have had a basic foundation in all the arts and have made various assessments about their likes and dislikes. Recreation is considered to be important but it is realized that senior pupils will not enjoy their one unit of expressive art unless their interests are taken into account. Staff therefore aim to encourage a happy, relaxed atmosphere, where pupils can follow their interests and take an equal share with the staff in the running, and in the fun which the course can give them. Pupils are therefore offered a series of short courses/projects in art, drama, dance and music, and pupils are asked to select the courses they most prefer. This allows the pupils to move from one area to another or to work in art, dance, drama or music all the time if they so wish. Pupils are asked to make a first and second choice for each term/half term, but it must be noted that their second choice is only used after consultation with them. Whether courses are of a term or half term's duration depends on the length of the term; for example, a Christmas term of fifteen weeks could well be divided into two courses of seven weeks each. On the other hand, a term of ten weeks hardly offers time for two courses.

Examples of courses offered to the fourth year for one term.

Art
1. Slab, coil and pinch pots – basic hand-building techniques
2. Kinetic art
3. Assemblage of found objects and matcrials (3D work)
4. Going into print
5. People

Dance
6. Each group deciding amongst themselves the type of work that they undertake. Some suggested starting points may be dancing for fun, working to music you choose, using dance in experimental situations, preparing for productions, lead lessons, sharings etc.

Drama
7. People

Music
8. Guitar
9. Experimental music
10. Making simple instruments

Fifth-year expressive arts has taken a general theme of 'Communication' for the projects offered in this year's course as an attempt to bridge gaps between pupils and others. Pupils are therefore encouraged to establish links not only with children in the school, but also with the community in which they live – taking work out for others, and working alongside younger children are just two examples of projects that seem to have worked. All the projects outlined are therefore to a lesser or greater degree concerned with communication, and where possible with building a bridge between the pupils and the community. It must, however, be realized that it is no good forcing this link; the desire has to come from the pupils. Indeed, throughout this year pupils are relied on to take the initiatives; it is very much their year and it is up to them and us to make it as exciting and productive as possible. Staff are always on hand to give technical assistance, teach new skills as and when applicable and to give any aid needed. We envisage a fifth-year expressive arts time being more of a 'workshop' session where staff and pupils work together, staff acting as advisors rather than teachers.

Examples of courses offered in one term
1. Illustration
2. Light environment
3. Carving in wood

4. People
5. Posters
6. Dance – the group deciding how and what they communicate
7. Drama – problems of our society
8. Music – music for young children
9. Composing music for dance.

Sixth form
Sixth-form pupils are offered an opportunity to participate in 'Arts Workshop' with art, dance, drama and music staff. This may take the form of working towards performance, or pupils may choose to follow a particular interest in one of the arts.

In addition, a one-year expressive arts CEE course is offered in the lower sixth. Pupils choose three modes out of five offered – that is, art, dance, drama, music, photography. Pupils will work in each mode for one hour per week for one year – total CEE time, three hours per week.

'A' level courses are also offered in art and music.

Perhaps it could be taken as a measure of the present interest in the arts within the school that some pupils have chosen to take a CEE course in expressive arts as well as participating within the 'Arts Workshop' which is offered as part of the 'Core' studies.

Departmental Organization

A large department such as this which involves a high degree of collaborative work cannot possibly function without careful organization: the organization of pupils within each year group, and the management of the teaching teams. The latter includes the organization of the department on a day-to-day basis, future planning, co-ordinating structure, timetabling commitments, deployment of staff, extra-curricular activities such as productions, festivals, open evenings etc.

Organization of pupils

All the pupils have expressive arts as part of their normal timetable commitment. Each year is blocked into two groups, and in the first three years each group has two lessons of expressive arts a week, each session lasting for seventy minutes. In the fourth and fifth years all pupils have one session of expressive arts a week – a wide choice of activities being offered to them. In addition, pupils who wish to can follow a CSE or GCE course in art, drama, dance, music and photography. In the sixth form, arts workshops are available as an option for all pupils in addition to the 'A' level courses provided in art and music and a CEE expressive arts course.

Years One, Two and Three
Each year is split into two half-year groups. Each half-year group is broken down into six smaller groups of approximately twenty-eight to thirty pupils. These are groups of mixed ability, pupils' intellectual and social traits, musical and physical abilities being considered when the groups are formed. All the pupils will have a session a week of art and music for two terms, and a session a week of dance and drama for one term. Each half-year group requires the following room allocation: hall, theatre, at least three art rooms and two music rooms. A system of rotation has been devised which makes all this possible and which allows pupils to be taught by all members of the first-, second- and third-year teams. Each half-year group meets together for 'lead lessons' and 'sharings' when these are appropriate.

Years Four and Five
1. CSE and GCE courses are offered in art, drama, dance, music and photography, pupils choosing their courses towards the end of the third year.
2. *Expressive Arts*
Each year is split into two half-year groups. Pupils are presented with a brochure of courses for each term and invited to make a first and second choice of activity. Working groups are then formed, these being dependent on the choices made. A high staffing ratio is essential, as is the use of all the arts facilities for each half-year group.

Sixth form
Pupils may choose to follow 'A' level music or art courses, or an expressive arts CEE course. Such courses, as well as the workshop sessions demand a high staffing ratio and use of specialist facilities.

The Teaching Teams

The expressive arts department could not function effectively unless it met regularly as an entire team. Over the years, because of heavy demands on time, the meeting structure has had to be redefined and it is now essential to meet weekly as a team. A rotational system of meetings has had to be devised so that all the present demands are satisfied. The meeting structure is at present as follows:

Week 1	Full Team
Week 2	Workshop
Week 3	Section Meetings
Week 4	Workshop
Week 5	Heads of Section Meetings
Week 6	Full Team

This meeting structure is essential if ideas are to be shared, lead lessons and sharings organized jointly, and the collaborative nature of the work utilized fully for productions, exhibitions, open evenings etc. Additional meetings of staff involved specifically in years one and two are also arranged. For those activities that are extra curricular, and which involve the whole area, meetings are also arranged outside the normal meeting structure, usually in an evening. Evening sessions have also been used for discussion of curricular innovation.

Section meetings are concerned with the topics which are of particular interest to specialist departments, and with the internal and everyday organization of specific departments. Heads of section meetings deal with topics relating to the whole area, mainly on an organizational basis, and help section heads to keep in touch with the overall working of the area. But the vital element of the whole of the expressive arts area is the full team meeting. These meetings tend to be divided into two sections, the first part dealing with issues relevant to the whole area, brought forward from heads of section, senior staff meetings: the discussion and organization of forthcoming events and other topics which might come under a general management heading.

The second section involves a more philosophical discussion based on any educational matter relevant to the expressive arts area. Such discussions have to be ongoing for unless the philosophy of the expressive arts area, the relevance of our curriculum to our pupils, curriculum innovation and consolidation, methodology etc., are reviewed frequently, new members of staff will not identify themselves with either the principles or the practice of the department.

Conclusion

It must be obvious that for the expressive arts area to have grown in strength over the last eight years the advantages for both staff and pupils have had to outweigh the disadvantages. It is difficult to define these clearly. Perhaps the most important advantage is the strength that staff gain through working very closely with one another. Strength is gained from both the success and failure of others if those experiences are genuinely shared. Staff therefore become supportive of one another – they understand the nature of that success and that failure, the latter being regarded as an experience that we all go through and need help in, no matter what our experience, age or 'title' may be. Discussion between individuals in small groups, practical help and working situations through together, all help to give a feeling of support. Support also needs to be on hand and given at times within actual teaching situations. This can be given by people who have practical experience within specialist activities and therefore who understand the particular problems that arise. Perhaps one of the biggest advantages comes from working with staff who realize and who acknowledge that they have a similar language. Too often art staff in schools are out 'on a limb', the special demands of these areas not always being either sympathetically understood or even recognized. We not only talk to each other, but work with each other, using a common language, and are sympathetic to the demands made on staff within creative situations. Perhaps, however, our main gain from the collaborative situation comes from the great deal of inspiration we gain from each other.

Too often arts staff become drained of inspiration, of the creative spark which is so necessary for their work. However, working in a collaborative situation seems to counteract this – ideas bounce from one another, growing, spreading and exploding in many different ways. This give and take, the feeding of one from another, the ignition of ideas, is essential to all that we do.

What more do children gain from working within an expressive arts situation, as distinct from working traditionally? We believe that they come to see the arts as being collaborative, rather than competitive; that they see a variety of artists talking, working, helping and arguing with each other. The very fact that they see their teachers in such close contact must, we believe, help them to realize that the arts do spring from common ground. To experience a similar situation, whether it be in paint, clay, wood, music, dance etc., will help our pupils to build an awareness of the problems, disciplines and limitations of media. But perhaps one of the most important aspects of this work for our children is the gradual awakening and awareness of the life of the senses. Exposure to, discussion of and participation in the arts is essentially important to these children, many of whom are starved of exciting stimuli and opportunities to express their feelings in their home environment. Our hope for the arts in the future lies in the children we teach. Perhaps if we can help them even to start seeing that the arts are dynamic, exciting, alive, enjoyable and worth being involved in, our efforts will have been worth it.

12 Dance

Susan Morris

Introduction

Susan Morris was associated with the 'Arts and the Adolescent' project from the start and her contribution conveys a vivid impression of her day-to-day encounters with her pupils through dance. In fact Mrs Morris describes almost exactly what I had in mind when writing about the 'good enough creative arts teacher'. That her own work is really distinguished there is simply no question – however I doubt that Mrs Morris would claim much more for herself than that she seeks to be 'good enough' for pupils with so much dancing in them. Indeed, reading her piece, it is the children who come shining through, and I only wish there had been the space here to illustrate their work more fully. Mrs Morris's account highlights in practical terms many of the points I have tried to make elsewhere – in particular I am grateful for her assessment of her own role within what she calls 'this magic encounter'. On the one hand she says, 'I act as an inspirer, enthusiast, and general encourager', on the other as 'an originator ... who builds a framework within which the learning process takes place'.

Mrs Morris's claims for creative dance in education are compelling. I hope there will soon be a more general acknowledgement of the power and appeal of this medium for young people – and that the boys will wish to assert their right to participate.

M.R.

I feel that it is vital for the arts to define themselves and justify their position in the school curriculum. Nevertheless, before embarking upon my contribution to this book, I must state that I find it both difficult and dangerous to commit myself to making statements about my work. The opinions which I express are those which have evolved from my teaching experience and which I have accumulated over the past nine years. They exist only for today, because I believe that a good teacher is always adapting, changing and refining his or her ideas. I would therefore like my contribution to be regarded merely as a statement of personal belief relevant only as a record of current thought and not as a matter of indisputable fact.

Dance in the context of the school

Although dance by no means enjoys the same priority over timetable time, staffing and resources as does art, it has over the years become a significant part of school life. There was very little dance taught in the school when I joined in January 1970, but now it is taught throughout the school, with a CSE and CEE Mode III course run in the fifth and sixth year respectively. I have sole responsibility for all the teaching of dance, which is quite a heavy load, and because of the limitations of time and the small space in which I work, the activity as part of the curriculum is limited to girls, a factor which I very much regret. The boys can only be involved occasionally in after school activities, so far as dance is concerned.

The first- and second-year girls get an average of one lesson per week. They are allotted a double period which is used for either gymnastics or dance. The third and fourth years have a block of three lessons per week and the fifth and sixth have a block of four. Again the limitations of time and space mean that after the fourth year, the activity is optional. As with every department I would find more time with pupils desirable. I believe movement is a form of expression which children need to grow up with. Dance is a language which they should use as often as possible, and I would be really happy to see a lesson per day for every child.

The facilities at the school are really quite bad for dance, but this disadvantage has never outweighed the advantage of working in a small friendly school. The hall in which I work is flanked by seven doors, three leading to classrooms, three to the corridor and one to the make-shift changing room. This hall is used as an assembly hall, thoroughfare and worst of all, a wet break assembly point. This means that it gets filthy, and dancing in bare feet upon such a surface is far from ideal and often hazardous, especially as we have no showers, not even a foot shower. There is one sink in the corner of my room. My musical equipment has improved over the years as has my capitation allowance, although, as with most teachers, I could wish for more equipment to help me in my work. I work almost every night after school.

The Dance Curriculum

As I run the dance department single-handed, I do not have too many problems of internal structure, organization and administration. I am fortunate to be able to spend most of my time teaching. I make all my own decisions, implement my ideas and make all my own mistakes, then adapt and change things as and when necessary.

From initially aiming to give pupils enjoyment and confidence through dance, my present aims are more complex and sophisticated. Through my pupils I have been made aware of the potential of dance as an educational medium. They have extended my concept of dance and helped me to understand its value, and forced me to devise a coherent approach to curriculum structure.

The curriculum is devised to sensitize and enliven the minds and bodies of the young people I teach. It relies on their creative individuality and upon my responsiveness to them and the situations in which we find ourselves.

Starting Points for Dance

In terms of curriculum content, the material I use from one year to the next will change almost completely. In fact I purposely avoid using the same material more than once, unless I feel that it will be of great value to my pupils. This is because I find that I am far more responsive, and that I can get involved more honestly in new material. I get enthusiastic about starting something new, and excited by the pupils' responses. My excitement seems to affect them, and I think this infectious enthusiasm is a very significant element in my work. The originality, inventiveness and imagination of the pupils never ceases to amaze me, and I am still constantly thrilled by their responses. I try never to underestimate their potential.

However, having said that the actual content is always changing, there are certain principles which are constant: I try to use as wide a variety of stimuli as possible so that all the senses are stirred into response, and dance does not become an activity merely inspired and accompanied by music: I use external sources of inspiration – music of all kinds from classical to progressive pop, sounds both natural and man-made, words, individually, or as poetry or prose, spoken or sung, English or foreign. I use visual sources of inspiration from the environment to works of art, slides; tactile stimuli including contact with themselves, each other and all manner of surfaces and textures, such as cloth, clay, sand, etc.; props, costumes, environmental situations of lights, structures, smells, atmospheres, anything can form a starting point for dance. I also tap the internal world of the individual for inspiration: feelings, thoughts, sensations, ideas.

The exploration of the medium is itself also a vital source of inspiration used when pupils can appreciate the intrinsic value of the activity, and accept abstraction.

Although I have listed external, internal and intrinsic sources of inspiration, the activity of creating dance always involves all three elements. They are inseparable, and are merely listed to illustrate that a starting point for dance can be found anywhere. Any child is free to suggest any idea which she finds exciting. Each element acts to inspire the other, sparking off excitement, and leading to an integrated and more meaningful experience. I have seen first-year pupils, engaged in exploring the idea of moving like a mechanical doll, feel the sensations of restriction, learning to understand its meaning through the experience, whilst being excited by finding a new way of moving their legs.

One of my sixth-form pupils recently created a solo. She began with the idea that when one speaks one's mind one is often hurt or hurts someone else in the process. She discovered the full strength of this feeling through the movements she evolved which in turn extended and excited her physical being with new sensation. Through the nature of the activity she had to organize her ideas, and having developed and resolved the movement form through discrimination, refinement and control, she realized that such discrimination, refinement and control were the necessary elements in helping her to resolve her problem of speaking one's mind which needs to be tempered with those concerns. She experienced the associated evocative elements of dance as inseparable and integrated.

Whatever the starting point for dance, it must be selected very carefully. My knowledge of the group is always employed to guide my choice. I have known situations in which I have listened to ten pieces of music and known that none of them would work for a particular group at a particular time.

Generally I have found that pupils will progress from external to internal to intrinsic starting points, as they grow and develop. To begin with I would use simple musical pieces like 'Carnival of the Animals' or the Waltz from *Dr Zhivago*. Music with a simple, easily definable structure or familiar music like TV theme tunes or ideas like playing in the rain, follow my leader, or laziness and business, familiar sources of inspiration which will give them the security they need in their initial stages of development. During this stage of development I am trying to help them to become aware of, develop, organize and control their feelings and ideas into meaningful form, helping them to discover, and recognize that they have their own identity, their own movement vocabulary which is distinctive to them. Hopefully they will lose their inhibitions and become confident in their ability to respond naturally and spontaneously.

I then slide pupils gradually into the use of more abstract starting points leading to dance, which evolves its own meaning, feeling and form and does not necessarily tell a story or express an idea. It can exist in its own right without associations. It can even break away from the initial starting point. At this stage we may explore shape and texture in movement, or start with a more complex musical piece like that of the group, Kraftwork or Focus, or Stockhausen's electronic music. We may explore the concept of prejudice or write a poem together, like the one below which was written by a group when we spent one of the many dance courses I have organized in the countryside. These courses have been very valuable ventures providing immediate inspiration for the pupils, and many very exciting dances have evolved.

Ulswater
Still in time the lake stands calm and motionless,
Robbing itself of the pleasures of life.
The mist rests its weary back on the hills,
While luminous patches on the hillside reflect an expanding pathway.
Dancing shadows skim along the water, plundering the unexplored.
The trees share their secrets with the wind
Yet all are united in ages of stillness.

I try to give all pupils this type of first-hand experience at some stage during their development. It always provides starting points which are immediate and uncontrived.

During this stage of development I am trying to help pupils to consolidate and extend their experience by very selective use of such starting points, some of which require them to use the knowledge which they already have; re-affirming their identity, and others which will evoke new experience and initiate exploration into abstract expression.

I have just finished a dance with my third-year group which aimed to achieve the latter. It has been an experimental venture with Manchester's North Centre electronic workshop. The starting point came out of discussion with the pupils and it was decided to base the dance on feelings. They threw out all sorts of ideas and we explored them through movement. I realized that they needed a structure to work within and I helped them to evolve this. We began with exploring what happiness meant. They selected excitement, joy, gratitude and contentment, and created movements to express these feelings, sharing, exploring and extending their understanding of these emotions, and evolving movements to epitomize their responses whilst manipulating the movements and group structure objectively to communicate their ideas. Having created the form the pupils then found sounds that would complement, accompany and reflect this form.

We discussed how happiness led to freedom, but that if everyone exercised freedom at the same time in the same space, it caused restriction and aggression, which would lead to greed, jealousy, malicious gossip and false superiority. Ultimately, frustration and isolation. I then thought it might be an idea to make a transition back to excitement and the first cycle of happy feelings. This involved tentative attempts to communicate with suspicion which gradually brought the whole group back together again. We repeated the first cycle, but joy and contentment were experienced as more of a group activity, finishing with complete togetherness, understanding and concern. The sound for the middle section of the dance was created first so that they experienced coming from the ideas into movement into sound, and from ideas to sound to movement. I feel that it has been a very valuable venture in that they have explored and extended their experience of feelings and learnt that one adapts and changes through what is learnt. Inevitably they have extended their personal movement experience and I have forced them into a more objective use of group relationship structure and organization.

With this particular group I will probably use a much easier starting point for the next piece of work, seeking more spontaneous and individual responses. I think they will need the freedom to re-affirm and consolidate themselves and find their new identity, recognizing what stays with them from the present experience, which bits really belong to them as individuals.

Finally the starting points for dance come from the medium of movement when the challenge is found from manipulating the elements of dance itself. The process of creativity becoming not a form of expression, of that which is part of oneself, or even that which is discovered about oneself in the process of extending one's capabilities, but is the creation of unique experience. The starting points at this stage are often found by the individuals themselves, or presented to individual students who can cope with the challenge of creating pure dance. I might suggest bits of music which will evoke the sort of response which a certain pupil needs to stretch her, or suggest that she work on transitions or images which I know are areas which will provide a challenge for her and extend her understanding. This is not to say that all starting points will be so pressurized. They have varied from movement sensation ideas like suspension and bounce, to choreographic considerations such as rhythmic patterns or development of basic motifs to manipulating group relationships and images. Hopefully the articulation of these elements extends their experience into purely abstract feeling and form. At this stage I think the process becomes an intellectual and soul-searching activity which employs all that has been learnt from the earliest stages of their development, in which analysis and discrimination are expected to control intuitive and spontaneous responses. The dancer not only creates but learns to become aware of the process she is going through so that she can control and articulate it more effectively.

Even at this stage the creative act employs external, internal, and intrinsic sources of inspiration, and the dancer is continually responsive to these elements. They naturally and inevitably interact and influence each other to give a richer and more meaningful experience.

A very significant development concerning my work with the sixth form this year has, I feel, been the growing control they have gained over improvision. The girls have learnt to consider the 'feeling idea' and the image created at one and the same time. I think this has developed through group improvisation in which the students have related to each other, copying, complementing, developing and contrasting with each other's movements. In this situation they have had to relate to the images projected by the rest of the group. We have done quite a lot of work of this type and as well as developing an awareness of the individual images which evolve, they are now more easily able to relate to the image created by the group as a whole.

I feel that such experience is developing a divergent mode of thinking which hopefully will carry over into the way they respond to other situations. In actually being forced to articulate about this development I realize its significance more fully, and I hope I will be able to use this knowledge in future. Again it has been the pupils who initiated this way of working, and again the value of the experience has been assessed afterwards. Only then can its true significance be realized. This is the process through which my philosophy and conceptual framework has evolved. This is what makes my commitment to dance education so strong for I have seen living proof of its value.

The Teacher's Role in the Creative Process

Many of the starting points suggested may seem obvious and predictably dull, and may not have worked for many teachers who have tried them. I think that it is indeed impossible to prescribe a curriculum for any group without knowing them, and inevitably it must be said that it is not the material which is selected which is of prime importance to the success of the lesson but how that material is presented. So far I have talked about the multitude of starting points one might take for dance, and about the development from simple representational work to more complex abstract and purposeful activity. I will now try to explain how I see my work.

To me each lesson is a magic encounter in which the pupils and I are engaged in an experience of discovery and learning. A time in which we can share feelings and ideas, experience things together, act out, listen, talk, discuss, accept, reject, experiment, explore, compromise, adapt, etc. We interact either spontaneously through improvisation or through careful consideration and analysis of our ideas. I have found that both ways of working are equally important tools for extending experience. Ultimately, both work together as I have described earlier but until that time I seek to keep the balance between the two. Each must be kept alive and given a chance to develop. The lesson is also a time for quiet and private exploration of personal probing into new experience. Individual and group work from duos to large group dances are experienced and both are seen as equally important.

So within this magic encounter I act as initial selector of starting points although the pupils very often suggest ideas which are taken up. As an inspirer, enthusiast and general encourager. As an engineer who not only keeps a balance between dance which evolves through spontaneous improvisation and that which evolves through analytical exploration or between individual and group work, but who also builds a framework within which the learning process takes place.

Initially I structure the experience quite tightly, leading pupils through the creative act, pushing them into discriminating and making decisions at each stage within the process. As they become more secure and confident the process gets more complex, involving them in many more considerations. As they learn to cope with these complexities, my role as guide diminishes and they begin to structure their own learning programmes. Hopefully they become autonomous and my role becomes one of helping them to resolve their problems, perhaps offering alternative solutions, making sure they consider all relevant factors but generally to help and encourage. Even older, reasonably confident students need as much encouragement as the little ones for they are continually treading new ground.

Generally I will lead my pupils from quite highly structured situations in which they make only a few decisions, to open-ended situations in which they make all the decisions, plus all the variations in between, according to their needs. In this capacity as engineer I am always seeking to keep a balance. Striving for a state of equilibrium between many factors is a vital part of my work. I seek to provide security and risk, consolidation and extension of experience, discipline and freedom, problem solving and problem finding, etc. I try to let them experience the extremes of these polarities and the gradations in between.

In and out of lesson time, my aim is to get to know and understand every child, so that I can temper my teaching to suit each individual. I try to establish a relationship with each one of them. My teaching relies very strongly upon this knowledge, the relationships we develop, and upon my sensitivity and responsiveness to them all. I am concerned about all of them and knowing that, for instance, one child's father is in prison, helped me to understand her behaviour. She felt she could share her sadness with me, because we knew each other well; such growing trust is necessary to my work. I believe that every child is capable of learning through dance and it is my job to spark off their enthusiasm. If by the end of the first year some pupils do not like dance then I feel it is I who have failed. Ironically it seems that those children who would benefit most from the experience of dance, usually find it most difficult to get involved. These pupils are always a challenge and have taught me much about teaching. My aim is also to let the children get to know me, learn to trust me and feel secure with me, for I believe that they can only truly be themselves in such an atmosphere. We become friends who can trust each other, share things, and not be frightened to make mistakes and show ourselves up. We can only then really learn and extend ourselves because we have the security of knowing that we understand each other. We share the uncertainty of putting ourselves at risk, knowing that we can accept the failures as well as the successes of each other.

One of my many such failures quite recently was with a second-year group for whom I had selected some music. I really thought it would inspire them and that an exciting group dance would evolve, but having tried a few ideas out I realized that it just was not going to work, so I apologized to them and we decided to look for another piece of music as a starting point. I did not push things because I felt we would not get anything out of it. I just responded to what happened and this responsiveness is the skill I employ most as a teacher, and yet it is the most difficult to explain. Essentially it recognizes the uniqueness of every child and every lesson, and the fact that one can never predetermine a response. It involves the continual monitoring of the pupil's responses which condition the course of action which is pursued. It controls the use of material, the way the material is presented, and it tempers my use of comment, it takes account of those intangible, but vital things which I have to consider, such as the state of the weather, which lesson the children have just come from, or the fact that Monica has fallen out with Pat etc. It means that I am constantly trying to observe, absorb and analyse the situation which I am involved in, and then take the action which I feel is most appropriate.

I suppose that I have acquired certain skills which help to inspire the pupils, help me to structure their experience and help me to respond to their needs, and I think that the teaching process involves the integrated use of these skills through which I try to make the best possible use of the situations which evolve.

I see this process as a creative learning activity, similar to that which I am helping the pupils through. As such, it is my aim not only to integrate my skills appropriately but also to develop an objective awareness of the situations which evolve whilst keeping alive my spontaneous involvement and responsiveness. I feel this is necessary, for I need to control and articulate myself effectively to suit the needs of the moment, even if it means keeping my mouth shut when I want to say something because I realize that my ideas may influence the activity too much and what they need at that moment is to make their own minds up. Only by developing this objective awareness can I really draw out the most from my pupils. This is ultimately what I hope to do.

My comments so far may seem to be over-considerate of the needs of the children, and one might envisage that the sort of work produced was very self-indulgent and undisciplined, but this is not the case. The discipline comes in with the objectivity, when decisions have been made, once the form has been created and sketched out. It is then that I will push each child and make her take things as far as she can. If a child has decided to do a certain jump which she cannot control, I will step in and suggest ways in which she might gain the control she seeks. If a child is doing a stretching movement but not taking it as far as she could, I will make her aware that she could take it farther and then make sure that she really tries to extend herself. I feel this discipline is very important because, although one learns a great deal from solving the problems set, making the decisions and organizing the ideas, these processes gain an importance and validity if the finished form is something concrete which the individual is proud to perform. I think that it is at this stage, when the form is repeated and refined, that the individual also re-affirms what has been learned in the process, at the same time developing her physical skills.

The uniqueness of dance is that its form is a living one involving the whole being moving in time and space. In perfecting and performing a dance the children will experience their form with different nuances and the experience gains in depth and subtlety. It is of course my job to make them aware of such variations so that they can control and articulate them. I do indeed spend much of my time just making my pupils aware of how they have responded.

Initially pupils' responses will be experienced, recognized and recorded in feeling form. Later the visual imagery which is projected by the body, moving in time and space, will be another means by which they learn to recognize the created form. Teaching children to become objectively aware of this visual imagery is, for me, very important. It is an element which I think has hitherto been neglected in modern educational dance. To recognize and record dance in feeling form alone can lead to vague and self-indulgent dance. I try to teach my pupils that within the making of dance they must develop the ability to oscillate between spontaneous and subjective activity, and involvement and objective awareness and consideration, so that they create movement whose feeling content and visual manifestation are articulated to achieve a state of optimum compatibility.

Hopefully, the skills developed by this type of process will carry over into the everyday lives of pupils. I believe that the ability to involve oneself emotionally, whilst keeping an element of objectivity in one's mind, helps individuals to make controlled and rational decisions about feelings and thoughts. It is hoped that the development of these skills of discipline and objectivity will help pupils to balance and integrate emotion and intellect, and I believe such a skill is of value to us all.

I believe that the use of comment needs very careful consideration. I have found that a simple smile can provide the impetus for an idea to blossom, whereas an expression of apathy can kill something which might never be reborn again. There are two basic principles which I follow. One is that my comments should always be constructive, and the other that I avoid making value judgements. I will comment openly about the concentration, involvement, commitment, effort and enthusiasm of my pupils but I try not to state that their work is good or bad. Any piece of work is acceptable if it is produced with sincerity. I believe that the pupils are the only true judges of their work. It is my job to help them to be honest with themselves, to get them to ask the right questions about their work so that they can make judgements which are valid. As they grow and develop, my questioning of their work increases in order to help them to be self-critical and better able to justify their actions. The use of such questioning will of course depend upon the child, the stage of development, and the situation. I have to be very careful not to push too hard or too soon, and not to make it too easy for too long. I do believe that dance education involves this continual discovery and realization. This fulfils a basic instinct in us: it evokes excitement and gives us much satisfaction. This in turn initiates our desire to search out new experiences of discovery and learning, and the process becomes a self-perpetuating cycle which leads to self-motivated inquiry and autonomous learning.

The way I operate within the encounter with the children is dependent upon my consideration of all the elements I have mentioned. However, there are other factors which may be significant. I am always on the move when I am teaching; I walk, run or dance from one place to another, all the time involving myself with the activity of the group. I join in with them, but I avoid demonstrating, for I do not want them to feel that the way I respond and perform is the right way. I want them to believe that their way is the right way. If I want to make a particular point, I will use two or three of the girls as examples. Needless to say, I avoid using the same person too often.

I talk a great deal, using my voice as an instrument, manipulating the pitch, tone and volume to keep the group interested and involved with what I am saying. I even sing out ideas with the music when it is appropriate. Such as 'Follow your leader off you go', as was the case in a recent second-year duo dance, other words I sang with this piece were, 'My feet are going to play to-day' and 'Look what I can do', 'I can do it too'. These silly sentences gave the children an idea within which to work, without telling them what to do.

The content of my comments will range widely: suggestions of movement ideas, such as 'you can reach up high', or backwards, sideways or forwards; making associations between these movement ideas and the external world, such as 'like the sun's rays breaking through the clouds' or 'a tree's branches reaching up into the sky'; identifying the movements and ideas with physical sensations and feelings, 'feeling tall and long', 'as though someone is pulling you by your fingertips'; pushing them into making decisions and structuring the movements which evolve; making them select a number of ideas, show them to me and link them together into a short pattern. I do this so that the whole experience is kept alive and steered towards an integrated process which has an end product, whether it be as short and simple as three movements which make up a motif or pattern, or a long and complex group dance. I hope that after every lesson the children will feel a sense of achievement from having created something for themselves.

Performance and Assessment

Although many dance educationalists at one time denied the fact that performance was a necessary part of modern educational dance, I have found that it is a vital part of my work. All the children I have taught have, at one stage or another, welcomed the opportunity to show their work to an audience. Within their lessons the children are frequently required to show each other their work, and I organize many displays for the purpose of letting pupils see other groups perform and to show their work to their parents and friends. These performances generate terrific enthusiasm and I have often found that the added pressure of this situation will help pupils to acquire that extra discipline needed to execute their ideas to the best ability. The whole experience seems to give pupils more confidence in themselves and a greater commitment to dance.

These displays involve all pupils, they are not organized to give the gifted few the chance to perform, but are for everyone. A great deal of solo, duo and small group dance work is done by the girls on their own, and these displays give them the opportunity to show this work as well. There have been so many people involved recently that the displays have had to be split into first and second, third and fourth, fifth and sixth, so that everyone has the chance to show what they have created.

As pupils get older the demands for more complex work arises and from this has usually sprung production work. This has meant that the girls have produced at least one major performance a year (although this year we have done four). These have included a dance

drama version of Shakespeare's *Macbeth*, a purely abstract piece
called *Structures*, a jazz cantata in conjunction with the live music of
The Michel Garrick Jazz Group, *Sea Change*, a piece which explored
some concepts from Shakespeare's *Tempest*, a dance drama version of
Lord of the Flies, and *Lord of the Rings*, in conjunction with one of
Manchester's youth orchestras, with original score and live music.
Most of these displays have involved the co-operation of other
departments, and I think all have been valuable ventures. Each has
provided a set of constraints within which the dancers have had to
work, and posed many problems which would not evolve in the
normal course of development, thus stretching our resources and
extending our experience. These productions have often resulted in
great personal revelation when dancers were limited by the conditions of a prescribed situation.

Such ventures have always lead to the development of real group
feeling and understanding, and this has often come out of initial
antagonism and clashes of personality. In fact, the whole experience
of co-ordinating, staging, lighting and performing to a large and
usually enthusiastic audience, has given these pupils an experience
which I am sure they will never forget.

As I have stated earlier, I believe the only true assessment of what
is learned will come from the pupils themselves, within whom it is
hoped to develop the skills of self-assessment, criticism and justification. I believe that the only way I might judge the real effect of
dance upon a group of individuals is to find them in ten or twenty
years, to meet them as middle-aged adults, at which time I would
hope to find individuals whose experience in dance, that initial
initiation into awareness and responsive sense of being, has sustained
them, and has matured as they have grown and is still alive.

However, one has to make more immediate assessment of one's
work and its effectiveness, and try to judge its significance to the
young people of today, so that one can adapt one's ideas to suit their
needs.

At my school, we operate an assessment system of grades 1–5 for
effort, and A–E for attainment. For me the former is the most
significant and the only one which I would reveal to pupils on their
yearly reports. The latter is kept as a guide on their record cards.
The distribution of attainment grades is supposed to fall within a
natural curve of distribution for each group, but I find it often unfair
to make accurate assessments within these limitations. I feel that it is
more important to make a record of how much progress a pupil has
made rather than measuring the skills revealed in more objective
terms.

Having said this it seems ironic to then say that I run CSE and
CEE examinations in dance,[1] which ostensibly seems to put my
previous premise in jeopardy, but these exams are Mode III and

[1] Details of those two courses appear as Appendix 1.

therefore were proposed by me, are set by me, marked by me and moderated externally. This has therefore meant no real compromise on my part and has indeed proved to be a valuable inclusion in the dance curriculum.

I introduced these examinations because I felt that my pupils deserved some sort of external commendation for their attainments in dance. I submitted a syllabus, the content of which was then the natural progression from the work which I was already doing, and in no way conflicted with my ideas. More recently I submitted an 'A' level proposal, which was rejected by JMB. Unfortunately I think that it will be a while before such examining boards realize that the skills fostered by activities such as dance are worthy of commendation at 'A' level standard.

The CSE and CEE examinations have in fact proved to be very valuable. The developing potential for analysis, discrimination and objectivity which seems to reveal itself most significantly in our fifteen-to seventeen-year-olds, is fed by these courses. These skills add a new dimension to the process of creating dance, and I believe they are what is needed at this stage of development. I have adapted and changed the courses when necessary, having made many mistakes, and I expect this process of refinement to continue.

At this stage in the development of my pupils I think it is quite fair to assess them with more objectivity because the correlation between the development of physical skills and that of the affective, intellectual and cognitive skills, for which I aim, has in most cases reached a compatible stage, and revealed itself. If there is any discrepancy between the two, caused perhaps by a physical disability, then the pupils can manifest their understanding in the written element of the examination.

The CSE exam requires that the students keep a written record of the work done in practical lessons and a written project. This task helps them to develop objective skills, within the context of the creative act. This is always an illuminating process for students, which, although initially difficult, proves to be very valuable, adding a new dimension to their work.

For the CEE exam students have to write three essays which require them to think more deeply about the whole area of dance and its significance to them. This work has also proved to be incredibly revealing and often given me much reassurance.

Some Examples of Pupils' Work

I obtain a great satisfaction through being able to be creative in movement, for example the movements and feelings created and expressed in solo. Knowing they are of my very own making, and using this developed ability with which I can use movement as a instrument to express my feelings and emotions to others and provide pleasure for others and for myself.

Yet; apart from all I have gained, I can still educate myself by defining, studying and selecting; the thinking process which has been developed through dance, the way in which to interpret that which I wish to show. Dance has therefore plenty of future potential as regards myself.

I am not saying dance is the only way by which people can obtain and gain that which I have, indeed there must be many ways, it is just that for myself Dance is the best way.

To end this essay I would like to summerise that which I have gained; unfortunately the following summary is poor for without showing what I am trying to say without dancing is very difficult.

In all I have gained by dancing; with simplicity I can say, I feel much more pleased with life and I am satisfied with that I possess, and that which I can see.

*   *   *

His movements became distorted. His body jerks forward. His movemenis become confused he rushes forward frantically and he leaps into the art.

Now the revenge has been taken.

His body starts to crumple. He clenches his fists and slowly leans to the side. His body becomes rigid and his limbs become numb. He rests his hands on the floor and lingers for a few minutes.

Then he rushes forword and moans in a regretful way. He reaches out his arm and tries to receive forgiveness.

Then he slithers to the ground with no life within him.

When he realises what he has done he is deeply sorry. In a way he can't accept it and wants forgiveness. When he does accept it he dies inside – he wants to suffer, for what he had done, was unforgivable.

Fig. 12.1

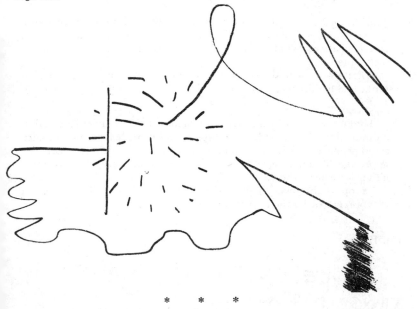

*   *   *

One part of the production which really thrilled me was the part of my solo where Piggy has his glasses stolen by Jack, Piggy gets up from his sleep feeling lost in a world of darkness. When i dance this part i relly got involved. This is how it would illustrate it.

Fig. 12.2

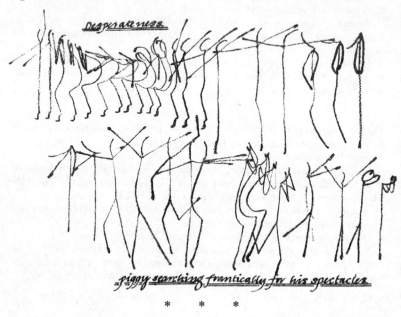

Desperateness.

piggy searching frantically for his spectacles.

*   *   *

The feeling I got when I wrote these three essays was not one of apathy but of great enjoyment. Dance is one of the masterys of great craft, and it is education. What I have experienced in my body, is my dance technique.

What drove me to dance? It was nothing but enthusiasm, obsession, faith, and endurance.

*   *   *

The most significant thing at the moment is that dance has made me into an individual, it has made me search for answers, helped me to understand people especially those that seem to be a little adrift from others. I appreciate life and love, and my problems sometimes are solved as easy as if they were never there.

I propose that every person should take an interest in dance, and maybe it can do for them what it has done for me.

*   *   *

Fig. 12.3

DANCE IS THE MOST IMPORTAIN THING in schooling.

13 Arts in Wonderland

Ben Bradnack

Introduction

Ben Bradnack writes from the point of view of the drama teacher in a sixth-form college, though, as his title rightly implies, a good deal of what he has to say is of distinct relevance to all the creative arts. In the first section of his chapter Mr Bradnack anatomizes an institutional situation that will be familiar to colleagues working at all educational levels. Where I have stressed the need for conceptual clarity Mr Bradnack points to the dangers that stem from what he sees as ideological confusion. The two are, of course, intimately connected. It is certainly crucial to the chances of the arts, assuming what we believe to be their true educational role, that arts teachers define themselves ideologically and collectively and then take the appropriate political decisions to safeguard and further their legitimate ideals.

In the second half of his contribution Mr Bradnack describes his own work. He exposes the irony of the situation of sixth-form drama: the drive to educational legitimacy, via the examination, frustrated in the end by the reluctance of universities to admit the student with an 'arts' qualification. The arts student (along with the arts teacher) is defined by the academics as having 'opted out of the main lines of English education'. Clearly, status is not necessarily going to follow examinability and certification. My own view presented elsewhere in this book, is that the arts have to establish their claim to a core position as a distinctive and essential way of knowing – as one of the basic languages of representation.

Teachers who write about their places of work run a number of risks: they are certainly lucky not to be thought either toadies or rats. In attempting to understand and pinpoint the tensions within which he works Ben Bradnack has felt bound to question certain philosophical assumptions and organizational characteristics of his own college. They constrain his actions since he perceives them in the way he does. The College Principal in this particular case felt that the impression given in this chapter was in some respects unfair to his College. I did not wish to see the article itself substantially altered so I invited him to contribute a comment of his own and that appears on page 232. I include it without comment.

M. R.

Attempts to describe teaching in sixth-form colleges face particular problems which derive from the novelty of the institutions: when I started teaching in one in 1972, there were only thirteen in existence, and rapid expansion since that time has not had time to be reflected in the Schools Council literature, which seems to be one's chief means of keeping in contact with changing educational structures. What follows is therefore not necessarily representative of institutions other than my own, and is indeed based on an extremely limited knowledge of all but a very few.

There are further difficulties in my own college in trying to describe practice in 'the arts'.[1] These difficulties, which may become apparent as I proceed, derive partly from what I take to be a lack of structural and ideological coherence in the college, which has placed all arts teachers within the institution in positions from which it is peculiarly difficult to get a general picture, much less detailed insights, into how arts teachers work. The difficulties also derive from the need to be detailed and particular in my observations, at the risk of appearing subjective and 'unprofessionally' critical. I believe that lack of an 'overview' tends to lead to implication of personalities and failure to identify structures and ideologies. I believe that these are failures common to many teachers of creative arts in secondary schools – and perhaps in other disciplines too. But the 'overview' which I hope to express, depends on particularities; and these are inevitaby drawn from an experience which is partial and particular; and cannot escape the problems of its derivation. I should make it clear, however, that my own college has a stronger commitment to the creative arts than many – perhaps most – sixth-form colleges. I am one of the few drama teachers in the country on a scale 4 salary. All the creative arts subjects have at least one scale 4 teacher attached to them – sixth-form colleges have, until recently, had an extremely high points allowance – and the principal of the college has gone on frequent record as attaching importance to creative arts subjects, particularly music and drama. Like most teachers, I have a healthy scepticism about such *ex cathedra* statements; but, though I feel that I have always lacked a clear sense of how far, or how, the creative arts are

[1] These I have taken to include English, music, drama, film, art and dance.

important in the college, they are clearly a great deal more important here than in colleges which do not employ specialists to teach
them at all.

Because I lacked a clear understanding of the place of the creative
arts in my own college, I asked the principal to write something
about his ideas on the subject. I was worried by his response, chiefly
for three reasons: that he gave weight to 'appreciation'; that he felt
it was inappropriate for him to have an 'ideological perspective' on
arts teaching; and that he wrote in the way he did, perhaps not too
happily, because he lacked, it seemed to me, the appropriate
language in which to discuss the place of the arts in education.

I am unhappy about 'appreciation' of the arts, because it leads
away from the 'felt' response, and towards blandness, when put
into educational practice. I am unhappy about the denial of the
appropriateness of 'ideology', chiefly because in this case it stems
from the questionable assumption that what is presently practised is
not informed by an ideology: the traditional liberal posture. And
there follows in the principal's comments, a commitment to a
particular structure which carries a profound ideological sub-text.
Under the general heading 'Faculty Department structure', he wrote
that he believes in the faculty of 'Creative Studies' in which art is
placed with home economics and technological crafts; specifically on
the grounds that without art, the faculty would be too narrowly
vocational or functional.

Music, drama, film and dance remain in a faculty called 'Communications', while art is in 'Creative Studies'; and the reason given
is – the 'balance' within the latter: a balance between vocation/
function and something undefined, but antithetical to vocation/
function.

The first thought that came to me was that structure had gone mad
at the expense of coherence. Is a faculty of Creative Studies which
needs the presence of art to prevent it from being 'too vocational or
functional', really a faculty of Creative Studies at all? It is arguable,
of course, that art is similar to home economics and technology, and
different from music and drama (in some forms) and film (appreciation but not making) in being committed to 'product' rather than
'process', but I doubt if many art teachers would accept this idea
happily: it creates a tendentious definition of 'creative'; and it seems
to imply that music, drama and film are *not* creative, or not in the same
sense. But then, in what 'sense'? What has this 'sense' to do with
'vocation/function'? I am not suggesting that strong significance
should be attached to the name of the faculty; but rather that significance *is* being attached to a concept of 'balance' which could specifically work against ideological coherence, since it seems to be
intended to make the faculty 'balance' between ideological contraries.

I begin to feel the ground opening up under my feet. Because there is
no overt ideological stance, and yet one can see strong evidence of a

hidden one, it is only too easy to imagine that there is a good deal more hidden away somewhere, which may be more sinister. Do I now detect that the 'Communications' faculty has been similarly 'balanced'; between English, in safer hands, and the nutters who teach music, drama, film and so on? Is it a subtle way of castrating faculties and preventing them from operating coherently? I become aware that a whole range of answers about faculty coherence, about function and vocation, which are assumed in the Principal's account, are operating without anyone knowing that the questions have been asked. Perhaps they never have been asked. Certainly a good deal of the account that I was given of the place of arts in the college, implied that they had not. Some of these questions I propose to ask because I take them to be central ones to all arts teachers; and meanwhile I hope enough has been said to indicate the grounds, for doubting the 'ideological coherence' of arts teaching and of the faculties in which the arts subjects are taught in my own college; and also for considering that a lack of such coherence, based on an ideology of 'balance', may constitute a serious threat.

The 'lack of ideological coherence' in my own college may be accounted for in a number of ways, some more threatening than others. It is possible that this particular principal simply has not the time to deal with knotty ideological problems about the nature and philosophy of creative arts teaching. It may be that he has an administrative structure, and that he is committed to making that work simply because it exists, whether it makes much sense or not. It may represent his ideology ('believing in what we have got') or, alternatively, his lack of one. It may be that he cannot see faculty structures as dependent on ideological coherence, for all sorts of reasons which I cannot conceive of; but whatever these reasons are, they can presumably be construed in two ways: either as deliberate strategies for avoiding coherence, or as failures to recognize the significance of coherence. In this respect, I have no doubt that arts teachers themselves are equally ignorant or culpable. For myself, I have rarely found it easy to enter into fruitful debate with other arts teachers, or to work with them on collective teaching projects. Now, the 'Arts and the Adolescent' project has suggested an area of debate which may be fruitful, and that the concepts of self-expression and personal development in arts education 'have not hitherto been well understood and in consequence have failed to provide the arts curriculum with an essential organizing principle'.[1] Whether my fears about the actual curricular place of the arts in the college are imaginary ones or real, there appear to be available now an opportunity and a rationale for making sense of that place, in Working Paper 54 and in *The Intelligence of Feeling*.[2]

[1] *Arts and the Adolescent*, Schools Council Working Paper 54, Evans/Methuen Educational, 1975, p. 57.
[2] Witkin, R. W., *The Intelligence of Feeling*, Heinemann Educational Books, 1974.

Clearly, the first thing to do is to try out the work of the 'Arts and the Adolescent' project on one's fellow creative arts teachers. I have tried this. The trouble is that it is not likely to be fruitful unless one has already established *a priori* some common ideological ground, and faculties which are structural rather than ideological communities are not particularly apt to do this. The evidence that there *is* common ideological ground may be established by a common interest in the project; but what if no such interest is forthcoming? Then, it seems to me, it is time to inquire with great curiosity into what a faculty *is*, and in particular, what the 'Communications Faculty' is, in order to challenge its perceptions of itself.

The Communications Faculty I am part of consists of four full-time and three part-time English teachers, one full-time and one part-time music teacher, one drama teacher, one part-time dance teacher, half a film/TV teacher who teaches other subjects, and assorted specialist instrument teachers etc., who are only marginally connected to any structure at all. The head of English is also head of the faculty, and therefore sits on the 'Academic Board', which theoretically makes curricular decisions. And that is about as far as it is susceptible to definition. It neither does, nor believes, anything in common. Why does it exist at all?

Certain decisions are made on its behalf. In particular, money is allocated on a basis which is theoretically a faculty one: so all faculties represented on the Academic Board in theory receive allocations corresponding to their relative needs; but in practice the Academic Board does not decide on the relative importance of these needs, nor does it define what they are. Instead, the individual faculty decides what *it* needs: again, in theory, *as* a faculty, but again, in practice, by subject departments defining what they need, and then, each and all, entering into departmental negotiation with the principal; so that, although faculties have a budgetary significance, that significance is only notional: a way of *identifying* what *is* going on; not at all a way of *deciding* what *should* go on.

Thus, if we take the budgets of the subjects within the Communications Faculty in the college for the academic year 1976/7, they stand in ratio to each other of English, 8.30; music, 2.50; drama, 2.00; film, 1.00; dance, nil; and these figures are a consequence of decisions which have been made by someone, and not, as I hope to show, by any means arbitrarily; but they were arrived at without the faculty ever having any sense of what was available *as* a faculty. They were overtly arrived at by individual negotiation between subject head and principal, mediating between the one's desire for maximum provision, and the other's knowledge of what was available altogether; but reflecting another, more far-reaching, influence at work.

What is available in these figures, I believe, is an index of the strongest force at work on the curriculum, certainly in this particular sixth-form college, and, I guess, in most 'student demand'. This, I believe, has largely superseded educational ideology, and replaced it with that of the 'market place'; and this, I suspect, is having a profound effect on the creative arts in schools. I am not suggesting that this is altogether remarkable. Nevertheless, an accurate description of what is happening may suggest the extent to which it is proper, or reversible.

The 'market place' seems to me to be located in three influences at work on students: in higher education requirements; in job requirements; and in secondary-school experience. These are the factors which condition the forms that student demand takes within the framework of curriculum planning. Curriculum planners then see their job as an essentially logistic one of fulfilling these demands by slotting them in to available spaces and staffing allocation; though it is arguable, of course, that this is actually an ideological exercise (making what students want fit into what already exists). Decisions about staffing and space provision rest with the local education authority and with the principal's logistic specialist, whose parameters are then mediated through the principal himself, in an exercise which is mystical, in the sense that only those two, out of the whole staff, can be fully aware of those parameters and their constituent features. The rest of the staff are inevitably committed to negotiation from the weakness of relative ignorance.

Now the 'market value' of the creative arts subjects is seen by students as limited: local employers are rarely interested in such attainments, and higher education frequently refuses to recognize even 'A' level art as a proper qualification. Consequently, secondary-school experience is the factor which most strongly conditions student demand for creative arts courses in a sixth-form college. There are in this instance at least seventeen secondary schools to draw from, and what is immediately noticeable is that much of what happens to students in the secondary schools is reflected exactly in what happens to them afterwards in sixth-form colleges.

All the secondary schools in the catchment area do art, so there is a considerable art intake to the college; staff provision amounts to three teachers, and room provision is also three. Music is done as a fifth-form option by (at my last count) about half the secondary schools; and this produces $1\frac{1}{2}$ staff and $1\frac{1}{2}$ rooms – inadequate provision because of the need for practice, and because it takes no account of the flourishing City Youth Orchestra, which has created a musical enthusiasm which needs to find some reflection in further education. Drama is only done in *some* of the feeder schools; and only two do CSE courses in fifth years in drama. Elsewhere, it is seen as suitable for younger children, or for 'less able' students who by that definition are unlikely to continue education at 16+. So drama merits one specialist and one room in the college and would have difficulty, as one would expect from the feeder figures, in making full use of this provision if it were not that a number of students tend to transfer into drama courses after a year in the college. Film and dance both merit less than a specialist and less than a specialist room because they are not done widely in feeder schools.

At 16+ students have decided, or been persuaded, as to what is serious; and that is what they are in college for, or so they tend to believe. At the beginning of a student's sixth-form life, persuasion can do something to fill up an empty set, or a student timetable which seems to contain more than a tolerable number of free lessons (the building cannot absorb more than a limited number of students in private study); and occasionally, as with those transferring to drama some way through their courses, students actually change direction. But, by and large, 'student demand' is accurately reflected in time-table provision. I set 'student demand' in quotation marks because I retain a scepticism about whether it is a *real* student demand, or a synthetic one created by the same sort of ideological failure that I have tried to identify earlier. The figures of space and staffing per subject, and the ratio of budgetary provision, coincide remarkably; though the space and staffing figures are, I have suggested, the result of student demand; and the budgets, the result of negotiation between subject teachers and principal. It is not clear to me whether the coincidence is real; or whether the student demand effectively manipulates the negotiation between subject teacher and principal, or that nego-tiation effectively manipulates the apparent student demand. But under either circumstance it is fairly clear that the correspondence between the figures is the result of passive acceptance by, rather than active negotiation within the *faculty* structure. In practice the faculty does little to affect staffing, nothing to affect room provision or resources.

If significant decisions are made by the faculty, I am unaware of them. The Faculty of Communications rarely meets; partly because it would not know what to meet for, even when there is a document like *Arts and the Adolescent* to discuss; and partly because it would have difficulty, because of extra-curricular commitments (particularly in music and drama) which tend to take these teachers away from faculty discussion into commitments to specialist student activities. And this entropic tendency seems to me signifi-cant: not least in that the curriculum is so organized that music and drama teachers find themselves having to operate outside the timetable to do the things that they want to do; and that this very tendency prevents them from being in a position effectively to modify the curriculum.

In fact, the one function which the communications faculty does seem to fulfil is in the handing down and ratification of unpleasant directives. If something unpleasant does have to be discussed, or there is a likely area of disagreement between principal and teacher, the head of faculty is expected either to be there for the discussion, or to mediate policy from on high; but since such occasions tend to produce bad blood rather than policy, everyone tries to avoid them. When they do occur, they most frequently revolve around public occasions: concerts, plays, open evenings, after exams: and the coincidence of these occasions with the attempts to make the faculty an effective policy-making unit, serves to underline a disjunction between what happens generally, when everyone goes his own sweet way, and what happens on those occasions when 'the college' is under scrutiny, when 'the faculty' must be seen to operate.

These are occasions when the work of subjects can come under the most severe strain. The expectation of them seems to be primarily a 'public relations' one. This expectation the faculty, invoked on such occasions, tends to underwrite. But arguably, 'communications', and indeed, the creative arts, will remain largely co-terminous with public relations, until an alternative language in which to discuss the place of the arts in the curriculum has been evolved. Such a language could, presumably, evolve, if a faculty of creative arts possessed any degree of ideological coherence to start with.

Lacking such coherence at a faculty level, each creative arts subject tends to develop its own ideology, and its own strategy for avoiding the deterioration into a public relations exercise. The strategy can never be fully effective, because all these subject areas do involve a public manifestation and induce a public response; but the strategy rests in the ways in which the pressures of the public response are mediated, either through setting alternative goals to the students involved in presentation, or in denigrating the public response, or both; but usually with an emphasis on process rather than product. Such complex educational operations make heavy demands on student time; there then develops a tendency for the subject area to attract to itself students who are prepared to devote a lot of time to the subject, see that subject as *their* discipline, the place where it takes place as their home, and the people who do it with them as their friends; so that there develops the 'music student', 'art student', 'drama student' (but fewer film or dance students, because they do not have either a geographical location within the college, or a member of staff representing that activity wholeheartedly). This separatism or specialist entropy amongst students is reflected in a tendency for those who pursue these subjects in their main studies programmes to become vocationally committed to them, going on to specialist further education in drama, music and art, to an extent which worries me a good deal. To take a sample group of ten students at the moment, doing one course in drama: two plan to go on to university drama courses, two to drama school, one to a performing arts course at a poly, one to do drama at a college of education; and of the remaining four, three are considering careers in the field of performing arts; only one actually plans to do something else: to go to art college. This is a frightening degree of specialization in a context which is not, in essence, vocational. It does not reflect decisions about careers made in secondary schools; on the whole, the option was chosen as an area which the student enjoyed; but in the pursuit of the course, the enjoyment has been converted into a commitment which may be satisfying for a lifetime, but which again may merely be the consequence of the failure of the creative arts to define what they are doing in other than vocational terms. *We are still failing to identify and operate a general function of creative arts within the curriculum for the majority of students.*

Such a 'general function' is supposedly fulfilled by general studies. This is the area of the curriculum which is not conditioned primarily by student demand. It is compulsory in outline, though optional in detail, and takes up rather less than one-fifth of a student's timetable, in the form of two one and a half hour sessions per week. It is also the area of the curriculum in which the creative arts subjects find a general, rather than a vocational function. Because of an ideological commitment on the part of the principal and those of us who teach in that area, the terms of the debate on what should be taught within general studies can be patronizing (based on the proposition: 'These are the things you *ought* to know') and occasionally sadistic ('This teacher is available. These students should be taught. Get on with it!'). Nevertheless the creative arts subjects operate most happily in this area, in that they all seem to believe that they can engage the enthusiasm of students within a framework which may be either a compulsory four-week course in the first year, or a limited option for eight weeks in the second year, but which has no recourse to exams, or to vocation.

Other sixth-form colleges do things markedly differently in the field of general studies. For example, Queen Mary's, Basingstoke, has a timetable organized on the contrary curricular assumption that non-exam courses are the first priority 'common core' of the timetable. The college advertises as many as eighty non-exam courses,[1] which suggests a completely different set of priorities from my own college. But in either circumstance, the creative arts tend to flourish in the general studies area of the curriculum, in which other subjects often have great difficulty. If this success clearly established a distinction between the creative arts and other subjects, one might be able to draw some conclusions about the nature and function of the creative arts in sixth-form colleges. But cookery, design technology, and needlework also flourish under general studies conditions; which suggests only that *practical* subjects do better than others: in circumstances where the delayed carrots of an exam and a job are not available, practical achievement becomes attractive. There is very little revelation in that. The only extraordinary thing is that such attractions do not play a larger part in the curriculum.

[1] For example an advertisement for Director of Linguistic and Literary Studies in the *Times Educational Supplement*, 23 April 1976.

So far, the direction of my inquiry has tended to suggest that arts subjects are either a public relations operation for the institution, a vocational frill for minorities, or a practical, and therefore relatively non-boring, aspect of general studies. These are depressing suggestions, but they are conditioned, I believe, by the form in which I have so far been couching the inquiry: the *general* conception of arts, and the nature of the *faculty*, are both in my own context, weak, and I have pursued them in order primarily to highlight their absence, because their absence is an important *condition* of my own work. But if I now retreat to a new and more embattled position as a drama specialist, I may be able to make clear what it is I do, in ways which may have some relevance to other arts teachers, without attempting to write on their behalf.

Professor Frank Musgrove recently suggested that 'we have a glut of so-called data, and we have a veritable famine of experience. The real problem of education is not the distribution of "objective knowledge" . . . but the distribution of experience, which is terribly scarce.'[1] I am not sure if this is relevant to all arts subjects; but for drama, it certainly outlines the territory usefully.

'Objective knowledge' is highly examinable, and examinability tends to confer high status within my own college: it is 'marketable'. General studies have low status among students because they are not strictly examinable (there is little relation between any general studies course and any general studies exam). But within the framework of general studies, the practical studies are preferred; and at this point, drama becomes a useful tool within areas which are not essentially practical, as a way of *experiencing* ideas, through simulation and role-play, forms of interaction and ways of working which are geared to solving some of the motivational problems of the unexaminable and therefore 'low status' subject areas. At Queen Mary's College, Basingstoke, they have gone further. The head of the drama department ran a course, open to all his colleagues, in which he showed them the sort of things he did, in case any of them wanted to use him as a 'resource'. The result has been extensive use in 'A' level teaching by Languages and Social Studies departments, and a long and interesting document of the results of co-operation. This suggests that a college which has, like Queen Mary's, a strong commitment to non-examined courses, is likely (to capitalize on Musgrove's vocabulary) to use 'experiential' rather than 'objective' teaching modes, even in *examined* courses; and when that happens, then drama becomes more properly a method of teaching rather than simply a substitute for the exam carrot.

The use of drama as a method is being increasingly explored;[2] but

[1] *Times Educational Supplement* report on 'New Themes in Education' conference at Dartington, 23 April 1976.

[2] See particularly Gibbs, G.I., *A Handbook of Games and Simulation Exercises*, Associated Book Publishers, 1974.

the use of 'drama as method' can have unsatisfactory consequences.
To take its use in general studies within my own college: I am aware
the use of 'drama as method' can have unsatisfactory consequences.
that it means that some pretty rubbishy ideas are being perpetrated,
and squeezed past a critical student judgement, simply because
dramatic methods are being used, and are fun; so that it becomes fun
rubbish. This is only ideologically acceptable for those who do not
make any larger claims for education or drama than that it *should*
be fun. In the past, students could at least reject the old rubbish,
because they were not being zapped out of their minds by 'experience' and 'involvement'. Clearly some sort of 'objective' judgement
must still be made by someone.

Another problem arises if drama is subsumed or submerged in
dramatic method: it loses its independent identity. *Arts and the
Adolescent* asks: 'What is the essential and unique nature of the
dramatic experience itself?', and goes on to suggest that 'in the
absence of an answer to (this) question . . . it proves impossible to try
and think about inter-subject relationships.'[1] This seems to me to mis-
state the case. It is only too easy, I would argue, 'in the absence of
an answer to this question', for one to think of drama as the hand-
maiden of many subjects, objective, experiential, and anything
else in between; and for it to cease to exist independently of them.
This does not happen to other creative arts subjects because their
special contents are so much more easily identified, while the content
of drama can be easily ignored because it is difficult to objectify. I
am well aware that my own special 'use' of drama may be an 'abuse'
of that which drama essentially is, or which other people take it to be.

This use, in part of the general studies programme for first-year
students, involving pastoral groups of sixteen students of mixed ability,
revolving around a circus of practical activities, in each of which they
will work for four or five sessions of one and a half hours, starts from the
proposition that, since the students may come from any or all of the
secondary schools in the area, they will have no common expectation
of what drama is or may be. Their experience may vary from advanced
improvisation work, through school plays, music and movement and
dramatic games, to total ignorance of the term; so one starts from a
position of common confusion, and often, with a pastoral group who
have only met each other for the first time at the college, of common
embarrassment.

It is unlikely that this group will, in four sessions, find expressive
forms of drama which can be sustained in any depth. It may seem then
that four weeks is a silly arrangement; but, though it is not of my
choice, I find this period serves admirably a specific function of 'social
engineering', so that at the end of the four sessions, certain significant
ceremonies have been observed.

[1] *Arts and the Adolescent*, p. 52.

The first week is spent almost entirely in the group talking about themselves. I have never subscribed very wholeheartedly to the school of drama teachers who believe that for it to be drama, you have to do it and not talk about it. I sometimes think all that means is that the teachers are the sort who get impatient listening to other people talking. In this first session, I outline the formal responsibility that I believe we are embarking on: that whatever we do, we should try and do it as a group; that since there are no desks, no books, no apparatus and no obvious information resources, what happens is likely to make use of us: them and me. I show that I am prepared to suggest things, but that they may change the course of events if they wish, so long as this is appropriate to the whole group. I ask them to do something initially which is more difficult probably than anything I shall ask them to do later: to enable us to find out what we have got in the way of 'us': i.e. for each member of the group to talk for a minute or two (left deliberately vague) about themselves. The question is formally put: 'Who do you think you are?'; and then we go round the group. I normally contribute only if I am asked to, about myself, thinking it better not to try to identify with them unless invited to. Some people have difficulties, chiefly of two sorts: those who think they have nothing interesting about them; and those who find a formula from listening to others (listing, for example, birth, schools, hobbies, ambitions) and use the same formula to avoid saying anything. In these cases, I sometimes chip in with questions, and the process may well take up the whole of a one and a half hour session.

The second session will involve games[1] such as Zoom-Screech, Matthew, Mark, Luke and John, and alphabetical passing the parcel, designed to elicit quick responses with minimal responsibility but maximal participation in a controlled ('game') situation. These will lead on to games which are called, more in hope than in earnest, 'trust games'.

I nearly always either precede games by suggestions as to what they are designed to elicit, or follow them with a discussion of what they may have elicited. For example, I am by no means certain that trust is elicited by 'trust games'; and some sort of description by the group of what is going on is probably more important than any overt pedagogic objective in perpetrating the game in the first place.

Trust games are followed by games which demand a verbal response which is personal rather than functional: in order to play, what is said must have intrinsic meaning although the rules governing what can be said are sharply definitive. These games are based on either a sort of 'pair-bonding' (where pairing may be instituted which exploits existent relationships between members of the group, or non-relationships, or may be random); or on whole group participation; but in either case, the intention is to prepare students to take part in

[1] For games, see Appendix 2.

improvisational role play; and since that role play will demand some contribution from their own experience, it is important to ensure that personal response is encouraged.

Improvisational role play is intended to discover something about personal strategies in everyday situations: how students cope with pressures which are more or less common to all; how they 'read' situations with which they find themselves faced, and how the 'project' versions of themselves.

And finally (if we have not spent all four sessions on this work, or been led off into some more or less productive byway – for I take it as central to these sessions that they should be susceptible to pressures to do that) we may get on to a freer idea of improvisation work, based largely upon a few very simple improvisation patterns which seem to me to be fertile and flexible: 'helping' and 'instant theatre'; which depend on the groups having, or developing, a sense of improvisation as being in itself a satisfying and worthwhile activity. But what I have done here is to describe a formal development which is a theoretical construct, to which I can resort if I am not interrupted. Sequences of sessions in which I am not interrupted are disappointing, and not only for me, but for the group as well, because what should become available to them in these sessions is a means for 'coping with' or 'expressing' their relationship to each other, to me, and to the world outside the door; but at the least, if we have arrived at the last point I described – the freer improvisation work – we have arrived at the starting point for what will be available to students in their second year option, when they can work for nine $1\frac{1}{2}$ hour sessions, with people who have chosen to do drama as one of three courses they must do during the year.

This second-year course has produced disappointing results so far. I am torn between the desire to work on 'projects', which may have an end-product event (performance?), and on the other hand a series of sessions in which skills and responses will develop in the sort of 'subject-reflexive' form defined by Witkin[1] and where the achievements will be less explicit, and therefore, I take it, more in danger of disintegrating into confusion, than is the case with a 'performance'.

The problems with either goal seem to be similar, and may be endemic to any optional aspect of general studies within the particular curricular framework of this college. We have used, in the 'performance based' sessions, nightmares, student jobs, a local development scheme, and an event now lost in antiquity – the 'India House massacre' – as subjects in recent years; and most of them emerged in some sort of performance at the end, but in sadly debilitated form. In the sessions based on the contrary assumption, we have used further developments of the games already used, and whatever material has

[1] Witkin, *The Intelligence of Feeling*, particularly Chapter 1.

been to hand as sources of group response; but neither I nor the students have felt happy with what we have achieved. I can locate the sources of dissatisfaction in, firstly, the probability that nine $1\frac{1}{2}$ hour sessions are not enough to establish a body of work which is worth showing unless it is done with students who are already experienced performers; secondly, the probability that a once-a-week session is too infrequent for there to develop a group identity which will produce either performable work or useful group interaction; thirdly, nine weeks fall very oddly into the patterns of terms which tend to be twelve to sixteen weeks; and the rhythm of a term tends to dictate rhythm of work: for example, you do not want a holiday to intervene before your culminatory sessions; fourthly, second-year students are nearly always exam-fixated students, and performances, or sustained concentration on non-examined activity, is only possible for those who are experienced in at least one, and preferably both: exams and drama. Fifthly, the logistics of the situation are such that in practice not everyone going round the general studies circus in the first year gets as far as drama; so a number of students opt for it in the second year to find out what it is about, while the majority have opted because they think they *know* what it is about; and the two seem to mix only on sufferance. Finally, the majority of my teaching is done with groups whom I know much better than these general studies groups; I do not know them because I see them briefly and infrequently; and my commitment to them is not as high as it ought to be.

In effect then, first-year general studies work in drama focuses on method; maximal participation, operations in group dynamics and encounter, within existent pastoral groups; while the second year focuses on dramatic content: improvisation or performance art. This is an answer to the curricular problem of what to teach when, but, of course, it does not face the responsibility of defining what drama is, except in terms of 'this is what I do'. Indeed, I find I really do not know how to mediate between those two versions of what drama ideally is, within a sixth-form college. I am not even very happy with the descriptions: 'method' and 'content'; I am aware that my tendency to fall into the 'method' camp is conditioned very much by my sense of the particular institution in which I am teaching, and I prefer to use a term like 'institutional' to describe the tendency, and to oppose it to the idea of drama as 'art' available in isolation from, and sealed against, the institution: almost a distinction then, between 'applied' and 'pure', as in the old designation of mathematics.

But these categories apply strictly only to general studies activities; and the curriculum gives much more time and significance to examined activities. In them, it is still more difficult to discover the sources of the subject 'drama'; the very problem of definition, which is created by the distinction between 'pure' and 'applied' versions of the subject, places it firmly in that area which Fred Inglis, in *Ideology and the Imagination,* describes as the 'new, informal curriculum';[1] and that area is right in the cross-fire of the contradictions inherent in the ideology of examinations. Inglis' description, though knotty, seems to me the best account I have read of what is happening to any subject which is able to be integrated into 'interdisciplinary' activities and is being examined. Thus, 'applied' drama becomes, in his terms, a tool of an exam-bound education whose significance is anti-educational; while 'pure' drama is simply hidebound within aesthetic structures which are irrelevant. Meanwhile, we end up, as I have already suggested, running exam courses, because that is what students want, and because we have developed no better ideology to justify any other practice.

At the moment, we run three examined courses in drama: a CSE Mode III; CEE; and (in an odd fashion), 'A' level GCE.

A CSE Mode III was first developed in the college in 1971; and has subsequently been modified a good deal. One of the reasons for these modifications has been increased experience on our part; but another has been the increasingly stringent conditions which have been placed on Mode III syllabuses by the local examinations board, the Southern Regional. Guidelines have been sent out by them, requiring syllabuses to conform on such things as aims, objectives, assessment grids and profiles of assessment. My response to these stipulations has been piecemeal, reluctant, and (recently) hostile; and as the pressure from the Board has grown more intense, so have my objections to the stipulations been clarified. It has taken me a long time to discover that these objections have respectable antecedents within the world of educational technology;[2] and I have had to think the position through for myself, in the first instance, before I could have recourse to respectability.

The problems first became apparent to me when discussions of drama syllabus aims and objectives got bogged down in terms like 'concentration', and the difficulty of measuring it. It quickly became apparent that teachers were expected to measure in terms of their objectives; and that they were, handy-dandy, setting themselves in their syllabus objectives only those things which could be measured. Immediately, the question which is isolated as being central by *Arts and the Adolescent*: 'What is the essential and unique nature of the dramatic experience itself?' was being superseded by the question 'What can be measured?'. Moreover, this measurement was expected to take a particularly crude form: a mark given in relation to the achievement of a defined objective.

But (to quote James Hoetker, Director of Research in the Educa-

---

[1] Inglis, Fred, *Ideology and the Imagination,* Cambridge University Press, 1975. Chapter 4, 'Social Mobility and the Examination System'.

[2] Stephenson, N. and Vincent, D. (eds.), *Teaching and understanding Drama,* NFER, 1975, particularly chapters and bibliographies by Hoetker and Brossall.

tional Laboratory Theatre Project in the States in the late 1960s)[1] 'We know too little to afford the luxury of objectivity, and . . . we will get nowhere if we restrict ourselves to techniques that are only suited to the ratrunner's model of the human being, which everyone knows by direct personal experience is comically inadequate, but which many of us have been trained to accept as a convention because it is "useful".' Drama teachers are still very unclear about their objectives. This is not necessarily a good state to be in; but it should not prevent them from doing that which they do in schools. They find difficulty in arriving at a common terminology; but that does not mean that they cannot describe what they are doing. *What they cannot be expected seriously to do, is to make sense of a model which demands objectives and common terminology as sine qua non, and then attempts to apportion numerical values to the achievements of their students on such bases.* What in practice teachers tend to do is to invent and cheat all along the line, defining their categories according to what they hope will be approved, and marking according to their own values, and then grafting their marks on to the approved categories as best they can.

I have been closely concerned with the evolution of the syllabus in Appendix 3. It has recently been submitted to the SREB. It incorporates certain advantages over other forms of syllabus: in particular, it is modular, and thus has some of the advantages of a Mode III, without the same isolation; and any school can make use of it, and graft on its own modules without too much difficulty. But it is clear from a glance at the marking scheme that there is some fairly arbitrary work going on in the name of objectivity. Some members of the consortium which worked on the syllabus preferred working only in marking units of 5 and 10 marks, on the ground that marking out of 7 or 19 was asking for impossibly fine distinctions to operate. (Who ever apportioned marks out of 19, for goodness' sake?) On the other hand, the '5 and 10 markers' are open to the charge of standardizing to fit their own laziness. Either way, the teachers, when assessment day comes, will mediate their categories necessarily to get the results they feel have been earned. Only in the possibility of doing this can they have any confidence in the whole operation. Moreover, the assessment grid is a form imposed by those whose concern for objective standards is not necessarily matched by a concern for good drama. As Witkin says in *The Intelligence of Feeling* about English teachers:[2]

> In devising ways of assessing people we usually think that we are providing information about them. Very often we are doing the opposite. We are losing what information we have about them by transmuting it into an examination grade. If a grade is to be a comprehensive summary

[1] Hoetker, James, 'Researching Drama: An American view', in *Teaching and Understanding Drama*, op. cit.
[2] Witkin, R., op. cit., p. 74.

embracing the entire quality of a person's mode of engagement with the world, then it will have to be arrived at by quite different forms of assessment from those used to establish examination grades.

Because of my concern about the pressure towards spurious objectivity in Mode III CSE Drama, I have moved sideways into CEE. In 1974, the opportunity arose to make proposals for a modular CEE Communications syllabus which would include some drama modules; and three of the modules from my own CSE Mode III syllabus were accepted, with minor modifications, for that syllabus.[1] There was little pressure for rigorous definition of aims and objectives, and less for these to be matched by measurement of them; so that my own assessment procedures seemed appropriate enough. I am not happy that a satisfactory assessment procedure has been arrived at in this syllabus; but there is room within the framework of the CEE assessment for me to consider and evaluate the work which has been done because I or the students considered it valuable, rather than manipulating arbitrary categories which bear little relation either to work done or to values which we hold.[2]

Clearly I have been lucky to have a CEE syllabus which 'went my way'. For those who do not have that, there is the AEB 'AO' level as an alternative, which is supposed to be particularly suitable for sixth forms. The syllabus seems to me heavily orientated towards written answers (40 per cent of total marks); it specifies that 'unrehearsed improvisation is not acceptable', which puts out of court what I take to be the central dramatic activity; it insists that no fewer than twelve candidates shall be entered, whereas I rarely have more than eight candidates in one year; and both syllabus and assessment remain too far outside teacher control to enable the work to respond to the people who are actually involved in the course. Moreover, a glance at the plays offered for study on the syllabus, which includes *Dandy Dick*, *The Rivals* and *Oedipus Rex* as some of its less digestible items, suggests that the criteria which are being operated are, if not entirely academic, certainly historical rather than practical.

[1] See Appendix 5.

[2] In fact, I have been able to run the two syllabuses – CEE and CSE Mode III – side by side, with the same candidates, without involving them in any 'double' work, for one year, because there was so little distinction between the two syllabuses (see Appendices 4 and 5). However, I have since been involved in preparing the syllabus at Appendix 3, as a way of encouraging Mode III CSE Drama in the area secondary schools; and a comparison of the various syllabuses shows that this new Mode III allows less freedom than the old: particularly in the disappearance in the new syllabus of part four of the old, which stipulated that the students should 'keep a file which contains material on topics of individual interest on which they would like to be assessed'. I could not see how to 'objectify' this part of the syllabus under the demands for the assessment grids demanded of the new syllabus, so I dropped it as a proposal. Lacking freedom as the new CSE syllabus does, and anyway having to consider now that some of the secondary schools have started doing the new CSE syllabus, it makes little sense to go on doing either CSE, old or new; so unless something extraordinary happens, I shall do only CEE from now on.

But as it is, I have, as I have suggested, relatively few takers for a course which offers CEE: usually about four or five students at the beginning of the first year, which may rise to seven or eight during the course. I might get more takers for the 'AO' course; but I do not believe the price would be worth paying.

During the time that the present CSE/CEE syllabus has been operating, groups have offered productions, on $2\frac{1}{2}$ hours a week over two years, of: *Cinderella* written by a member of the course; *Woyzeck* by Buchner (teacher produced); *St. Patrick's Day* by Sheridan (student produced).

And group projects: *Going Up in Smoke* – a performance timed to coincide and comment on an anti-smoking campaign in the college; *As Far As Who Goes Farthest* (the college motto) – a consumer's guide to sixth-form colleges; *Passing the Buck* – about abortion; *Just cause? or Impediment* – about marriage; *Monopoly* – a game about life.

The emphasis in all the work done has been on presenting material to audiences in the circumstances which are available, which are very limited, as there is no proper studio, only either a hall for which there is competition for use with other departments, or a drama hut which cannot take an audience of more than twenty. The emphasis is not on theatrical technology; but beyond that it is difficult to generalize, which is a modest way of saying that groups have been able to work in totally different ways within this framework, as has suited their own group identities.

I wrote on p. 223 '(in an odd fashion), 'A' level GCE'. The London University English 'A' level syllabus makes it possible to do entirely plays on one of its three papers; another consists of Shakespeare and Chaucer; and the third, of practical criticism. We have taken advantage of this syllabus, to enable those who want to do drama and get an 'A' level, to pursue a course which, although heavily circumscribed by the lit. crit. aspects of the actual exam, allows, even if it does not encourage, more practical work than the AEB 'AO' Theatre Arts syllabus; because, in curricular terms, an 'A' level is allowed twice as much timetable time as an 'O', yet the syllabus demands study of only eight texts; and what else is done is not prescribed. A play can be read fairly quickly if reading competence is high: after all, it should only take three hours or so in the theatre: and that leaves an enormous amount of time for practical work, which, though not examined, has the fairly predictable consequence of maximizing involvement and providing some sort of 'experiential' relationship to plays in general, and those on the syllabus in particular, such as (in recent years): Miller's *Death of A Salesman* (student produced); Farquhar, *The Recruiting Officer* (staff produced); Wilde, *The Importance of Being Earnest* (student produced); Wilde, *Lady Windermere's Fan* (student produced); Shakespeare, *Measure for Measure* (staff produced); Stoppard, *Rosencrantz and Guildenstern are Dead* (student produced).

There is, of course, a considerable problem in trying to mediate between dramatic, and Eng. Lit. examination objectives; but my experience has been that a strong sense of the play has always created a *desire* to think critically; and that while this criticism has tended, in my view happily, to see the play as primarily a thing to be performed, it has not been difficult to transfer concern to, for example, Shakespearian imagery, or levels of reality in *Death of a Salesman*, because the sense of the play can be assumed amongst those who have taken part in its presentation.

I am slightly ashamed, nevertheless, to admit how much I have enjoyed teaching such a bastard course. I think much of this enjoyment has come from the commitment it has been able to capitalize on from students. Many have signed on for it because, in the words of one university professor of drama, they 'are interested in drama as an activity . . . and . . . opted out of the main lines of English education'.[1] Some have hoped it would be a course without essays; it has had its fair share of illiterates, dyslexics and skivers; and as a matter of policy those with academic pretensions have been discouraged from joining the course; yet exam results of those doing this course have been only marginally worse than those for other English courses in the college. Meanwhile those who have failed 'A' level do seem to me to have got something out of the course, of the kind that is traditionally associated with drama: a sense of group activity, a development of their own not strictly academic resources in solving practical problems, and a very strong sense of the institution of which they are a part; and usually, I believe, a developed critical sense. What they are unlikely to have overcome is their own preference for this course over other types of English course; and they may still be finding essays difficult, and traditional academic processes dehydrated, if they chose the course in the first instance for that kind of reason. That, again, is a problem which is posed by student choice.

But I doubt whether such a bastard course can ever find sound ideological foundations. I think it likely that it will be superseded by the new AEB 'A' level Drama syllabus, devised by Gordon Vallins of South Warwicks College of Further Education and now being piloted in a number of F.E. colleges.[2]

The virtues of this syllabus are that it has been devised by a practising lecturer in drama, that it has a strong practical content, is flexible enough to allow variation for individual teachers and students, and unlike any other syllabus, concentrates a good deal of attention on dramatic theory. It does present some simple curricular problems: it is based on Vallins' own teaching timetable, and expects students to devote nine hours per week to the course: necessary in terms of the comprehensiveness of the syllabus, possible in the F.E. context, but presenting considerable difficulties to the sixth-form college, or ordinary sixth form of a comprehensive. One of the justifications of the nine

[1] Professor Peter Thompson, of Exeter, in a letter to the author.
[2] See Appendix 6.

hours is that it incorporates a general studies element and attempts to cover the ground between other academic disciplines which may be relevant to students on the course. Again, the sixth-form context might not so easily adjust to those doing 'A' level drama, opting out of the general studies courses.

But there are more serious ideological problems than these; and they have been expressed by Vallins himself, particularly in a correspondence with Michael Walton, of Hull University Drama Department.

Walton wrote in the *Education Guardian*:[1]

The battle for acceptance of drama as a subject in schools has almost been won. What it still appears to lack is status, and the introduction of 'A' level studies is seen as a way to improve this. But many teachers believe that even in 'respectable' academic subjects, 'A' levels are a poor reflection of the standards of teaching and achievement. Why then regiment drama, whose value in schools lies precisely in its freedom from rigidity and the competitive nature of working to an exam structure?
Concentrate on it as a subject that develops emotional and social responses, which is aesthetic and imaginative, and even good exercise, and which can enrich the community life of a school. Encourage an interest in the theatre as part of the artistic life of a country, and the drama of any period as a reflection of its preoccupations and its moral attitudes. But at least in schools let us preserve the subject from being submerged in the qualifications lottery!

This is much the case that is argued by all anti-exam progressives, of course, focused on drama firstly because that is Walton's specialist area and secondly because drama seems to be the last outpost of the unexamined; but he is also arguing for a specific definition of drama as being free from 'rigidity and . . . competitive nature'.

In an unpublished letter, Vallins replied:

I agree with Michael Walton that 'the play's the thing' and that drama can help develop emotional and social responses which are aesthetic and imaginative and fun and can enrich the life of any community. . . . It's true that to examine a basically free, open, expressive, anarchic and highly personal subject can be limiting. However, all examinations have their limitations, which must be accepted if we approve the examination system which the universities exploit for entrance qualifications. . . .
In the meantime, I should like to assure Mr Walton that Drama at South Warwickshire is far from rigid. We have an inbred dislike of what has been called the 'tyranny of subjects'. We try wherever possible to arrange for subjects to interact. . . .

Vallins goes on to describe areas of interaction: English, history, art, music; and he ends:

The reason why South Warwickshire proposed an 'A' level in Theatre Studies was simply to give sixteen to nineteen-year-olds following a

[1] Walton, Michael, 'The Play's the Thing', *Education Guardian*, 14 January 1975.

course in Drama and Liberal Arts the opportunity to gain some kind of qualification which may help them to gain a place in an institution of higher education should they wish to apply. For some of them, an 'A' level in Theatre Studies may be more interesting and personally more fulfilling than an 'A' level in another subject.

Walton's classic case against exams has been matched by Vallins' equally classic liberal response to them: 'We don't like it, but it's the way things are, and if we have to have it, let's make it as enjoyable as possible.' Meanwhile Vallins was writing privately to Walton, making this position more explicit. 'Basically, I agree with you . . . I will be the first in the protest march that shouts "Down with exams", but you know as well as I do that you would not be lecturing at Hull without some kind of qualification. . . .'

Finally, Vallins, in another letter to Walton, outlined the problem which I believe was in his mind all along, but which remains unresolved still. 'I shall be very interested to hear the outcome of discussions between lecturers and drama departments on the value of 'A' level Theatre Studies . . .', he writes; before restating his position with a *cri de coeur*: 'I don't really want to know about examinations, but I feel trapped.'

Now this problem of university drama departments which Vallins mentions, is one that holds considerable interest at this stage, because it may well be crucial to the success of 'A' level Theatre Studies. Vallins has suggested that the exam was proposed to enable students to gain a 'qualification which may help them to gain a place in an institution of higher education'. The question is, will universities accept it as such?

The indications that I have been able to discover suggest that several, at any rate, will not. There seem to be three sorts of objections on the part of universities to 'A' level Theatre Studies. The first is implicit in what Michael Walton suggests in his *Guardian* article and correspondence with Vallins: that drama will be more hindered than helped in fulfilling its proper educational function if it is examined. This is, I believe, the position which is taken by a number of university drama departments, partly, no doubt, because they know they can survive without *any* drama going on in secondary schools. This position was put obliquely by Peter Thompson of Exeter University, in a letter to the author: 'There has never been a shortage of good drama students. Good drama courses, on the other hand, are thin on the ground.' Because, again in Professor Thompson's words, there are always plenty of students who are only too happy to 'opt out of the main lines of English education', and get a degree for doing so, it is easy for the university drama departments to fill their courses without admitting any particular responsibility to courses in schools. Professor Thompson himself concedes that this is not enough; that the drama departments must work to some extent on behalf of drama in schools; and therefore he concedes (reluctantly) the case for an 'A' level exam.

But he is by no means representative of other university departments of drama, let alone of university admissions officers, who are so far not accepting the AEB 'A' level as grounds for exemption from matriculation; but on other grounds than those on which Walton stands as representative. These grounds are, firstly, that an exam with such a large practical content is unacceptable as evidence of academic ability of the sort a university requires; and secondly, that the actual process of practical examination will be carried on by people who are incompetent to judge adequately for university purposes. This account may be garbled, and it may no longer be up to date; but it is the best account I have been able to get from the drama departments of universities themselves of the present position; and indicates that there are serious problems in the way of the 'A' level Theatre Studies exam fulfilling Vallins' intention of providing a university qualification; and it seems at least unfortunate that universities should not admit responsibility for, or obligation to, the new 'A' level.[1] It is, in my experience, very difficult to get universities to admit such a responsibility. For example, I wrote in 1975 to all university drama departments, asking: 'What criteria does your department operate in selecting candidates for your courses? What do you consider schools, and school exams, should expect to achieve with those of their students who wish to apply to enter university drama departments?'

Just over half the departments replied; some of the answers were putative because their courses were not yet off the drawing board; one or two others were circumscribed by their connections with other departments which left them without effective control over admissions; but I was rather surprised to discover that, of the answers I got, none of the departments was specifically interested in prior practical achievement in drama, and only one – Exeter – was aware of the irony of this, in selecting applicants for a practical course in drama. None showed a flicker of approval of the idea of 'A' level drama, and not many, even a flicker of recognition. Above all, I found it surprising that the letter got so few responses; until I got the letter from Professor Thompson, with that sharp observation on the plethora of good students and lack of good courses; and this remark, both he and I agree, illustrates the lack of a sense of responsibility on the part of university drama departments for what happens in schools, which seems to me manifest in the universities' response to the AEB syllabus.

Clearly, on the place of drama examinability, as on most of the other crucial issues in drama teaching, I am in two minds. Art and

[1] Professor Thompson has pointed out to me that my picture of university admissions is oversimplified; that some universities have positively refused to accept 'A' level Theatre Studies, and that Hull University is the only one that so far has accepted it as exemption from matriculation. However, this situation shows signs of changing, not least as the result of pressure from the principal of my own college.

music are both examined at 'A' level. Did they once have all this heart-searching? Did the subjects themselves suffer when the exams were validated? How do they cope with universities which will not accept their exams as qualifications? Which universities will not accept them and why? These seem to me crucial questions to ask, if we are to discuss the place of the creative arts in the sixth-form curriculum.

What will be the consequences to drama, if and when the 'A' level Theatre Arts syllabus becomes generally available? A nine-hour course allocation would throw my own college into turmoil; and the implications of the brief Vallins set himself are that it would replace the common general studies course. Moreover, Vallins has written that the course depends on sixth forms to 'have the facilities – i.e. like a science laboratory for physics'; and in that case, demands are going to be made for physical resources well beyond what I, for example, have in my own department (a scruffy room 25ft by 25ft, without blackout or a roof high enough to mount spotlights).

But more importantly, I think that what may happen will be that sixth-form drama specialists will have to commit themselves much more firmly than they have had to so far, to a received notion of what drama *is*, because an 'A' level syllabus will be both a definition in itself, and a challenge to further definition. I suspect that neither Vallins' 'dislike for the tyranny of subjects', nor the work of Albert Hunt[1] will protect us from the demands of the examiners for objectified criteria and measurement of that which I, at the moment, value without measurement, and do not know how to measure without destroying. When that happens, I shall no doubt be forced back to what I take to be still the staple diet of many drama teachers at all levels: the non-curricular work, which revolves, expands and contracts at intervals around weekly workshop sessions, productions after school, and 'messing about with ideas'.[2]

For I have just been trying to work out the relations between the amount of time I spend working in timetabled lessons, and the amount of time I spend altogether in contact with students; and there is no comparison between the two figures. If this sounds complacent, I hasten to add that I do not think much virtue attaches to it: it is quite largely the result of my incompetence at using timetabled time as well as other teachers, added to the greater enjoyment that I get out of teaching outside the timetable; and above all, the knowledge I have that if I get bored, as I do at times, it is possible out of timetable to shove off home; and that is not (yet) a solution properly available to either students or to me, in the timetable.

[1] Hunt, Albert, *Hopes for Great Happenings*, Eyre Methuen. See also, by the same author 'The tyranny of subjects' in *Education for Democracy*, Penguin.

[2] With all my reservations I have, in fact, agreed to teach the course at my own college from 1977, under some pressure from the principal, and from the knowledge that it is, in our current climate, the one way of 'marketing' a subject. The indications are that the course will be full, and perhaps over-subscribed.

And yet. . . .

Is this all? Is it a full account of what happens, as well as being an account of what does not, or ought not, or may not in the future? I am aware that somehow I have failed to answer the question: 'Why teach drama in a sixth-form college?', in any way which can make my continuing to do so, anything but a continuing act of bad faith. Is art not being created, amongst the compromises that are being made and the institututional pressures that are being absorbed? Where, in all this is 'good drama'?

Again, I find myself resorting to my distinction between 'pure' and 'applied'; and finding in 'pure' drama some of the values I am hoping to foster in improvisation work, in which one is aware of seeing something happen which will only happen once, when a student offers, and at the same time risks, the unknown, to others, in order that they together may make it known. I am aware of events which can be described in exactly the same terms, which have been performances: perhaps one performance of several, of one production among many, or one rehearsal among many; when an offer is made, and a risk is taken; and these are taken up and used by others: actors and audiences alike.

And the 'applied' version can be described in exactly the same terms: when a student offers, and risks (and this often means risking official disapproval, and offering the unacceptable), and catches an echo in the college at large: a student on the college council who will challenge an official decision; a group who define their existence in the college as hostile to the prevailing ethic, but who find in a public response, that which accepts the offer and gives absolution to the risk.

If the terminology sounds ceremonial, that is intentional: drama consists of significant ceremonies; and if the terminology is subject to irony, that is also important.

The Principal of the College writes as follows:
Sixth-Form Colleges are complicated places: 80 staff and 700 students' separate timetables cannot easily be summed up. Nearly 50 'A' level subjects and as many 'O' levels and (separately) CEE subjects make a complicated timetable.

There is a doubt over the meaning of 'market places' as used in this chapter. I am not averse to market places. They may be real and they may have important values. But if the College were a market place, then we would no doubt have filled it very full indeed with students who were allowed to do just what they pleased – including perhaps more Drama. We do not do that; for example we make them all do more Maths almost without exception and we tell them beforehand in their schools that this is what they will have at the College.

Of course if you use 'market places' and 'values' to mean a large number of examination levels, subjects and choices which will lead to careers that students want, then that will be right. You can be sure that we persuade them to do a mixed diet ('A' level or sub 'A' level) of different kinds of subjects, and that we include every kind and type of subject in an effort to liberalize the examination time-table. Of course, Arts have claim to a 'core' position. At the College, Art and Music for instance are central and large-scale.

The General Studies scheme is an attempt to introduce all students to specialisms they would not otherwise meet and, in any case, with all its options, it is an attempt to introduce students to a very many-sided view of life in which Arts are central. The scheme is compulsory in the first year. The group taught is the mixed-ability Tutor Group, so that we are trying some mixed-ability work in each age range, though of course the target is non-examinable.

As for Faculties, I feel the writer's account is wholly exaggerated. 'Why have them at all?' is one question. Some HMIs want only three; or one could have 15 departments of the old kind, or simply deal with 50 subjects. Of course, it is a question of administration and finance and it will never be perfect and suit everybody. We chose six and obviously the smaller subjects in each Faculty might often be in some other Faculty. Geology, for example, is with Social Sciences – although I know it to be a Science, only the Geo-graphers teach it; and Secretarial courses are in Social Sciences be-cause their teachers also teach Commerce which is connected with Economics. We decided on a 'making' or 'practical' Faculty where Art would be central and the Home Economics and Technical Crafts would connect with it. I don't agree that the new Design Technology is not a Creative Art; indeed I believe Dress and Fabrics to be one also. There may be a debate about Drama; there is a case for putting it with Art. But the best case, I thought, was with English, Music, and Film because at a Sixth-Form College level, I consider Drama to be more academic than it is with younger children.

But the really important question about Sixth-Form Colleges will not be answered in these kinds of way. The important and underly-ing questions are those to do with compassion and tolerance, with treating each and every individual, whatever his or her ability, belief, race or background, as a separate person with 'God-given' rights to his or her own individuality; quietude and loving kindness also have an important place; we have to look for 'that of God in every man'.

We should be proud of the fact that such a Sixth-Form College is open-access and thus many young people have been given a second chance. They may have achieved at CSE only targets of grade 3 or 4 or 5 or U, or not have been entered for CSE at all, and for them the CEE is providing a very great advantage. The College motto as fully expressed reads:

>You speak to Casca, and to such a man
>That is no fleering tell-tale. Hold my hand:
>Be factious for redress of all these griefs,
>and I will set this foot of mine *as far*
>*As who goes farthest!*

and does express a reasonable point about the College in so far as
any quotation can!

14 A Note from the Back of Beyond

Elemental music is never music alone but forms a unity with movement, dance and speech.

Carl Orff

School Music

The experience of those of us who worked on the 'Arts and the Adolescent' project has always been that music teachers are something of a race apart as far as the creative arts go – a fact we have already elaborated upon elsewhere. They tend, on the whole, to regard their subject as a special case, with singular problems of organization, discipline and technique. And I have a good deal of sympathy with their situation: they inevitably advertise their presence (albeit unwillingly) wherever they go about their work, and what they are doing is usually common knowledge because universally attended. When they are not restricting themselves to the production of melifluous and familiar sounds they are liable to be disturbing everyone within ear-shot and, worse still, being maligned for doing what they will regard as their proper work. Music teachers are often in an exposed situation, are often under pressure to measure up to other people's misguided and inappropriate expectations ('I know good music when I hear it'), and have to contend with pupils ill-disposed to accept that what they are doing is either relevant or useful. As I say, the difficulties many secondary-school music teachers face in their schools are real enough.

However, I cannot let the matter rest there simply because that is not all there is to be said about it. Music in secondary schools frequently falls well short of fulfilling its expressive and creative function. Despite considerable efforts by enlightened teachers, local advisers, college lecturers, HMIs, the Schools Council, the BBC, and societies and associations promoting the ideas of composer-educators such as Kodaly and Orff, music in our secondary schools is still, by and large, in the hands of traditionally trained instrumental musicians, many of whom have neither composed nor improvised a piece of music since they left college (if they even did so there). Their first priority is to contain the bulk of their (as they see it) reluctant learners in a disciplined routine that involves the singing of a few old folk songs and learning about the lives and times of the great composers. Sometimes, as I saw in a primary school recently, a class will spend a whole term writing out all there is to know (from books) about the history and mechanics of the instruments of the orchestra. Having occupied the masses by some such means as these the teacher then feels free to indulge his sense of what a real musical education means for the benefit of those relatively few boys and girls actually capable of reading music (or of learning to do so) and, hence, of singing in a choir or playing in a band or orchestra.

Now I hasten to add that this is not a situation that prevails universally: there are, as there always have been, teachers and schools where music (even traditional music) is a vital factor in everyone's lives, and there are nowadays a growing number of young teachers working in the schools who have benefited from the kind of influences I have already referred to and, perhaps even more to the point, actually share many of their pupils' out-of-school musical tastes. They have, of course, a real advantage over the old guard who, Canute-like, sit facing the irresistible tide of their pupils' actual musical preferences. Even the 'new' teachers of music are not wholly to be relied upon however when it comes to using music as an expressive medium – *much of what is apparently new in music education today is more 'novel' than different.* There is a dreadful sense in which the musician's motto is like the scout's – 'Once a musician always a musician' – that means always a reader and renderer of someone else's scores.

That I have not found it easy to obtain a specimen music curriculum close to the purpose of this book will of course testify to the poverty of my acquaintance: nevertheless, I guess there will be few secondary-school music teachers who will find the foregoing assessment of the role of the creative arts in school either immediately recognizable in their own practice or attractive and compelling enough to stimulate radical change. And it has to be said that if I am right about the general picture then it is a crying shame because, as I have frequently insisted, music has to be *the* basic, because it is the most immediate and most instinctive, expressive experience. I cannot conceive of an expressive arts curriculum of which music is not the bedrock and foundation, and yet my experience is that we should not look to the specialist music teacher to provide it. More usually the kind of musical experience I have in mind is provided by an English, drama or art teacher. Regrettably most musicians either do not see their work this way, or, being totally unprepared for a creative approach, will have none of it.

A Special Case

I recently had the opportunity of discussing her secondary-school teaching with a young musician on a course at my University. She

agreed pretty much with the *Arts and the Adolescent* assessment of
the state of music in schools today, though she hastened to point out
that there *were* schools one could go into where teachers and children
were actively engaged in creative music-making, and in which full
account was being taken of the living tradition of the children's
popular culture (meaning, of course, not just the world of Western
pop itself, but, in districts with large immigrant communities, the
world of contemporary Indian, West Indian and African music).

She drew my attention to Tom Gamble's work at Manland
School, Harpenden, (described by Nicholas Soames in an article for
the *Guardian*). Here is a brief extract from that article:

> One of the first lessons with the first formers, for example, will involve the
> children finding out how many sounds they can make just by using their
> hands. An imaginative class will come forward with about ten or more.
> He then moves on to the voice, and again pupils move rapidly into double
> figures. Following this he will perhaps play a work like the Voice
> Sequence by Berio which uses a wide variety of basic sounds instead of
> just the singing voice. Soon Mr Gamble and the first formers are moving
> on to instruments, exploring them, listening to music, which uses them in
> different ways. By the third or fourth lesson, the pupils are organizing
> sounds themselves into short two-minute pieces . . . The result is that all
> pupils learn through their own experience; yet all, not just the 'musical'
> ones, have composed and performed frequently by the time they come to
> the end of the third year.[1]

We went on to talk about her own teaching and I want to quote some
passages from our tape-recorded discussion (tidied up to turn speech
for talk into writing for reading) because she raises most of the key
issues in music education today and her own working solutions are I
think not without general significance. Like Gamble she unashamedly
gives pride of place to music-making, to participation. Given this
gravitational pull at its centre, her own music curriculum hangs
together, and it allows her to teach many of the traditional skills and to
introduce knowledge about music and new musical experiences that
might be felt to be beyond the likely interests of the 'average' child.
And this is perhaps the key in appreciating what she is saying: she is
talking about *music for all children*, about music-making with large
groups of boys and girls of average and below average academic
ability and with no special interest in or talent for music. Many of these
children give their other teachers a hard time, and they are unlikely
to make an exception for a young music teacher. Yet it is not hard to
believe, from her own modest account, that there is learning, as well
as enjoyment in her classes.

MR: Starting where the kids are – what does that mean for the secondary-
school teacher?

T: They ask 'What is the point of learning about crotchets and quav-
ers?' They are thoroughly bored by musical 'knowledge' that is so

[1] *Guardian* 16 November 1976

remote from their own experience of music, and, because of its largely abstract and academic character, so remote from their interests and abilities as learners. I'm talking of course of the majority of kids in my own 'creamed off' comprehensive school, and of classroom music, not of music for the musically bright or gifted ones. My own kids just don't relate to all those black marks on paper, and they cannot connect the traditional study of musical notation with their own feelings about music. They're not going to use it. Should they choose to learn an instrument or decide they need to notate their own compositions then they'll want to learn to 'write' and 'read' music. Music in school has to mean something other than musical literacy for the majority.

MR: The children you are talking about reject the traditional music syllabus lock, stock and barrel.

T: They don't see the point of learning to read music; they don't want to know about the lives of the great composers and the fact that so and so wrote sixty symphonies, and they don't really want to sing songs out of the *Oxford Song Book*.

MR: What do you answer when they ask 'What's the point of it all?'

T: They usually only ask that question when they've got a lot of irrelevant learning to do. And that doesn't just mean in music.

MR: How do you provide a musical syllabus that doesn't provoke that question?

T: I try to get them creating their own music – and that means having plenty of ideas myself about music-making. Eventually, once you've really got them involved at first hand in musical experiences some will certainly want to learn conventional instruments and will see the point of learning to read a musical score and improving their technical skills. For instance lots of kids want to learn the guitar – perhaps because the guitar is *the* instrument of their own culture. It's not an easy instrument to master but you'd find they spend hours and hours practising and quickly become very knowledgeable about the traditional language of music: they'll learn about modulating keys and chords and so on, simply because they're interested in learning to play the guitar. But that's by the way really – my syllabus is relevant (I hope) because it engages them here and now.

MR: So if you don't teach the world of traditional music what do you do? How do you arouse their involvement and commitment, how do you create a sense of relevance?

T: You have to forget about your own musical training for a start and begin with their enthusiasms in music, and their own immediate knowledge and interests. For instance I often take the idea of football chanting or the jingles girls use to accompany their skipping and ball games with. By making rhythmical patterns out of words (I don't mean writing poetry but just stringing words together in purely rhythmical patterns) you can provide the basis for quite sophisticated work in rhythm, movement, accent, series and so forth in a completely non-technical way and using the voice which is of course the one musical instrument every child has already come to terms with. Though some of them would probably be wary of actually singing if that's what you asked them to do they very soon find that's what they're doing anyway. I like to begin my work with

the first years using the most immediate means to hand – that is to
say voices and bodies exploring rhythms and tunes – simple chanting.

MR: Can you give me an idea of how such a piece of work would go? You
begin with voices...

T: Well, here's one little exercise I do. We begin by collecting words
with different numbers of syllables in them and we identify their
natural patterning of stresses: I usually write the words they suggest
on the blackboard, taking a connecting theme such as football
teams for instance. The 'bank' can be freely added to as new words
occur to the class – we end up with something like this –

1	2	3
Spurs	Cambridge	Liverpool
Stoke	Chelsea	Middlesbrough
Hull	Norwich	Birmingham
Crewe	Arsenal	Huddersfield
Saints	West Ham	Sunderland

4	5	6
Queens Park Rangers	Manchester City	Newcastle United
Bristol City	West Bromwich Albion	Manchester United
Leeds United	Sheffield United	
Plymouth Argyle	Coventry City	7
Crystal Palace	Nottingham Forest	Wolverhampton Wanderers

We then select words from different columns to make coherent
rhythmical patterns – building 'verses' or chants line by line.

Leeds – Liverpool – Queens Park Rangers

Manchester United – Chelsea – Hull

Spurs – Birmingham – Plymouth Argyle

West Bromwich Albion – Huddersfield – Stoke

I then help them pick out an ostinato to form the base for the verse
rhythm – we find a single word from the verse itself (e.g. Chelsea or
Huddersfield) or from the 'bank' for this purpose. The class then
divides so that some of the children repeat the ostinato word while
the rest say the verse. This arrangement can be elaborated several
times so that you achieve quite complex patterning: you can have
three or four different ostinati going at the same time. The effect is of
a word orchestra playing a rich rhythmical tune! Then you can
use the same principle to produce material for binary and ternary
forms and so on. When chanting takes over, dancing has to follow.
Having broken into the field of musical rhythm and rhythmical patterning you can isolate the pulse from the words by substi-
tuting clapping, body slapping, finger clicking, and so on. The step
from there to working with percussion instruments of all kinds –

tuned and untuned, traditional or home made – is a very short one. It's musical, it's fun and everyone can get into it. By choosing different themes and finding words to match you can achieve considerable variation of mood or feeling.

MR: You say that dance need not be far behind. Is creative music as straightforward a subject to teach as say dance, drama or art?

T: There are special difficulties for the music teacher who wants to work in this creative or expressive way. I'm not thinking merely of keeping a class in order but the art studio for instance can look the picture of good discipline and industry with everyone doing their own thing whereas if everyone does just what they like in the music room it's bedlam and sounds like all hell let loose. Music uses the medium of air for its making and you cannot easily provide every child with his own insulated supply of it. More usually each class shares the same air-space and there's no way of insulating the children from each other – or the class from the rest of the school for that matter (and thereby hangs another tale). So for the music teacher who genuinely wants to encourage each child to create his or her own musical forms there are real technical difficulties – and the danger all the time of either over-directing the work in the interest of good musical order or letting the kids have their head and risking anarchy. There has to be compromise and I've found it helpful to provide a basic sound structure (ostinato pulse or pentatonic scale for instance) that will allow individuals some freedom for personal expression and yet more or less guarantee that the total sound will be interesting and musically coherent. Kids know what they mean by 'music', and they want to be able to produce notes that harmonize and rhythms they could move or jig or dance to. As their experience develops, they can tolerate a greater range of experimental music and will be ready to participate in group happenings in which playing with sounds gradually becomes genuine pattern making with a feeling of its own. But not right away. So it's up to the teacher from his knowledge of the way music works (as flow and tension) to provide learning experiences that are structured in a way that will allow the musically unskilled, unsophisticated child to make his own meaningful contribution to a shared experience. You have to scale down the complexity of the musical situation so they don't have too many variables to work with at the same time.

The smaller the group or ensemble the greater the scope for the individual. Class work more or less means that school music has to be a social occasion, as to some extent school drama and dance must also be, I suppose. But as with these forms of art unless what the individual is contributing has something useful and significant about it, unless there's scope for the personal expression within the group activity, you'll soon find you're in for trouble. They will just lose interest and start 'improvising' in unhelpful ways.

I try to make the sound the kids actually end up producing like them – vigorous, bloody-minded, dramatic, muscular and so on. It's so easy to distort what they offer in the interest of musical 'correctness'. Teenage boys don't get into tinkles and chimes – they expect their music to be manly, aggressive, even savage at times. It's got to have the right feeling.

MR: I wanted to ask what you do about bringing in the children's own music – their interest in pop music and dancing for instance.

T: Well, in an ideal situation, I would want to have music and dance (and drama as well for that matter) as closely linked as possible. I very often start with a drama exercise to suggest a mood, or situation, and then move into a musical expression of that experience. And it's the same with movement: from movement into music and then, if necessary, into movement again. To have to divorce music from movement as is so often the case in the secondary school is really crazy. The two are indivisable really, you only have to think of the so-called primitive music-making of the Africans or West Indians for instance. In many ways our school music should take that kind of musical experience as its model and not the more traditional Western one of the concert hall and the cathedral. The kids' own music is social and ritualistic – it is truly popular in its feeling. It's got little or nothing to do with the mainstream of the Western élitist musical tradition. I'm really happy for instance, when one of my kids gets a rhythm going that he's picked up from a jazz or pop record; we've then got something to work with that is immediately involving for everyone.

There was a case in point when I was working with a mixed class of fourth years. Now they'd had no music lessons before and really only had music on the timetable now because they couldn't do all the academic subjects and had to be occupied somehow. I was very sure that unless I could really get their interest I'd have a bad time. I chose a pretty obvious idea: we set about looking at the history of pop music. They brought their own records and were soon able to show me that they knew a good deal about the subject. Then one day one of them took up a set of drums (I'd always dreaded their raiding the instrument cupboard as I was by no means sure I'd be able to handle the situation). But he quickly established a confident reggae rhythm and before long all 25 were into it and we had a really terrific session. Subsequently I was able to help them make their own music using a variety of pop rhythms and I was more than happy in my own mind that they were developing their musical know-how as well as enjoying themselves. Of course I could have offered to set the sessions going myself but it was infinitely more acceptable to them that one of their own mates did so. I could then try to help them elaborate, control and develop the sound they were producing so that they moved away from mere imitation into forms that were more and more their own. They made no objection to my actually teaching them the techniques of music-making and of musical form. These big boys were really scarry – but I was so glad afterwards that I'd decided to give them a chance when all my instincts told me to get the instruments back under lock and key before the head arrived to find out what all the row was about. After that I found that I could often rely on them to provide the basis for our music-making from week to week. A more formal approach – even to creative music – would never have worked with them. They just wouldn't have accepted it. What actually happened was that their musical enthusiasm and native musical talent provided an endless fund of ideas and material for us to work with. But I have to say that I had to rely enormously on them – and of course they helped each other. Their music 'lessons' were very often real jam sessions – and I'm sure that's where school music so often fails. It's too much about the teacher, or about some irrelevant notion of musical knowledge. In the art room they make paintings. In the music room they should actually make music and learn how to make it better. But what has both surprised and reassured me is the discovery that so many of these ordinary children of mine have an instinctive feeling for musical form, for rhythm and melody. They have an inborn feeling for it. My job is to tap their instinct.

MR: How do you feel about the tradition of instrumental playing in school: performing or interpreting scores? Singing from sheet music seems to have been the staple diet since the year dot – nowadays I notice children are being given modern unconventional scores to work on and that appears to take the tears out of learning to play an instrument properly but is this kind of music-making any different from the old stuff?

T: It certainly can be. I take it you're thinking of the kind of scores produced by the BBC for the series *Music in Action*. There's certainly enormous scope for expressive or emotional response on the part of the children – and provided the teacher as conductor helps the children to get into the feel of the piece then the instrumentalist interpreting these new scores has just as much opportunity to play 'with feeling' and to find his own feeling through the playing itself as in playing more traditional music. However the danger of presenting the children with scores to follow is always that musical correctness (doing exactly what the score says) will come to dominate everything else and the session becomes a trip for the teacher with the kids as dummies or automata trying to get it right for him. There's a chance of a real breakthrough for everyone if the new scores are really used intelligently: but a Brian Dennis piece can be as remote and as uninvolving as slogging away at a five-finger exercise. The point about these new scores is that they provide the basic structure for a group improvisation. To follow them rigidly as if they were definitive scores of the old type counting time on a stop-watch is entirely to miss their point. But some of the material *is* very complex and *does* strain the endurance of the not especially musical.

Your general question about encouraging interpretive playing – of course it can be 'expressive'. Once the technical skill is adequate to allow a reasonably faithful rendering. Many children in the past have been denied instrumental music-making because they've failed to master the necessary techniques. The new music sets less store by technique and gives everyone a chance to contribute. Mind you, my own feeling is that this more experimental music-making is best attempted when the children have already gained confidence in their music-making through more traditional forms. I would use these free scores – and if I had the equipment available, electronic media – with older children in the fourth and fifth years. By that age they soon become really interested in acoustics and the whole technology of making music. But with them again, as I've said before, it is the music-making that really works – using your voice or an instrument to let your feelings flow in music. If I digress to talk about some technical or historical matter or to introduce a record as an illustration it is always to return as quickly as I can to the main business of each session – making music together.

MR: What about singing? O.K. not the *Oxford Song Book*!

T: I don't specially want to knock the poor old Oxford Book – there's lots of lovely stuff in it. It's just that, as you say, for donkeys years kids have been sat in rows and made to go through the motions of singing these old songs week after week. Just as if they were doing Latin unseens or conjugating irregular verbs. Kids really like singing – they like four part harmony: I know someone who gets them to sing simplified versions of Bach for instance. When they hear the sound they're making they actually like it! But I must confess for most of my singing I turn to contemporary folk songs, or the rock and pop musicals like Superstar or Joseph or Oliver. There's so much singing going on on the radio and the box that the children are already into, there's no problem over material. There can be problems of inhibitions though and this I try to overcome by singing with and for the kids myself, joining in with their music-making – and by setting a momentum in the early years strong enough to carry us through the problem years in the third and fourth. For me singing and moving will always be at the heart of the music curriculum: that's how they get the music that's in them out into the world.

Since this conversation I have had to set up a number of what I call 'basic music' sessions on my own account. The Arts Curriculum Team has lacked a specialist musician and having dabbled at a fairly primitive level in the other expressive arts I felt it was time to try my hand at music. My idea was to put relatively naïve groups into expressive contact with acoustic media. To do this I had in the first place to decide what might constitute an overall programme for a general musical education for all and sundry. My music syllabus is such a programme and I offer it here because I think it chimes well with some of the ideas already advanced in this chapter and because it has enabled me at least to find and organize material for expressive and impressive learning in music, movement and drama.

A Music Syllabus for All and Sundry

I have in this book largely avoided prescription about the actual content of the arts syllabus preferring to emphasize the importance of a teacher's grasp of the general expressive 'theme' inherent in the arts curriculum as a whole. There's a sense in which any 'content' will do provided it is relevant to the needs and capabilities of the class in question and allows the creative process we have been exploring to be implemented. However, arts specialists will all have their own ideas of what constitutes a basic education in their own discipline and most would probably argue that education *through* the arts is not incompatible with education *in* the arts – indeed some would insist even that the former requires the latter. Nowhere in this book have I suggested that there would no longer be a place for art appreciation or the skills of craftsmanship for instance. Rather I have tried to provide a theoretical framework which fits all the standard aspects of arts education into an integrated set of activities, interdependent one upon another in relation to the underlying expressive function of the arts.

As I say, I have not given much attention to the nuts and bolts of the arts lesson, and some readers may feel disappointed about this. One of the dangers of being too specific is that material offered simply to illustrate a point or to suggest one among a number of possible approaches can all too easily acquire a quite improper and wholly unintended significance. My feeling is that most arts teachers can weave the 'particularity' or form of an educational encounter from their own repertoire of experience and expertise. The help I felt we could best provide was in terms not so much of the 'particularity' of the encounter as of its structure or 'generality'. I have said that any content will do. That may be too sweeping. I do however believe absolutely that the specific content of the encounter – whether it be an encounter with an individual child or a group of children – can and should be conjured 'out of the air', and built from moment to moment. The present moment, Now, contains all the particularity we need, if we can see it and grasp its potential. With practice we gradually acquire the skill to do so.

That said, I confess that I rarely confront a class empty-handed, however, simply waiting for inspiration or impulse. I like to have done my 'homework' and to have come to some conclusion, based upon reflection on what happened the time before, about possible growth points, lines of development, call them what you will. Invariably these decisions involve the selection of one of the four curriculum elements as the starting point for the encounter, and that may also mean the preparation of stimulus materials, the provision of media, the organization of information or instruction. When I speak of a syllabus I suppose what I have in mind is neither the generalized conceptual framework that I have been setting out in this book, nor the actual content of particular encounters, rather a curriculum fleshed out as an intermediate programme specific to the representational medium I am concerned with. My training, and my continuing concern with my own discipline, usually provides me with the material out of which I make this 'syllabus' – I call it that for want of a better term. Again it is not a programme I would slavishly follow – indeed it is not conceived strictly, with a beginning, middle and end. I want to keep classroom decisions as alive and spontaneous as I can. Nevertheless, it is good to be able to refer to such a programme – for ideas when ideas are not forthcoming and as a way of checking the essential balance of the education in and through art, music, dance, drama, English, that I may be trying to provide. My 'syllabus' is not to be read as either sequential or developmental; it will provide the substance and objectives of music education at all levels. Concepts, experiences and activities will be geared to the mental, physical, emotional and cultural levels of the different groups involved. It is rather a repetoire than a programme.

Four Elements of the Music Curriculum

1 *Sensation*:
Investigate *responses* to patterns of sound and silence – encourage listening and educate hearing (perception). Musical *expression* (enaction) as a *sensuous* experience (vocalizing, sound-making and kinetic movement).

2 *Medium*:
Sound in all its aspects as the primary (presentational) medium – representational media include all the means of sound production (voice, body, instruments, 'natural' phenomena). Musical 'conventions' and music's social or group character. Our study of the medium will include an appreciation of the particular character of sound as an expressive language. Such concepts as timing, rhythm, beat, volume, pitch, tone and timbre. Musical form and rules (beginnings, middles and ends) can also be considered as an aspect of the medium.

3 *Craftsmanship*:
All aspects of the control of sound production and reproduction (including study of notation systems). The performance character of much music-making has also to be taken into account.

4 *Imaging*:
Listening to, making and participating in the performance of realized musical forms.

These are the basic elements of a musical education. We notice especially:
(a) that music is a strongly social experience – it is often shared in the making and in the responding and due weight must be given to this element of the medium. In particular we shall need to generate group impulses for group improvisations. A group impulse is a mood or feeling shared by the participating partners.
(b) The concepts and the learning required must be appropriate to the mental and emotional 'levels' of the children involved.
(c) Children should learn about the physics of hearing (acoustics) as well as experiencing and controlling sounds. They would learn about sound production and control (vocal and instrumental) as well as the shaping and forming of sound patterns. They would learn to discriminate between different sound sources, different musical 'instruments', the sound characteristics of different ages, peoples, places. They would learn the

basic concepts of musical structure so as to exploit them for their own expressive and recreative ends. They would learn the skills of sound production and reproduction and become culturally aware.

Seven Major Themes of the Music Syllabus

1 *Noise, Sound and Silence*
Sound is meaningful or intelligible noise; the object of music education is the development of aural intelligence and imagination (not to be confused with musical literacy in the narrow sense). It means being able to make sense of aural experience, impressively and expressively.
Noise and information: the semantics of sound (signs and symbols). The properties of sound in time and space – energy in action; beat, stress, volume, pitch, percussion, tempo, timing, pace, accent, melody, timbre, tone.
Octaves, registers, range and sequence.
The emotional as distinct from the conceptual meaning of sound.
Learning through games; matching sounds to object sources and sounds to sensuous reciprocals (e.g. Wagner and Turner).
Musical (sound) Responses (tastes) of young and old differ due to developmental (affective and cognitive) factors as well as cultural ones – explore this and base learning upon what we know of the representational and expressive capacities and needs of the children we are teaching.

2 *Voice and Speech*
Basic resources for work on sound production:
Explore different kinds of information conveyed by normal speech as sound. Sex, age, social class, state of health.
Race, native/foreigner.
Feeling character of the situation and non-verbal communication. Feeling state and intention of speakers.
Explore uses of voice – communication, expression (reactive and reflexive).
Talk, singing, humming, coughing, gasping, tut-tutting, etc. All in relation to the properties of sound.
Anatomical and physical study of voice in action; relation of breath, vocal chords, mouth, lips, bone structure, etc., etc.
Relation of voice production/control (concentrating on sound qualities) to specific communicative and expressive purposes; (singers, news readers, sports commentators, politicians, crowds, air hostesses, different races (families of languages), people in day to day situations). Plenty of scope here as elsewhere for dramatic simulation as well as study of documentary material and produc-

tion of audio and visual tapes. Relation of Physical and Emotional condition to voice production.

3 Musical Instruments

Physics and technology of sound production: taut strings and surfaces, cavities, resonators, amplifiers.
Identification of conventional instruments (native and foreign).

4 Sound Reproduction

Notation systems, discs and tapes and electronic technology.
Mass media.

5 Tension and Continuity in Music and Movement

Space: tunes and textures.
Time: rhythm and tempo and timing.

6 Performance and Ritual

Here we would investigate the social use of music as realized form – such topics as:
Folk song and folk music in its original form and as an inspiration to composers: rooted in life cycle, work, passage of the seasons.
Sound in relation to religious, mystical, and ceremonial purposes – hymn singing, royal and state occasions, sporting spectacles; also more primitive forms (African, etc.).
Music and death (dirge, lament, requiem mass, etc.); other cultures besides Western.
The concert (classical, pop, recital, jam session, spontaneous event).
The emotional programme: film music, music in shops and planes, political music, national anthems, military music, love songs, nursery rhymes, rugby songs, pop.

7 Music in Action

Music as the expression of an era, a people, a period – relation to changing ideas, social habits, economic situation, politics, work, new modes of thought and social behaviour. Music that embodies the spirit of a people, a culture, the times (America in the '30s, England in the '60s). Musicians whose music seems to anticipate (even bring about) changes in sensibility. Here there would be opportunity to relate music to other art forms whether we took music, art, and literature at the end of the eighteenth century in Europe or examined examples of primitive tribal music and art. Musical forms have to be seen as equivalents of other representational forms – forms of thought and forms of action as well as feeling forms. Someone said that it isn't that artists are ahead of their time – it is simply that most people are behind the times.

These would be some of the key elements for inclusion in my music syllabus. Again I would probably move amongst them fairly freely – i.e. nonsequentially – except where the understanding of one concept presupposed another. I would think in terms of curriculum 'sequences' though, rather than individual lessons. There would hopefully be a manifest logic about the musical development I was looking for – involving the education of the senses, conceptual grasp of the language of the acoustic medium, technical skills and a growing repertoire of realized forms. However, the emphasis and direction of each sequence would be expressive; I would be seeking to arouse expressive impulses (individually and in groups) and realize them in improvised musical images (both ephemeral and repeatable). Most of my music teaching would be enactive – i.e. dramatic and kinetic – and would be inseparable from work in the other arts. The concepts would be discovered heuristically through exploratory experiments, and reinforced through participatory action. The conceptual would always be at the service of the expressive.

From this syllabus I have developed a number of curriculum sequences. Readers might be interested in a series of sessions I did with one particular non-musical group. They were not 'unmusical' – it was just that most had little serious musical experience and all were very nervous at the idea of 'doing music'. It is not offered as a model – simply as an example of curriculum making in 'basic music'. The sequence relies heavily upon group work but the development is towards increasing individualization of response and image making. Severe restrictions of space and resources tended to dictate the range of activities (one lecture room and no conventional musical instruments).

A Curriculum Sequence in Music

Aim:
Working in groups to stimulate individual expressive responses to the concepts of acoustic *continuity and tension*. In particular to get individuals to listen to and lead each other in a series of group improvisations. (The sequence spans several weeks.)

Class:
20 non-arts teachers on full-time courses in curriculum, counselling, etc.

Development:
towards individual improvised composition.

1. Whole group in a circle.
   Issued Football Team Word Game Sheet (see interview page 239) and worked from word patterns to the beating and stamping of metrical rhythms. (20 minutes)
2. Talked briefly about rhythm and metre and timing – pulse, beat, etc. as an essential to patterning acoustically (sound and silence). (5 minutes)

3. Introduced idea of the semantic rhythms of verbal language – rhythms related to meaning and the content and 'direction' of verbal encounters. Illustrated by reading excerpts from plays, poems, speeches and tape of children's play-talk.

   Issued copies of piece from R. D. Laing's *Knots*. We read it first all together, then in verses by groups but with all reading at the same time. With the utterances thus overlaid and the whole 'reading' recorded we were able, during play-back, to discern the deep waves of pulse and counter-pulse active below the verbal surface.

   Two soloists were then invited to improvise within the context of ensemble whispering of the text; the piece achieved a dramatic tension this way that was clearly dependent upon the sound texture and deep pulse, not merely upon the meaning of the words themselves. By adding percussive vocal sounds the tension and drama were increased. The piece was recorded, played back, analysed and discussed in terms of the main aim of the sequence – i.e. 'acoustic continuity and tension'.

   This was a truly expressive experience in the terms of this book as group feeling was evoked and an adequate improvised form developed to match the group's response. (40 minutes)

   (Listened to Stockhausen's 'Contact')

4. Group broken down into 3 sets of 6/7 persons but remained in the same room. Using voices only they explored (and taped) improvisations on the following simply contrasted ideas.

   WARM – COOL
   BRIGHT – DARK
   LINE – POINT

   The sensate themes were all chosen as, in the first place, not obviously connected with hearing. After momentary dismay all went well and some interesting pieces were produced. (30 minutes)

5. As relief and refreshment a highly structured and imitative exercise. Played record of African drumming (complex on the surface but with simple and pronounced ostinato bass) and invited class to 'join in' using whatever was available. The value lay in the sustained character of the piece: 'drumming' continuously for 15 minutes or more is an unusual experience (and an essential one).

6. Group brought home-made and improvised 'instruments' and, after 'introductions', explored them in terms of acoustic

   Time: Flow, pulse, beat, rhythm, etc.

   Space: Pitch, volume, texture (30 minutes)

   (Listened to Messenger's piece from end of Stravinsky's 'Oedipus Rex')

7. They sorted themselves into groups of 4/5

   First of similar-sounding instruments

Next of compatible or complementary instruments
They continued to explore the concepts of time and space, continuity and tension – undirected as to either feeling or form. Used
two extra rooms on this occasion.

They were instructed to 'Let the music discover itself'. (30
minutes)

8. In discussion the physical side of music-making, was picked out
and we agreed that bodily and mental 'posture' were important
factors in sound patterning (following Orff's ideas here). We
then tried to find the best way of playing our various instruments
and concentrated on becoming physically and mentally sympathetic (not easy when you are playing a watering can!). (30
minutes)

9. Further group 'doodling' now led to increased sense of physical
involvement – one group 'processed', another danced as it played.
With increasing confidence voices played a greater role.
(45 minutes)

10. By way of a change issued simplified score of harmonized Bach
chorale.
Achieved reasonable rendering. (15 minutes)

11. Major expressive project in same groups (6/7 instrumentalists).
Expressive Problem: FAREWELL – SWEET SORROWING
DIALECTIC
Stimulus Material (images): Donne's 'A Valediction: Forbid-
ding Mourning'–Botticelli's 'Pieta' (Alte Pinakoltek, Munich).
I especially drew attention to the dialectic between 'leaning
and hearkening' (i.e. flowing out and flowing in). (90 minutes)

12. Performed improvisation based on written score produced by
group member entitled 'Blue Notes from the Back of Beyond'.
Went on to consider its dramatic, kinetic and graphic possibilities. (90 minutes)

This musical piece grew out of a drama exercise involving the
exploration of spatial – situational idioms such as to be 'down in
the dumps', 'over the moon', 'out on a limb', 'under the weather'. The
student took the expression 'at the back of beyond' and chose
'contrast' (broken-flowing) as her problem form: to be at the back of
beyond meant a feeling that was both frightening and yet somehow
acceptable, consoling. The holding form she created contained
'finite' swelling droplets of sound gathering and falling against an
'infinite' wash of voices (Eliot's poem 'Eyes that last I saw in tears').
Figure and ground.

She worked initially on paper (i.e. in abstraction) sketching the
effects she wanted in words. She described a journey in sound from
here and now (harsh and broken) to there and then (oily and insistent). Words gave way to signs-for-sounds and in a series of written
scores for ensemble playing she reduced and refined her ideas. The

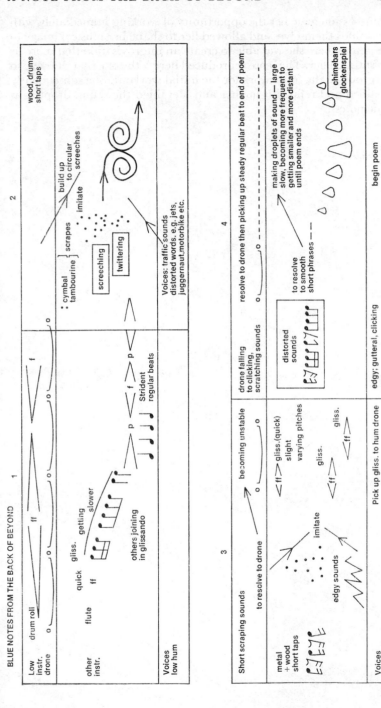

group session gave her the opportunity of working immediately with the sounds themselves and allowed her to shape her musical image to the point where she was able to create an improvisation that more or less satisfied her. The score reproduced here is the one that she gave to the group as the framework for the initial workout. She subsequently modified and refined it further and identified the sound droplets as 'blue notes'.

15 Evaluation, Assessment, and Certification

This is a vexed matter for the arts and not one, having studied a mass of current syllabuses and papers, that I yet feel very composed about. I shall try to strike a balanced view, recognizing the strong case for certification at the present time, and yet I feel concerned about the damaging effects that exam 'pressure' can have upon the arts curriculum. Among the CSE papers Susan Morris sent me I found the following comment by one girl – she makes a simple but significant point:

> I didn't realize how dance had changed me or what dance really was until the exam. This demanded that I think about what I did: I had to write and draw about it. This opened a very important door because I began to realize, in an exciting, practical way, the meaning of dance. This has improved my dance because I have become more aware. It always goes hand in hand with practical work and in fact it has made me value even more the practical aspect of my work.

Mrs Morris found no contradiction – advantages even – in creating the means of public assessment for her children's work. I suppose every intelligent and sensitive teacher, given a responsive examination board, could do the same.

Evaluation and assessment are terms often confused with each other. I want to use them to signify two quite different ideas. By evaluation I mean those procedures designed and deployed to feed back to the participants in an educational encounter information about the character and effectiveness of that encounter so that informed decisions might be made by the participants about their future encountering. Evaluation is a formative process: it affects the form the curriculum will take from there on. Evaluation needs to be comprehensive and regular; its aim is to keep curriculum action and curriculum objectives aligned.

By assessment I mean those procedures designed and deployed to rate operational competence. In schools, assessments are usually made of pupil competence only: through specially devised tests and the monitoring of course work a pupil's level of educational performance is rated. Whenever possible these ratings involve some element of measurement and either imply or specify an absolute standard of attainment that will allow ratings to be compared. Assessments are made of present and past competence as a means of predicting future performance. Evaluation often subsumes some form of assessment; assessment does not necessarily imply an overall evaluation of the educational encounter. Much of the information regarded as essential to evaluation is deliberately left out of assessment.

Certification invariably requires some form of assessment: it does not necessarily arise out of the process of formative evaluation. The certificate is a negotiable token of social worth: school certificates betoken levels of scholastic attainment and are granted to children who successfully measure up to certain 'legitimate' levels of performance. As far as possible certification aims to transcend circumstantial considerations and lays some claim to absolute value. Certificates specify the nature and level of accomplishment. Essentially they provide a basis for symbolic interpersonal discrimination. They are a special form of social currency issued to the young by the adult section of the community and exchanged by the young for the opportunity to work or study or participate in other reserved or privileged activities. Certificates therefore carry and bestow prestige. As things stand certification is a fairly powerful educational inducement and exercises considerable influence upon decisions made about the point and content of the curriculum. Where certification depends upon assessment and assessment upon the rating of educational products (children as products or as producers of products) the curriculum can become heavily committed to the idea of productivity. Teachers as much concerned with knowing as knowledge, as much concerned with process as product, tend to find certification something of an embarrassment.

However, if you work in a college or a school you cannot ignore or merely turn your back upon the certification business. In education generally, examinations are a boom industry. The impulse behind the boom comprises a number of different elements: the teacher's feeling that an examination gives his subject status, that being examinable gives a child status and that no children should be declared unexaminable (and so, educationally worthless) if it can be avoided. Parents and children clearly regard examination success as a passport to a decent job as well as providing an entrée, for some, into higher education. There are many schools who have adopted a kind of 'examine or bust' philosophy as a way of dealing with pupil disaffection. Whatever the reasons – and there are probably many more – the boom is on, and today you can get a CSE in fell walking and French, sports and Spanish. The prodigious examination machinery is almost overwhelming. The advent of teacher assessment (the Mode III examinations at CSE and GCE level) has enormously increased pressure on teacher time, and organizing the examination timetable in a large comprehensive school frequently rates a special graded appointment. The good sense of all this it is not my concern to question here.

Arts teachers have to come to terms with the situation as it is, and must find their own answers to the following questions:

1. What evaluation procedures are appropriate for my own teaching or for the department I organize? How may internal and 'public' forms of assessment be reasonably accommodated?
2. Which children should be assessed in my subject, upon what basis, when and by what means?
3. What level of certification will be most appropriate for a particular pupil?
4. Who should be informed of the results of evaluation and assessment, and by what means?

Evaluation

Given the kinds of objectives that I have been suggesting in this book for the arts curriculum, these questions could provide a framework for evaluating the teacher-pupil encounter:

TABLE 15.1

A. Subject Reflexive Action

	GENERAL COMPETENCE	PARTICULAR TASK
1. Playing	Is there a readiness to play, to relax, to doodle, have fun? Can we relax and respond playfully together? If not, why not? Is there an appetite for experiment and invention, improvisation and speculation? Do I bring these things about or inhibit them? Does he? Am I too often too heavy? Solemn? Do we always need to be able to play before we can resolve an impulse?	Is there scope here for fun, 'formless functioning' as well as more serious, focused creative activity? Where in this task is the area of play to be located? Has play occurred? Should it?
2. Impulse	Is there a deep reluctance to admit to feelings, to show me his feeling, to project a feeling impulse? How active are inhibitions– his and mine? Where does feeling flow fairly freely that confidence may be gained between us?	Does this idea (exercise, task) arouse intrinsic expressive motivation? Is the child 'involved'? How far and for how long should I provide motivational support?

How frequently is the expressive response reactive?
In what kinds of feeling area are we most comfortable?
Are his expressive impulses varied or obsessive?

3. Expressive Problems	Does he understand what an expressive problem is? (Gestalt) Does he always need me to set the problem or can he set his own?	Has he got hold of the expressive problem? Can I set it some other way?
4. Centring	Does he know how to go about centring the impulse in a medium? Does he know when he is centred? How successful are his holding forms? How accurate are my assessments?	Is he centred? If not, what can I do to help?
5. Resolving	Does he know when he is finished? Do I? When resolution is not achieved, can we discover why? Are we tackling increasingly demanding problems? If so, in what respects?	Has the impulse been resolved? If not, why not?
6. Sharing	Does he welcome sharing opportunities? Is he receptive to criticism? Does he know how he feels about his own work?	How much of this evaluation will we be able to share? What is his own estimate of the piece of work (process as well as product)? How does he rate my part? Has the product public value?

TABLE 15.2

B. Curriculum Elements

1. Sensation	Can he see, hear, feel, move? Which modes are strongest? Can the weak ones be strengthened?	What senses are involved here? Are we playing to strengths? Are we challenging growth and change?
2. Media	Which media does he respond to most successfully? Where is there scope for development? What is the extent of his cognitive understanding? Am I getting my ideas across?	Again, what about strengths and weaknesses, growth and change? Is the medium appropriate to the expressive task? What instruction is needed from me? Are the necessary media available?

3. Craftsmanship	What skills does he have, does he need, has he some chance of mastering? Can I teach him the skills he needs? Can someone else? Are we adequately equipped with the necessary resources? What particular difficulties does he have?	Is the task within his capacity? How good a craftsman is he? How can we make the most of the skills he already has? Is he sufficiently motivated? Are we properly equipped? Is the task itself an appropriate one for him?
4. Imagery	Does he enjoy using his imagination? Is he imaginatively fluent, creative, spontaneous? Does he respect his own imagining? Do I share my imaginative life with him? What is the character of his personal imagery? Is it distinctive? Do his made images seem to please, surprise, satisfy him? What kinds of realized form does he most easily and most satisfyingly respond to? Can I widen the scope? Do we share imaginative experience? Does he grasp the principles of aesthetic meaning?	Have I stimulated his imagining? Do his own images relate to feeling impulse? How do his images work as public as well as private forms? Can I help him increase the power and meaning of his image? Is there a firm structure within the form? How sophisticated (accomplished) are his products?

It would be silly to imply that this were either a comprehensive or an adequate check-list – but it is at least a start and it does suggest a fairly methodical procedure for thinking about and so planning and modifying the individual encounter. Each encounter has to be built mutually, and teacher and pupil must find some way of locating the problems together before a strategy can be worked out that might resolve them. Both the participants have to be party to the strategy for it to have any chance of success – which is why I suggest that a good deal of encounter programming should occur as overt teacher-pupil discussion and emerge from personal interaction. In practice this is often the case in many arts classes.

Where ideas and instructional situations seem to have a wider application there obviously exists a basis for a group or 'class' activity. But the essence of the arts curriculum has to be the individual child–teacher encounter.

This check-list could perhaps serve as the basis for evaluating the ongoing encounter and so for curriculum decision-making. It will also provide a sensible structure for reporting on a pupil's expressive abilities and aptitudes, either in the form of case material to be passed on to colleagues within the school or of assessment to be offered to parents and others external to the encounter itself.

Assessment and Certification

I wrote recently to a number of examination boards to inquire about developments in arts examining. The response was almost 100 per cent. Looking at the many explanatory and helpful replies I received, one could not but be impressed by the seriousness of the examiners and in very many cases the painstaking and sensitive work that had gone into the devising of the syllabuses and the assessment procedures. There is the strongest evidence that the teachers are being thoroughly involved in the examination process and that their priorities and practices are being respected – only one correspondent sounded a faintly sinister note – 'We are *not* amongst those Boards who are prepared to believe that *every* teacher knows what he is doing!'

By and large, whether we are talking of dance or drama, music or media studies, art, craft or design education there is a reassuring emphasis upon practical work of a personal and creative kind, upon the taking account of course work (sometimes extending over the entire five-year span of secondary schooling), and the keeping of written work and written examinations to a minimum. This rubric from the East Anglia Examinations Board is not untypical in spirit of a great many of the instructions and syllabuses I received:

ART AND CRAFT (Course Work 100 %)

Art is so closely involved with the development of the individual that the course must cater for the individual evolution of each child. The course is designed to give full scope to Art education's many facets, and it is possible for candidates to enter work of any kind, of any size and in any medium.

The areas of visual and aesthetic experience have widened considerably in Art education, and it is hoped that within the broad framework of the course will be found ample scope for creative experiment and much lively and expressive activity. It is suggested that the discoveries the pupils will be making through their Art should be related to the large world of Art and Design, both past and present, and the interests and discrimination that can be exercised in all kinds of ways in the course of their daily lives.

There will be no set examination, candidates being judged on the work produced in the course of their studies . . . The form of presentation will depend upon the facilities available to the school. In some schools it should be possible for candidates to present their work in the form of an exhibition. In others, where space is limited, the assessors may look through a folio of work. A small exhibition arranged by the candidate will, of course, be most helpful to the assessor and will also give the pupil the satisfaction of seeing his own work grouped. Candidates may be present during the assessment and may be invited to discuss their work, but this is not obligatory.

The Art and Craft course should encourage all that is best in Art education with no restriction on media, subject, size of work, or breadth of study. It should encourage teachers to broaden the scope of their courses and should provide inspiration rather than limitation.

There were of course exceptions – an astonishing CSE music syllabus, for instance, insisting upon knowledge of a single work by each of twenty major composers from Bach to Britten ('the candidate is expected to have some knowledge of the composer, his general achievement and his position in musical history'). However for the most part the emphasis was unmistakably upon stimulating children to be resourceful, inventive, wide-ranging in their interests and enthusiastic in their commitment to the arts. Assessment procedures were often informal and positively oriented to make the most of individual strengths and interests. In short it would be difficult to accuse any of the Boards of reactionary practices or of doing anything but support and indeed prompt innovatory teaching methods in the classroom. The Boards repeatedly insist that they wish as far as possible to examine what is taught – they resent and resist the insinuation that used to hold good that the schools only dared to teach what the Boards said could be examined. As I say, the overriding impression is of an enlightened and experimental approach with no pains spared to produce a syllabus and an assessment procedure acceptable to the schools, relevant to the teachers' work and fair to the children.

And yet, certainly where arts education is concerned, I have to say that the most serious doubts about all this well-meant hustle and bustle remain. As I have said elsewhere in this book there is absolutely no question but that examinations *of a kind* can be devised for arts education. You can teach specific skills (manipulative, critical, problem solving) and see whether they have been mastered and to what level of attainment. You can examine understanding and the memorizing of factual information. You can treat educational drama as 'theatre studies', examine a course on media using a mainly 'traditional literary criticism approach'. You can run a photography course that does not go much beyond examining the pupil's 'understanding of the use and working of common photographic equipment and chemicals in present-day use' – supported by 'research . . . undertaken in a book and regularly marked'. When you have worked your way through the rubric and arrived at the course itself it is often to find that the subject has suffered a frightful sea change – or merely gone soggy. A really carefully thought-out dance syllabus often boils down to a course file and one or two rehearsed practical pieces assessed – ice skating-style one suspects (all those over-coated little people with numbered cards held over their heads) – for 'skills, sensitivity, shape, physical development and personal qualities'.

There are so many problems. First of all in the categories of behaviour or qualities of production to be assessed. (Is 'evaluation of situations' in drama really worth six points – whatever that means – and 'use of sound' four, while 'flexibility and grace' can get you eight?

Seventeen rated factors making up the total 100 marks.) It is so diffi-cult to decide what the right terms are for making a judgement about whether or not a pupil is 'good at' drama, or dance, or media, or art and so forth. English as a subject is in similar embarrassing straits when it comes to assessment. Despite the blandishments about com-munication skills, listening and talking as well as reading and writing, to say nothing of 'helping pupils appreciate something of the beauty expressed in our language and to express beauty through their own experiences' we still know precious little about language behaviour and language development that will allow any serious assessment of linguistic competence beyond the traditional assessment of certain rather limited kinds of formal operation. One Board – experimenting with assessment interviews of children discussing topics in groups – makes this rather lame admission: 'We accept the essentially sub-jective nature of assessment in English. Our concern should be to arrive at a consensus agreement . . .'

Examinations in art inevitably concentrate upon rating a finished product – though the Boards make prodigious efforts to set topics that will appeal to the pupils. However this kind of an offering from an 'A' level paper in 'Sculpture' has a long way to go in terms of the 'setting of an expressive problem':

> Through the analysis of some aspects of movement that have interested you in some other area of your academic studies, develop a piece of free standing, relief, mobile or kinetic sculpture. Some suggestions:
>
> (a) air, wind or water currents
> (b) rock strata or volcanic eruption
> (c) mathematical progress or sequence
> (d) circular or bodily movement

With the criteria for making assessments in the arts still so much of an open question it is very hard for a Board to decide precisely what it should be examining. And when the Boards ask the teachers, the teach-ers do not know either! The matter is further complicated by the difficulty of actually arriving at assessments, given that you know what you are trying to assess. One Board cheerily speaks of 'exploring the candidate's ability to communicate easily and successfully in both writing and speech'. How, one wonders? And is that really what you are doing when you mark his essay and discuss a poem with him? Another Board declares of its Mode I CSE Art and Design course:

> The aim of the examination is to measure the extent to which candidates show they are able:
>
> 1. to display creative thinking and ability;
> 2. to express personal ideas through as wide a range of media as possible;
> 3. to exhibit technical skills, powers of judgement, sensitivity and dis-crimination through the disciplines of crafts and the limitations of materials.

How one wonders will they set about their 'measuring' – and what criteria of attainment will they adopt?

As I say, there are probably certain aptitudes, abilities, and levels of attainment that are amenable to measurement in the arts as elsewhere in the curriculum. The question arises as to whether what can be so measured is really what we want to measure – and the answer, at least where the arts are concerned, would seem clearly to be largely in the negative. On the other hand there might be some abilities and attainments that arts teachers really did wish to assess – the question then is what are they and how might they be measured. So far most of the Boards, for all their good intentions, seem well wide of the mark. Arts teachers could certainly help them – and I have tried to indicate earlier some of the criteria that might apply. Essentially assessment in the arts:

1. Has to be non-competitive as between one pupil and another.
2. Has to emphasize process skills rather than product finish: knowing rather than knowledge.
3. Must aim to retain rather than loose information about the pupil: is he becoming more himself?
4. Must be arrived at through a joint pupil-teacher dialogue. The moderator's role would have to be totally re-thought.
5. Must balance public with private criteria.

When we consider public examinations in relation to arts education, we have to admit that we still have it all to do. In the meantime, until the teachers come up with something valid, we are well advised to take a very sober and very critical look at the syllabuses available before deciding they are 'good enough' for our pupils. There are radical changes to be made, and it is the teachers, not the examiners, who should initiate them.

There is no easy or obvious way for the arts teacher to resolve the examination dilemma. If we do participate in public examinations we run the risk of allowing our work to be wrested from its legitimate roots; and if we do not, we seem to push the arts even farther out on a limb. The more the arts become exceptions to the rules of schooling the less relevant they are likely to appear. Or so we are led to feel.

Nevertheless I feel we should beware of compromising ourselves. While being prepared to go a long way to meet those who do not understand the nature and purpose of our work, welcoming them to our classrooms, involving them in our activities, making them aware of what we are doing and inviting them to share experience with us, there comes a time when the price for 'acceptance' or whatever one might wish to call it, becomes simply too high. There are certain lines we have to draw if we are to preserve the character and integrity of our work, and this book has tried to establish some of them. As things are – and I base this conclusion on a fairly thorough reading of current examination syllabuses and regulations – there seems no hard

evidence that the special concerns of arts teachers have been accommodated. The moves to include the teachers in the examination procedure and to give increasing weight to course work, though obviously
welcome, can easily blind us to the fact that very little may have really
changed. There is still a strong emphasis upon pupils producing
written work in support of less easily assessable material. The art product is seen, if not as the most significant element of the course, then
certainly as the most useful from the examiner's point of view: being
good at art means being able to make a presentable or effective drawing, painting, sculpture, etc. In short, what is deemed to be valuable
by the examiner, because ratable, may not have such significance
within the curriculum as we the teachers see it, and the equation that
allows an examination rating to stand for a general level of attainment and ability in a subject is all too easily adopted. We all know
that ratable evidence of progress made may well be important within
the context of the educational encounter as a whole but when it is
taken out of that context and then loaded with spurious meaning, we
are bound to feel that the assessment picture is being distorted.

I have already raised the issue of rating procedures so I will not
dwell upon it further except to say that many of the examiners' claims
to be able to 'measure' this and 'explore' that may be very ill-founded
indeed. What from our point of view is perhaps more to the point is
the difficulty over assessing creative process as distinct from creative
product. Few examinations manage this issue with any conviction.
Course work properly monitored is clearly the best way – and the
teacher's evidence would be all important.

Children might be asked to 'improvise' for an outside assessor and
then questioned intensively about what they had been doing, but this
could be very time-consuming and would pre-suppose considerable
understanding of the creative process and an ability to establish an
effective rapport with the children on the part of the visitor. However,
this might be done on a sampling basis just to allow some kind of an
assessment to be made of the teaching and of the course itself. Given an
appreciation of the teacher's thinking and approach to the course,
the examiner would at least be in a reasonable position to understand
the conception of arts education within which a child had been
working.

The emphasis of the examinations could probably be corrected, to
allow a truer reflection of the priorities of our work. Legitimate
methods of assessment might also emerge – given a really careful and
critical exploration of the problems involved – that would really
register attainment and ability relative to the declared aims of a particular arts course. But even with those aspects of the examination
dilemma resolved, there remain other, more intractable issues. At
present the grading system of the CSE examination that ties it to
GCE builds in a high level of interpersonal competition. It is not that
we are necessarily opposed to all competition in any circumstances

(some of us probably are) : the point for arts teachers is that we seek to match our pupils against themselves. To help them become more themselves – creatively, expressively, emotionally. That does not – as we have already seen – mean that they remain narrowly focused upon themselves and their own work to the exclusion of everything and everyone else. We actively encourage comparison and sharing – and the children will certainly be aware of their different talents, levels and kinds of accomplishment. But we object (a) to restricting the range of our work to what is examinable, and (b) to introducing notions of personal acceptability among our pupils based on their getting a certificate, or obtaining a high or low grade of pass, that reflect acknowledge-based rather than a behaviour-based curriculum, one dominated by objects and productions rather than one organized upon some general notion of the affective and expressive development of children and of the particular growth of an individual pupil. It is of course at least questionable whether the present examinations are any more acceptable in other subjects than they are in the arts.

So there are no simple answers. In the end individual arts teachers must make up their own minds. As I have said, some Boards are really very willing to accommodate the wishes of the teachers and a little careful investigation of what is available or possible in your area could pay off handsomely. But we must keep a clear distinction in our minds between the wholly legitimate business of internal course evaluation and the maintenance of pupil-records that may promote and inform a child's education on the one hand, and the external assessment of the child for quite different purposes on the other. The notion that an assessment of an individual pupil can be rendered as a mark, and that this mark can then have general significance among all other such similar marks is idiotic in the area of education we are responsible for. Vocational preparation – and associated tests – is one thing. Quite another is the proliferation of personal rating procedures that seems inevitable for children whose schooling is a kind of dreadful paper chase. (Shades of *They Shoot Horses Don't They?* and *Rollerball*.) The arts certainly have no place in such scrambling. If a piece of paper is necessary, in the arts our certificate would need to say simply that, in terms of the aims of the course (stated), boy X or girl Y has continued to develop satisfactorily. Each certificate might list briefly the kinds of aptitudes the course has been trying to develop. We should not pretend to measure achievements that may not, literally, be measured.

A Modest Proposal

If pupils completing our courses successfully are to be given the public rewards that go with schooling – rewards to which they are surely entitled – then we must provide our children with the same opportunities for certification as are offered by our non-arts colleagues.

When adult society drops its admission charge upon the young, the arts teacher will probably be among the first to encourage children to work for the sheer joy of knowing. Many arts teachers are dealing constructively and responsibly with this issue. The more cynical among us play the examination game and allow so much of their teaching time (depending on the intelligence of the children they are dealing with) for exam preparation and making the best of the time remaining. But this is not a line I have much sympathy with since it denies any chance of real change or development to the examination system. It rather endorses the view that several Boards take: that the teachers do not really care. I would like to feel that arts teachers were making more and more of an impact upon the arts certification business – there are increasing opportunities for them to do so and these opportunities must be exploited.

We should insist that we are assessing *achievement* rather than future potential, and then ensure:

1. That the assessment process reflect as much of a child's experience of the course as possible.
2. That inter-pupil competition be reduced – possibly by allowing only one grade of overall pass – and failure (no pass) reserved for pupils who did not effectively participate (in any reasonable sense of the term) in the course.
3. That a variety of means of assessment be employed in order to reveal as much relevant information about the pupil as possible, and that teacher-pupil ongoing evaluation of the educational encounter play a significant part in the outcome.
4. That the means of assessment be suitable to the course to be assessed (no undue weight given to written work, course files, etc.).
5. That the course, once accepted by a Board, should be regularly evaluated by an 'outsider'. Continuity of standard would be ensured by evaluating the course rather than merely by assessing the pupils. All pupils accepted for a certificate course would normally be granted a pass having completed it – there could be some leeway given over the precise amount of time allowed a child. *Arts courses would aim to establish subject-reflexive action as a basic way of knowing and to encourage the acquisition of increasingly sophisticated levels of competence.* To pass the course and obtain the certificate, the child would need to have satisfied the school (the more teachers involved in the teaching and the assessing the better) that he or she had reached an acceptable basic level of competence and was continuing to develop the appropriate skills. The Board would nominate an external assessor to help a school arrive at a fair measure of detachment in evaluating its course. Certificates would be awarded on the basis of the school's recommendation. Assessment would take account of the pupil's competence in handling the process of subject-reflexive action –

there would also be some assessment made of attainment in relation to the four curriculum elements (possibly expressed as three grades: A = exceptionally good; B = good; C = adequate). Certification would take all this information into account though it might not all be reported. Where a combined arts certificate was offered it would not be difficult to develop the simple criteria I have suggested to include a wider range of media – always remembering that it is subject-knowing that is the point of the certification and that it is basic competence in this process rather than in a range of ancillary skills and knowledge that we are testifying to.

Finally there should be room on the assessment form for a descriptive piece by the teacher bringing out the pupil's future prospects and particular qualities – in the way a good critic helps us 'see' a picture or a book. Eliot Eisner[1] suggests a future for this kind of assessment where absolute standards do not exist, and where simple measuring is out of the question anyway.

> The vivification of perception which it is the critic's office to further is carried out by a particular use of language. It is quite clear that our discourse is not as differentiated as our sensibilities. We experience more than we can describe. Thus what the critic must do is not to attempt to replicate the visual, dramatic, or musical work verbally but to provide a rendering of them through the use of poetic language. The vehicles the critic employs are suggestion, simile and metaphor. Those poetic vehicles carry the viewer to a heightened perception of the phenomena . . . Much of what goes on in schools can be illuminated by the tools of criticism.

It is among lines such as these that I feel arts teachers should be tackling the assessment issue. Since we cannot beat them we may have to join them: But our 'surrender' should not be unconditional. We should state our terms and take the initiative to a considerable extent. There are many Boards ready to welcome teacher initiative – so we have to choose our Board carefully where we have a choice, and fight for the assessment and the certification we want for our pupils. We must also recognize however that certificates in 'expressive representation' may not satisfy the demands of a higher education organized upon the principle of impressive learning, dependent on the skills of impressive representation and the use of impressive symbols – a point made by Ben Bradnack in Chapter 13. We should consider what price we are prepared to pay for certification that may ultimately be of questionable 'public' value.

[1] In Taylor, P. H. and Tye, K. A., *Curriculum, School and Society*, NFER, 1975, p. 105.

Conclusion

We are beginning to develop a 'science' of arts education. Having proposed an hypothesis to account for the relationship between emotional growth and subject-reflexive action and found, from submitting the idea to the test of expert opinion on the one hand and experimental trials on the other, that we may have some confidence in it, we must now begin to work out in some detail the practical implications for the teacher, whose professional expertise lies in the devising and managing of 'learning' environments (curricula). We have a conception of the intelligent process we wish to foster and a strategy for engaging with that process.

Our basic model of subject-reflexive action (the creation of sensuous forms) holds good for all the children within the years of secondary schooling though every pupil passes from childhood into adulthood by way of adolescence while he or she is with us. We know that each of these stages of development is characterized by general patterns of behaviour, need, and interest, and would not be too hard-pressed I suppose to assign most of our pupils fairly easily to one of these broad categories (with the reservation that at times they swing somewhat wildly from one extreme to the other). The psychological and social needs and the 'developmental tasks' associated with each of these phases, though related, are different and not at all closely aligned with chronological age. As yet our knowledge and understanding of the way the emotions and the imagination grow is frighteningly sketchy – we have no such model of affective development as Piaget has provided for conception, to base our arts syllabus on. So trying to match curriculum with any idea of emotional or imaginative 'readiness' is still very much a hit or miss affair – and those teachers of the arts who actually see feeling and imagining as central to their work have to rely very much upon experience and intuition to guide them in their decisions. If you know children you develop a sixth sense which helps you to avoid making gross mistakes. However, it is a very regrettable state of unenlightenment that we have to work in, and research in these areas is most urgently needed if as teachers we are to achieve a better 'fit' between our curriculum and the developing emotional and imaginative life of the pupil.

In the writings of Caleb Gattegno and Robert Witkin there are many helpful ideas that arts teachers can use to support the distinctions they already make between the developmental stages we are concerned with. Certainly Witkin's suggestions concerning pre-adolescent and post-adolescent strategies for organizing sensate experience are extremely valuable and could prove crucial in helping to define our expectations of pupils' expressive behaviour. As we have seen, he suggests that the pre-adolescent organizes sensate experiences discretely: in juxtaposition (space), sequentially (time); the post-adolescent orders sensate experience holistically (space) and simultaneously (time). Unfortunately this important idea has still to be properly investigated, but it accords with experience and can inform a teacher's curriculum decisions and actions. We can be on the look-out for the shift in consciousness and support this new intelligent behaviour as it occurs.

Even in our present state of half-knowledge, however, it does not make sense to organize the arts syllabus on a year-by-year basis. We can really make no distinctions of personal development finer than the categories already referred to. While some of the children coming into the secondary school are certainly still very much 'children', others are already adolescent (emotionally and physiologically). As for fourth- and fifth-year pupils, we are often dealing not with adolescents so much as with young adults. Emotional development does not proceed by year of birth – nor can we make any rigid distinctions between the needs, say, of third- and fourth-year pupils, or of fifth- and sixth-year. So the arts curriculum has to work vertically rather than horizontally. What we need is a 'rolling syllabus' for every child.

The children will all be working with the four elements of the curriculum already outlined, developing their expressive know-how. What they will need from us will be expressive problems set in the *particularity* of their own experience and the skills and experience to resolve them in their own terms. That is where our task as curriculum makers becomes perhaps more complex and more demanding than it has been. And this can only be achieved by the teacher working from within particular relational encounters. The work load may seem to be greater than under the old ways – though with pupils engaged in individual projects and increasingly managing their own learning, this may not in the end prove to be so. We underestimate the strain on the arts teacher of trying to get whole classes to keep in step. It goes against the grain of subject-reflexive action itself. This new approach means the teacher has to be floating among all the learners – 'reading' each situation and participating thoughtfully in each enterprise. But if this book has made sense, he should at least be better equipped to work that way.

This approach is radically different from the way most arts teachers have traditionally thought about the arts syllabus. For all that they may have been committed to the idea of the individual child's personal development, most arts teachers do not base their syllabus upon such a notion. The subject is felt to be the only 'constant' and so the only point of departure for the syllabus maker. Content, coverage, technique sampling, factual knowledge and 'basic' skills are the features of the traditional arts curriculum as they are the features of the 'academic' curriculum. It really is nonsense, though, to produce a stepped subject-based syllabus in the arts: the creative process does not follow the laws of logical progression. Arts teachers who have a firm conceptual basis for their curriculum can establish the basic 'experiences' that will give a pupil know-how in a given medium. Then they can easily specify the basic materials and resources they will need. But they will not rush to write a traditional subject-based year-by-year syllabus. What they might offer as a legitimate alternative (and, what for many teachers will be a new departure) will be on-going *evidence* of the expressive development which individual pupils are undergoing together with a coherent and comprehensible assessment of aptitudes and abilities relative to their maturing intelligence of feeling. (Arts teachers have been especially handicapped in this latter respect.)

In the arts every child will be engaged on his or her own individual programme (and there will be sixth-formers doing work that will not necessarily differ at all, except in its particularity, from the work of a child in the first year). Emotional development does not follow a single track and cannot legitimately be organized step by step – it goes forward on many fronts at once, and must always be as open to regression as to progression. Trial and error is the creative way for most of us. A child's secondary-school arts education must be conceived of as a whole, and built from moment to moment. So curriculum-making becomes a creative activity requiring a creative teacher. Intensity of experience will be the keynote rather than breadth of cover. The pace of development will be erratic rather than steady. We expect to sense a growing confidence on the part of the pupils in their own expressive powers and increasing emotional and organizational independence in relation to their art work rather than the mere memorizing of information or the learning of skills (simply because they are thought to be easier to teach and to make the class easier to control and examine). The child's experience of the arts should be NOW: impulse is the touchstone. The rewards of working upon impulse are immediate – our actions have meaning as they occur. Engagement is absolutely of the essence in our work: to work with feeling you must be feeling. Which does not mean you should not be thinking too. And that goes for first years, fourth years, sixth-formers, the lot. There can be no defending the mass shedding of the arts that occurs in so many schools for so many pupils at the end of their third year. This is the arts curriculum they must have. And they must have an arts curriculum.

Towards a Whole Curriculum

Because the relation of the arts to representational action has not been properly understood, the arts are generally misplaced in the school curriculum. Their role has quite incorrectly been seen as practical – they have been thought of as belonging to the group of 'practical subjects' (see the Newsom Report, *Half our Future*, for instance). That the arts also operate symbolically has not been paid sufficient attention, with the result that they are felt to lie beyond the pale of the academic curriculum.

This is not the place to penetrate very deeply into the question of a whole or integrated curriculum in the secondary school, however it might be interesting just to sketch in one possible line of development even if only to illustrate the proper position, and so the proper role, of the arts. There have been several developments recently that have attempted to give a greater sense of coherence – perhaps most notable among them have been J. S. Bruner's project 'Man', and I. Goodlad's project 'A Mankind Curriculum'.

In re-thinking the secondary-school curriculum we must first distinguish between ways of knowing and fields of knowledge. The average school curriculum confuses the two at present, and schools are finding it increasingly difficult to maintain any sense of balance in the curriculum as the number of subjects goes on proliferating. (I was recently in a school that had decided 'personal development' and 'careers' were subjects in their own right.) My own formula is a simple one: you select what you feel are the essential fields of knowledge for any group of children and then project them as problems (projects) through the three media of representation. There are, as I have suggested in this book, two basic ways of knowing: impressive and expressive. There are three media of representation: iconic, enactive, and symbolic – all three common to the two basic ways of knowing. The principle of my Whole Curriculum is that key concepts would be identified and worked as projects drawing the various subject disciplines together and ensuring a full, rounded response to the expressive and impressive aspects of human experience. The key concepts (the problems to be projected) would be decided by the teaching staff as a whole and the particularity of the curriculum for specific groups of children worked out by the teams of teachers responsible for their learning. For example, a school might decide that the essential subject disciplines (fields of knowledge) were

Languages
Maths and the Sciences
Creative Arts
Humanities and Religion
Technology

These would constitute the school's teaching faculties. A concept such as 'Power' might be selected for investigation by all five faculties, with each giving the work a characteristically expressive or impressive emphasis. All five would be expected to make use of enactive, iconic, and symbolic media. With the creative arts given their due share of curriculum time and some of the non-arts subjects aware of the expressive potential of their own discipline we might be confident that there would be *a substantial amount of expressive learning going on*. We might expect work in history, geography, and language for example to issue in personal or group expressive images, and it would be true by the same token that there would be some impressive learning going on in the creative arts faculty. It would, of course, be up to each school staff to decide exactly the ratio of expressive to impressive learning for the curriculum as a whole.

The advantages of this proposal seem to me to be many. It guarantees that children become steeped in the basic ways of knowing and the different modes of representation and so become equipped to carry on their own learning. Such a curriculum could also effect a more balanced outlook on life and a much higher level of intrinsic involvement in learning itself, one of the by-products of which could well be fewer 'discipline' (alienation) problems. All projects would allow linked learning; some would inevitably achieve the level of genuine integration.

A Whole Curriculum includes expressive as well as impressive learning.

Good-enough Schools

We want those we teach to develop a deep respect for themselves – especially to feel deeply towards themselves. We want them to make their environment rich and significant (perhaps beautiful, certainly personal and personally meaningful). We want them to have the confidence to express their feelings and the openness to share their feelings with other people.

Arts teachers educate intelligent feeling: they help children acquire adequate expressive behaviour. To do so they need to work in schools that are 'good enough'. Good enough not just for children, but good enough for teachers too. And teachers cannot make them so on their own.

Selected Reading

Arguelles, Jose A., *The Transformative Vision: Reflections on the Nature an History of Human Impression*, Shambhala Publishers Inc., 1975.

Arnheim, Rudolf, *Visual Thinking*, Faber, 1970.

Bebey, Francis, *African Music: A People's Art* (trans. Josephine Bennett), Harrap, 1975.

Bruner, Jerome S., *Beyond the Information Given*, George Allen and Unwin, 1974.

Bruner, Jerome S., *On Knowing – Essays for the Left Hand*, Harvard University Press, 1962.

Cage, John, *Silence*, Calder & Boyars, 1971.

Cassirer, Ernst, *An Essay on Man*, Yale University Press, 1944.

Dewey, John, *Art as Experience*, Minton, Balch & Co., 1934.

Ehrenzweig, Anton, *The Hidden Order of Art: Study in the Psychology of Artistic Imagination*, Weidenfeld & Nicolson, 1967.

Fagan, John and Shepheard, Irma Lee (eds.), *Gestalt Therapy Now*, Penguin Books, 1972.

Fromm, Erich, *The Art of Loving*, George Allen & Unwin, 1975.

Gattegno, Caleb, *What We Owe Children*, Routledge & Kegan Paul, 1971.

Gattegno, Caleb, *Towards a Visual Culture*, Outerbridge & Dienstfrey, 1969.

Getzels, Jacob W. and Csikszentmihalyi, Mihaly, *The Creative Vision*, Wiley, 1976.

Giedion, S., *Mechanization Takes Command*, Oxford University Press, 1948.

Glasser, William, *Reality Therapy*, Harper & Row, 1965.

Itten, Johannes, *The Art of Colour*, Van Nostrand-Reinhold Co., 1973.

Itten, Johannes, *Design and Form – the Basic Course at the Bauhaus*, Thames & Hudson, 1964.

Langer, Suzanne K., *Mind: An Essay on Human Feeling*, Vol. 1, Vol. 2, John Hopkins University Press, 1972.

Maslow, Abraham H., *Toward a Psychology of Being*, Van Nostrand-Reinhold Co., 1968.

Paz, Octavio, *Conjunctions and Disjunctions*, Wildwood House, 1975.

Piaget, Jean, *Play, Dreams and Imitation in Childhood*, Routledge & Kegan Paul, 1951.

Read, Sir Herbert, *The Redemption of the Robot: My Encounter with Education through Art*, Triden Press, New York, 1966/Faber, 1970.

Rogers, Carl, *On Becoming a Person*, Houghton Mifflin, 1961.

Ross, Malcolm, Schools Council Working Paper 54. *Arts and the Adolescent*, Evans/Methuen Educational, 1975.

Winnicott, D. W., *Playing and Reality*, Tavistock Publications, 1971.

Witkin, Robert W., *The Intelligence of Feeling*, Heinemann Educational Books, 1974.

Appendices

Appendix 1
Examining Dance

Two examinations prepared by Susan Morris and operating at her school

A. Outline for CEE Examination Mode III Modern Educational Dance, July 1976, Associated Lancashire Schools Examining Board

Introduction

Movement is a mode of expression immediately available and inherent in all human beings. It is evident from studying the development of dance over the ages that the changing forms which it has taken have been very much influenced by the constraints of the environment in which it developed and have in fact been a reflection of the people and an expression of themselves.

Dance aims to use this readily available vehicle of expression, and through it to foster and develop the individual personalities of the pupils.

The areas of development sought are those which it is felt will be important and relevant in the future lives of these young people.

Aims

There are a number of overlapping and interrelated elements of personality development encompassed within the following aims: it is hoped to foster emotional, social and intellectual development, through movement where the body is used as the medium – through which these facets of development are realized.

1. To give individuals the opportunity of gaining experience, knowledge and understanding of those aspects of human behaviour lying within the affective domain. To help them to gain the skills required to realize their potential in this area.

   To help individuals to use the skills thus acquired to gain awareness and understanding of themselves, their fellow humans, and the environment in which they exist.

2. To develop the capacity for total involvement of mind and body, co-ordinated in a learning process.

3. To develop an enthusiasm for life and a living joy and delight in the real and imagined world, through awakening and fostering the inherent desire to be excited and stimulated by new experiences and the ability to control and learn from them.

4. Development of modes of thought which will be of use to individuals in their future lives, through placing them in situations in which they are required to take decisions, make judgements, solve problems, process information, etc., and take appropriate action.

5. To give individuals confidence in, and respect for themselves and for the individuality of others.

6. To give individuals the opportunity of experiencing the satisfaction and fulfilment gained from autonomous and corporate activity and achievement, leading to self-motivation and self-discipline.

7. To develop personal commitment to honesty, sincerity, and truth within the creative process.

8. To develop the intellectual capacity to articulate about the creative act, adding a new dimension to this intuitive activity.

9. To develop powers of recognition and association to enrich and re-validate the created form.

10. To develop powers of tenacity through the struggle to execute ideas to the best of one's ability.

11. To initiate individuals into finding form for their feelings in other modes of expression.

Specific areas of experience

Below is a list of specific areas of development which will be sought in the process of attempting to realize the stated aims:

1. (a) Development of perceptual skills.
   Awakening and enlivening channels of stimulation through the senses.
   (b) Manipulation of perceptual skills.
   Awakening and enlivening powers of observation, contemplation, exploration, analysis, discrimination, etc., through the search for, and use of, internal and external stimuli, and to enrich aesthetic awareness by this means.

2. Creative development.
   Developing the inherent potential for spontaneity of response, imagina-

tion, inventiveness, originality, etc., by providing situations in which these things are expected, accepted and commended.

3. Intellectual development.

Developing the ability to be able to control and manipulate perceptive and creative capabilities within the process of doing and making, using recognition, validation, justification, assessment and re-assessment, etc., involving objective monitering of one's own subjective responses and the ability to articulate and control these. Thus evolving a form of essence and truth embodying the activity of the process.

4. Development of self-concept.

Through the areas of development stated, to give individuals the opportunity to establish their own identity in the scheme of things. The chance to externalize their feelings, thoughts and ideas in movement, and explore their inner responses in a controlled way, amongst others who are also striving to find themselves.

5. Social development.

Fostering social development and awareness of group relationships and group interaction through providing situations in which communication between individuals is essential to solve the task set.

Objectives

To develop skills which will enable the individuals to gain optimum control of mind with body, when movement is used as the medium of expression.

Study of specific areas of movement experience should:

(a) be used to give inspiration or stimulus in order to initiate a creative response.

(b) arise out of the individuals' desire to find the appropriate movement form to embody the feelings/ideas which they are striving to express.

(c) be sought to extend the individuals' movement vocabulary and take them into new areas of experience.

Basic movement skills

1. Mobility of the body as a unit and of its individual parts.
2. Co-ordination of whole body movement and of different body parts one with another.
3. Balance and control of body weight.

Expressive movement skills

To enable individuals to give life and meaning to movement. Ability to create and recognize that movement has a feeling content created by the tension, speed, and use of space.

Development of this awareness of feeling content should be experienced:

1. Firstly through the natural and spontaneous expression of emotions, moods, atmosphere, etc., in a representational context.
2. Secondly as inherent elements of any created movement, representational or abstract.
3. Thirdly be articulated to create innovation of movement experience in a purely abstract context.

Skills of relationship

Ability to create relationships and set up channels of communication:
   (a) within the body between one body part and another.
   (b) between dancer and space, sounds, words, objects, etc., in all situations in which the dancer is solely concerned with herself.
   (c) between one dancer and another through improvisation, exploration, analysis, etc., of the possibilities encompassed within a particular situation (duo, trio, group), (i) within the context of responding personally to the situation or (ii) within the constraints of identifying with a particular attitude of mind.

Choreographic skills

Ability to manipulate, movement skills, expressive skills, and skills of relationship, and from them to create form, through the recognition that movement has shape, imagery, rhythm, pattern, structure, dimension, etc.
   (a) to discriminate in movement exploration within the context of the afore-mentioned choreographic elements.
   (b) to select and organize the movement ideas into choreography.
   (c) to recognize the finished form in the four stated facets.

The integrated process

These areas are experienced as one activity and will all be equally significant within any creative process. All these skills will be important right from the beginning of the individual's experience in movement; no natural progression from one skill to another is sought, but rather a clarifying and deepening of the individual's understanding, which will enable him to confidently carry out the creative process. It is hoped that eventually the process of manipulating these skills becomes a natural and self-steered activity in which individuals eventually become autonomous.

The subjective/objective balance

Within the making of a dance the dancer should develop the ability to oscillate between spontaneous and subjective activity and involvement, and objective awareness and consideration, being able to create visual imaginary whose feeling content and visual manifestation are articulated to achieve a state of optimum compatibility.

The Examination

This will be in three parts: marks awarded will be directly related to the aims and objectives stated.
1. Practical work — 60%
2. Written   — 30%
3. Oral   — 10%

1. Practical
(A) Prepared work:
  (i) *Solo (10%)*. Marks will be awarded for:
    (a) indication that the source of inspiration has been explored, analysed and understood
    (b) the response to the stimuli is interpreted clearly
    (c) creative use of movement knowledge and understanding
    (d) movement ideas given clear form
  (ii) *Duo or Trio (10%)*; *Group (10%)*. Marks will be awarded for:
    (a) originality in use of the relationship to express the ideas
    (b) inventive use of movement
    (c) awareness and control of the images created
    (d) imaginative use of choreographic skills in creating forms
(B) Unprepared work:
  (i) *Solo (15%)*. Marks will be awarded for:
    (a) spontancity of response
    (b) involvement in exploring the idea
    (c) establishment of movement ideas
  (ii) *Group (15%)*. Marks will be awarded for:
    (a) ability to pool ideas, select and adapt them to suit the group
    (b) setting up of relationships within the group
    (c) own identity within the group clearly defined
    (d) creating of organized choreographic structure

2. Written
This will consist of three essays based upon the areas of experience stated in the aims and objectives. Marks will be awarded:
(a) for understanding of experience and knowledge gained through movement;
(b) for exercising of perceptive skills in the collection and presentation of work;
(c) for creative use and presentation of ideas;
(d) for clear discussion and communication of ideas;
(e) for individuality of approach and self-identity with the ideas presented.
As with all aspects of the work covered by this course these essays should allow for the individuality of the pupils. The statement of fact is not to be sought but rather the communication of realizations which the student has made and which she feels are significant. Allowing for the individual to

explore and extend her knowledge in whichever area she feels motivated towards.

3. Oral
To take the form of a discussion in which the pupils will have the opportunity to explain their work, answer questions, and generally clarify their ideas to the examiners.

Moderation
Prepared practical work: the moderator will be required to confirm or adapt the teacher's assessment.
Unprepared practical work: the moderator will work with the teacher on the day of the examination.
Written work: the moderator will be required to select a cross-section of work and confirm or adapt the teacher's assessment.

CEE Dance

Written work – 30 % of the total marks awarded.

Three essays must be completed and submitted for assessment. Below is a list of essay titles. Number 1 is a compulsory essay question – two other titles must be selected from the list. Each essay is marked out of 10 % of the total marks.

1. Discuss the role of dance in the development of the individual personality in relation to developing awareness of sensitivity towards and understanding of (a) oneself; (b) others; (c) the environment in which we exist. You should also note any other significant areas of development which you have experienced. Give examples of your own experience and that observed in others.
2. Select an idea for dance and explain how you would work out a solo dance based upon that idea.
   Describe (i) The source of inspiration and why it was selected.
           (ii) The movements created to embody the ideas.
          (iii) The expressive quality of the movements.
           (iv) The relationships established (1) within the body; (2) between the dancer and the chosen space; (3) the choreography.
   In terms of words and notation include a description of music/costume/chosen space/make-up/props, etc.
3. What skills do you feel it is necessary for a dancer to master before she is able to express herself adequately?
4. Choose one of the group dances which you have created recently and describe the process involved in the evolution of that dance.
5. Consider the following words in relation to Dance:Stimuli/Inspiration/Transition/Climax/Image/Momentum/Mobility/Co-ordination/Balance/Control/Flow/Rhythm/Mood/Texture/Colour/Quality/Relationship/Form/Shape/Pattern/Structure/Dimension.
   Either: Choose one word as an essay title, e.g. Shape in Dance, or: Select a number of words which are relevant to your own movement experience and describe what they mean to you.
   (2 essays may be selected from the above question.)

6. Describe how you would choreograph a group dance based on an idea
   selected by you. Describe (a) Movements
                         (b) Expression
                         (c) Use of group relationships
                         (d) Choreographic forms
   In terms of words and notation make a description of costumes, make-up,
   props, lighting, etc. Imagine your budget is limitless.
7. Discuss the relationship between dance and other art forms. Give examples of your own experience of such relationships.
   You may choose one art form, e.g. essay title 'Music and Dance' or divide
   your essay into small sections, e.g. Art, Music, Poetry, Prose, Drama,
   Photogaphy, Sculpture, or any combination which you feel might
   interest you.

B. Outline for CSE Examination Mode III Dance, Associated Lancashire Examining Board

Dance is one of the earliest and most natural forms for the expression of
feeling and is a powerful means of integrating internal and external stimuli.

It has a long and varied history, changing its form according to the
prevailing ritualistic and other demands, and has always been strongly
linked with other art forms.

The recent widespread revival of interest in dance reflects both its lasting
revelance and its particular contemporary importance in servicing as a
direct and immediately available vehicle for creative self-expression for
large numbers of young people striving to find their identity in an increasingly sophisticated formalized world.

Aims

To develop the capacity for, and delight in, creative self-expression through
imaginative movement based upon kinaesthetic awareness, and control of
the body as the expressive medium.

To develop sensitivity and refined intuitive responses to stimuli by this
means.

To develop self-awareness and esteem for personal skills and creativity.

To give pupils confidence in their own individuality through the controlled exploration of their responses.

Through this and group work, to develop respect for the individuality of
others and the significance of the added dimension of corporate forms of
expression.

To enrich aesthetic awareness of the environment through the search for
and use of external stimuli in dance.

To add vigour and richness to intuitive response by systematic and progressive exploration and analysis of movement.

To deepen enjoyment of, and powers of discrimination in other art forms
through their integration with dance, in terms of both direct experience and
of the increasing use of dance in visual mass media.

To initiate pupils into finding form for their feelings in other modes of
expression.

Objectives

1. To establish an awareness of the pupils' natural movement vocabulary.
2. To extend and challenge individuals to continually increase their vocabulary.
3. To develop skills which will enable them to gain more control of the body as a medium for expression:
   (a) basic movement skills;
   (b) expressive movement skills;
   (c) skills of relationship;
   (d) choreographic skills.
   Study of such skills should arise out of the pupils' desire to find the right movement form to embody their ideas, or be used as a stimulus for creative activity.
4. To develop the ability to use and manipulate movement abilities:
   (a) as a means of self-expression;
   (b) as a means of communication;
   (c) as a way of objectively relating an idea;
   (d) as a form of expressing a subjective response to a situation.

The Examination

This will consist of three parts.
1. A practical examination carrying 30% of the total marks.
2. Course work carrying 55%:40% practical, 15% written.
3. Individual project carrying 15%.
Marks may also be awarded to pupils for explanation and discussion of work with the examiners on the day of the examination.

Part 1
Practical examination 30%.
(*a*) Unprepared work 20%.
Spontaneous improvisation on a subject set by the teacher or moderator. A wide variety of stimuli may be used, e.g. music of any type, words, poetry, sculpture, slides, props, etc.
In this section two dances will be created:
1. A solo carrying 10%.
2. Work with others a duo, trio or larger group – to be stated on the day of the examination carrying 10%.
Marks will be awarded for the following:
1. Solo – Spontaneity of response.
             Sensitivity to the stimuli.
             Involvement in movement exploration.
             Establishing of movement ideas.
2. Group – Sensitivity and adaption to the group situation.
             Establishing of relationships within the group.
             Manipulation of the group in the expression of ideas.
(*b*) Prepared work 10%.
A solo on a theme to be chosen by the candidate.

Marks will be awarded for the following:
    sensitivity to the theme;
    inventiveness;
    compositional awareness and clarity;
    communicative quality;
    general impression.

Part 11

Course work 55%.

(a) Practical 40%.

This will consist of four dances prepared by the pupils under the guidance of the teacher. One of the dances to be shown on the day of the examination.

Marks will be awarded for the following:
    Movement knowledge and understanding and appropriate use of such in self-expression.
    Awareness of one's own identity in a group, and one's role and adaptability in such a situation.
    Involvement in group choreography.

(b) Written work 15%.

The pupils notes on the work covered in practical activity, during the fifth year of study, should be submitted for assessment.

Marks will be awarded for the following:
    Understanding and analysis of movement, both individual and group.
    Individual interpretation and presentation of work.

Part 111

Individual project 15%.

The pupils will be required to make a study of some specific subject related to dance, e.g. primitive dance, gesture, music and dance, abstract expression, choreography, etc.

Marks will be awarded for:
    Extension of the pupils' own knowledge and understanding of the subject.
    Depth and/or range of study.
    Pupils' use of powers of discrimination in selecting ideas.
    Imaginative use of information collected.

Moderation

The moderator will be required to assess pupils written work.

The moderator will also be required to attend the practical examination and assess the pupils' work independantly, finally moderating the teacher's marks in relation to the standards required.

Appendix 2
The First-year General Studies
Drama Course

Prepared by Ben Bradnack

What follows is only an outline of the minimum of activities which are used consistently with these groups. Within and beyond them are a large number of variations and extensions, some of which can be found, for example, in *Improvisation for the Theatre* by Viola Spolin (North Western University Press) and the Appendices to *Hopes for Great Happenings*, by Albert Hunt (Eyre Methuen); but most of which depend more on use of material which can be drawn from the students themselves, and the local environment in which they are working. The more one works with a group, the less one is likely to want to resort to strict 'game' situations, and the more to the material of observable everyday life. Clearly, other uses can be made of this material than that which I make of it; clearly, other games are appropriate to pursuing the same ends. What I have tried to describe is what I actually do, insofar as that can be described accurately; and insofar as I am consistent in the things I do.

Games

Starters
Matthew, Mark, Luke and John
The whole group sit in a circle, and are named around the circle, Chairman, Matthew, Mark, Luke, John, One, Two, and numbers down to the last player in the circle, who is Hell. Chairman starts the game by sending the message, which can only consist of 'Chairman to. . . . . (name or number of player)', and it is then that player's turn to send the message '(Name or Number) to (Another name or number)'. Nobody may send messages to Hell. If a player when it is his/her turn, hesitates, stumbles, says something which is inappropriate or says nothing, that player goes down to Hell; and everyone below the player who boobed, in the hierarchy of the circle (Chairman at the top, Hell at the bottom), moves up one chair, and takes

on the name or number of the player who was immediately above them. The object of the game is for every player to struggle up the hierarchy to get the Chairman's job. No pauses are allowed.

Zoom-Screech

A game of two words, and the problem is to be looking in the right direction to say whichever word you choose to say when it is your turn. Sit in a circle. The player due to start has to say 'Zoom' to one of the two people sitting on either side of him/her. It is then that player's turn. The response must be immediate, and one of the two words. If 'Zoom', then it must be said to the third person round the circle; if 'Screech', then back to the first person. Whoever was being looked at, it is now their turn. But then (the tricky part) the word chosen depends on where it came from. For example; A to B – Zoom, B to A – Screech, it is now A's turn, and A must say either (to B) – Screech, or to the player on A's other side (Z) – Zoom. The analogy is with driving a car. The driver looks in the direction the car is already going, to make the noise of continuance – Zoom – and back towards where the movement is coming from, for the sound of brakes – Screech. It is possible for two players to spend the whole time saying Screech to each other, leaving everyone else out. The object of the game, though, is to try to get all other players to have 'accidents' (i.e. make mistakes), when they have to drop out (it can be played so that more than one accident is allowed per player; but sudden death is better in closing stages when some players have been 'killed'). Once all but two are dead, you cannot go any further.

Alphabetical pass the parcel

Sit in a circle with one player out and not looking at the circle. The players in the circle pass round an object (parcel), and the player out says a letter (not X). Whoever is holding the parcel when the letter is announced has to pass the parcel on, and say three words (not proper names) beginning with that letter. Meanwhile the rest of the circle hand on the parcel to get it back to the player before he can say the three words. If they succeed, he goes out, and the previous player out takes his place. If the player succeeds in his three words, the same player out stays out, the parcel passes again, and he names a new letter, still not looking at the circle to see where the parcel is. When players find the number of words too easy or difficult (it depends on the size of the circle of course) the number can be changed. It can also be changed for individual players, so that one may be trying for seven or eight while another is trying for three; targets can be made increasingly difficult individually.

Trust games
Falling about

A group of about six players stand in a circle, surrounding one player who stands with eyes closed, feet together and arms folded, and tries, without bending legs or taking feet off the ground, to fall over. The rest of the group have to earn the trust of the player in the centre, enough enable him to fall without opening eyes or moving feet, however late they leave their catching. Each player has a turn in the centre.

One word each

Many versions of this, but the central features are that everyone (in a circle) contributes one word at a time, round the circle, to a story, and that there are no rules about what can or cannot be said, except that it must be said fast. Use is thereby made of *whatever* is offered, and contributions are not evaluated because the story must be kept going without pause.

Variations include group letter-writing, and group interrogation of an individual, or by an individual, in which the group offer one word each round the circle, as questions or answers to the individual.

Mirror Games

Many versions of this too, but the central point is that, in pairs, one player mirrors the other; thus responsibility is taken for others, and individual behaviour is merged in group (of two) behaviour.

Pair-bonds

Passing the baby

A pair have an object between them. A holds it, and gives all the reasons available why B should have it rather than A; and then hands over the object. B cannot refuse to receive it, and having received it, must give all the reasons available why A should have it, not B, without using any of A's reasons; and then hands it back to A. The object is to try to get the other player holding the object, incapable of articulating any reasons for handing the object back.

Fortunately/unfortunately

A tries to describe in one sentence arrival at college one morning. After that one sentence, B can say one sentence, prefixed with 'Unfortunately . . .', to suggest how the arrival at college never quite happened; A can then reply with one sentence beginning 'Fortunately. . . . .', to make the arrival happen; and it goes on until one player cannot compete any longer.

Meeting and parting

A and B meet from opposite sides of the room, playing characters other than A and B, in a situation other than the room, without any prior planning, and try to create a real situation, in which these characters

(a) meet, have a conversation, and part, going on in the direction they were going, and

(b) meet, have a conversation, and part, each going back in the direction they came from.

This is an introduction to basic improvisation, where central importance is attached to receiving and giving information in a social situation in which parameters are established, but detail is not.

Simple role play

A play's A's own parent, teacher or employer. B plays A, in a situation in which the parent/teacher/employer tries to exercise authority over the other, and the other tries to resist the exercise of that authority.

Improvisation in groups

Helping

A player goes into the centre of the circle. The others try to give the player in the centre a role, by identifying what he is doing; and that identification is made, not by saying what is happening, but by going into the centre to help the first player to do it. The object is to get the first player out of the circle, but in the process, of course, the second may be left in; and it is the responsibility of the others in the circle to make sure that the activity which the first player was identified as carrying on, is carried on successfully, and that all players get 'off' (i.e. out of the circle), by 'helping' in the activity till it is brought to a satisfactory conclusion.

Knock knock
One person leaves the room and knocks on the door; the remainder create the situation and the identity of the outsider by their reactions in admitting (or not) the outsider to the room.

Status
There are all sorts of variations of this, but the central situation is one in which the players are given status within a defined social situation (a family, a firm, a school staff), and then either operate that hierarchy, or disrupt in such a way as to get themselves to the top of it.

Instant theatre
This is an activity which requires skill on the part of the teacher. From any name, gesture, newspaper story, or idea of the group, all suggestions of causes and consequences are accepted *from* the group, to build up a background from which a set of characters and a situation are created for improvisation. This improvisation is then used as a further source of discussion of causes and consequences, leading to another improvisation; building all the time towards some satisfactory climax or consummation, by asking the right questions of the group, and knowing when to switch from discussion to improvisation. Very difficult, but demanding above all that *all* suggestions are accepted: otherwise the effects of discrimination are to limit contribution.

Appendix 3
A Modular Mode III Syllabus (Amended)
Southern Regional Examinations Board
Drama and Theatre Arts
First Assessments 1978

Introduction

The Modular Mode III proposals which follow result from a course which has been designed by a symposium of teachers for groups of children beginning the course in September 1976. Due to the wide range of ability within these groups it is to be expected that gradings may range from 1 to 5 and 'ungraded'.

In each educational institution at least one teacher will be responsible for the course.

Aims

(a) To provide a socializing factor for developing children.
(b) To provide a course of instruction leading to a greater awareness of the individual.
(c) To provide a means whereby a greater awareness and appreciation of drama may be gained.
(d) To offer scope to the developing adolescents' imagination giving it an outlet in constructive exercise.
(e) To extend the students' communication skills.

Objectives

Candidates are expected to achieve the following educational objectives which are to be assessed throughout the course.
Basic skills:
  1. Use of the voice
  2. Use of the body in space

3. Use of the whole person in a variety of situations
4. Use of resources
Response:
  5. Personal contributions in group situations
  6. Communicative relationships with others
  7. Spatial relationships with others
Sensitivity:
  8. Sensitivity to the ideas of others
  9. The ability to respond appropriately to a stimulus
10. Growing awareness of the need for good timing
11. The ability to recognize dramatic shape and to use contrasts
Personal Qualities:
12. The degree of personal involvement in a particular dramatic activity
13. The ability to concentrate (and eventually total absorption)
14. The ability to evaluate one's personal contribution
15. The ability to be constructive in any group discussion
    To: (a) justify what has been attempted
        (b) to distinguish and clarify ideas and objectives
        (c) create further opportunities for exploiting ideas
        (d) recognize unavoidable barriers, ceilings and limitations
16. The ability to relate character organically to situation.

Content

Module 1 – Compulsory Improvisation (Objectives 1–15)
This is envisaged as a continuous module leading, by means of continuous assessment, to a practical and a discussion with the external moderators.
Module 2 – Optional Dance (Objectives 2, 5, 6, 8, 9, 10, 11, 15)
This is envisaged as a one-term Module to develop style and the ability to move creatively and purposefully in order to interpret and communicate ideas, whether concrete or abstract, of character, mood or atmosphere. Examination is by continuous assessment leading to a practical presentation and a discussion with the external moderators.
Module 3 – Optional Characterization (Objectives 1, 2, 3, 4, 8, 9, 16)
This is envisaged as a one-term module to build a store of physical characters, to develop a versatility of the spoken word in dialect and accent, and a realization that most people play several different roles in their everyday life; the playing of family roles and the exploration of characterization by placement in different situations. Examination is by continuous assessment leading to a practical with the external moderators.
Module 4 – Optional Plays (Objectives 4, 5, 8, 9, 10, 11, 12, 14 15abd)
It is intended that this Module be continuously assessed and marked in the following four categories:
    (a) By reading at least four plays from the list (objectives 9 and 15b)
    (b) In working on plays with written work, models, etc. (objectives 4, 10, 11, 15d)
    (c) Performance at external assessment, by taking some part in some aspect of the production of one play on the syllabus (objectives 5, 8, 12)
    (d) In discussion of the performance at external assessment (objectives 14, 15a)

It is suggested that the categories of plays may be used to compare or contrast plays within a category or between categories; but it is strongly recommended that not more than two plays should be drawn from any one category. Examination is by continuous assessment, evidence of work on each play, performance of one play, and discussion after.

1. (a) Any one-act play by Chekov
   (b) *In The Zone* by Eugene O'Neill
2. (a) *School Play* by David Howarth
   (b) *Ernie's Incredible Illucinations* by Alan Ayckbourn
   (c) *The Rising Generation* by Ann Jellicoe
   (d) *Ars Longa, Vita Brevis* by John Arden
3. (a) *The Exception And The Rule* by Bertolt Brecht
   (b) *The Measures Taken* by Bertolt Brecht
   (c) *Woyzeck* by G. Buchner
4. (a) *The Underground Lovers* by Tardieu
   (b) *The Bald Prima Donna* by Eugène Ionesco
   (c) *The Hole* by N. F. Simpson
   (d) *The Martyrdom of Peter Ohey* by S. Mrozek
   (e) *Zoo Story* by Edward Albee
5. (a) *The Erpingham Camp* by Joe Orton
   (b) *The Kitchen* by Arnold Wesker
   (c) *The Dumb Waiter* by Harold Pinter
6. Any other single play of not less than 20 mins.

Module 5 – Optional Group Project (Objectives 1, 2, 4, 5, 6, 8, 11, 12, 14, 15abcd)
A group presentation is to be devised and performed collectively, and a record should be kept of the part played by the teacher and students in developing it. The performance must have an audience of at least one person, and last not less than 20 mins. Examination is by continuous assessment on work towards the performance (objectives 4, 5, 6, 8, 11, 12, 15bc), by performance (objectives 1, 2, 10), and a discussion after the performance (objectives 14, 15ad).

Module 6 – Optional Mime (Objectives 2, 5, 6, 8, 9, 11, 13, 15, 10, 7)
The Module will be continuously assessed. The students will be expected to work up to a standard of mime which will enable their work to be understood. The work will involve the students' emotions which they should be able to convey easily and comprehensively. The students will work on two levels. One level is of speech communication through mime, using situations, e.g. involving playing at being foreigners in strange countries. This will also, as a side issue, be able to be used to help an understanding of deaf and mute people and their frustrations in trying to understand and be understood by speaking, hearing people. On the other level, the students will use mime to portray their emotions rather than using their mime to take the place of speech. This part of the module will lead to the students using their mime skills to aid their speech skills in theatrical and improvisation work.

Module 7 – Optional Stagecraft (Objectives 4, 5, 6, 9, 11, 12, 15)
The students should gain practical competence in ONE of the following, the use of lighting, costume design and construction, make-up, set design and construction, the uses of sound or stage and theatre structure. They may work either as a group or solo, and could produce a possible stage production. They will be examined by a practical demonstration before external

moderators in ONE of the above areas which THEY will have selected, followed by a discussion on the artistic possibilities of their chosen aspect. They must show evidence in discussion of a firm factual knowledge of both technical and artistic aspects of their chosen subject. Although this module culminates in a demonstration and discussion, it will be continuously assessed.

Module 8 – Optional Solo Project (Objectives 4, 8, 11, 12, 14)
Subjects for the project will be chosen by the individual candidate. The project may be presented in the form of a written study or as a miscellany of photographs, drawings, recordings, models, etc., linked and unified by written notes. It should incorporate an inquiry and should not be a major undertaking but on a scale manageable by an individual.

The examination of the project shall also include a discussion between the external moderators and the candidate, as this will help to remove the pressure on the less able candidate to offer written work.

Module 9 – Optional Speech (Objectives 1, 4, 6, 10, 11, 12, 13, 15)
This should be either a group or solo presentation and the module should consist of basic speech training, class repetition, intonation and inflexion, and voice characterization. It should be examined by a polished, spoken, scripted or unscripted, solo or group presentation, followed by a discussion of the work and techniques presented. It must be stressed that all choices affecting the presentation should be made by the candidate and not the teacher.

Assessment

All candidates must take Module 1 – Compulsory Improvisation – and 2 of the remaining 8 Optional Modules.
The 9 Modules are to be assessed as follows:
Module 1 – Compulsory Improvisation
This module will be continuously assessed by the teacher over the entire course. During moderation, the external moderators will see the candidates doing improvisation work and may discuss such work with the students. The demonstration and discussion are merely an attempt to aid the moderators by giving them a tiny personal knowledge of each candidate.
Module 3 – Optional Dance
This module will be continuously assessed by the teacher over a period of one term and moderated by external moderators through a practical present-ation and a discussion with the students in an attempt to aid the moderators by giving them a tiny personal knowledge of each candidate.
Module 3 – Optional Characterization
This module will be continuously assessed by the teacher over a period of one term and moderated by means of a practical demonstration by the students before external moderators so as to aid the moderators by giving them a tiny personal knowledge of each candidate.
Module 4 – Optional Plays
This module will be assessed in four ways. First, by reading at least four plays from the prescribed list and being continually assessed by the teacher. Secondly, in working on plays with written work, models, etc., and contin-uously assessed by the teacher. Thirdly, in performance at external assess-ment, by taking some part in some aspect of the production of one play on

the syllabus; being marked by the teacher and moderated by external moderators. Finally, in discussion of the performance at external assessment; being marked by the teacher and moderated by the external moderators.

Module 5 – Optional Group Project
This module will be assessed in three ways. First, continuous assessment by the teacher of the students' work towards the performance. Secondly, by performance at moderation, which is marked by the teacher and then moderated by external moderators. Thirdly, by discussion after the performance, which is marked by the teacher and then moderated by external moderators.

Module 6 – Optional Mime
This module will be continuously assessed by the teacher and moderated by external moderators by means of a practical demonstration by the students. This will aid the moderators by giving them a tiny personal knowledge of each candidate.

Module 7 – Optional Stagecraft
This module will be continuously assessed by the teacher and moderated by external moderators by means of a practical demonstration by the students clearly indicating their expertise in their chosen aspect of the module. This will be followed by a discussion in which the candidates must also show their knowledge of the artistic potential of their chosen aspect.

Module 8 – Optional Solo Project
This module will be assessed in a written project form by the teacher. At moderation the external moderators may discuss the project with the candidate as an aid to giving them a tiny personal knowledge of each candidate.

Module 9 – Optional Speech
This module shall be continuously assessed by the teacher and moderated by means of a polished, spoken, scripted or unscripted, solo or group presentation, followed by a discussion of the work and techniques presented, as an aid to moderators by giving them a tiny personal knowledge of each candidate.

It is important to stress the following two points:
(a) *The Moderator's function is to moderate the teacher's assessment of each pupil* and not to act as an external examiner. Such performances, practical demonstrations and discussions included in the modules are intended as an aid to the moderators by giving them a tiny personal knowledge of each candidate, not an excuse to award marks.
(b) *Before arrival of moderators, the teacher must have undertaken and recorded internal assessment.*

Moderation Arrangements

It is recommended that moderation and marking should be as follows:

Term One   — Foundation Course assessed by teacher only.
Term Two   — Foundation Course assessed by teacher only.
Term Three   — Foundation Course assessed by teacher only.
Term Four   — Foundation Course and assessment of 2 modules moderated by external moderators.
Term Five   — Foundation Course and assessment of 1 of the remaining 7 modules then moderated by external moderators.

Assessment Grid

The following assessment grid indicates the weightings of the various objectives within each of the 9 modules. For simplicity it is indicated in marks rather than percentages. The module percentage grid which follows the assessment grid, indicates the percentages and the 28 choices available to teachers within this syllabus. Finally, there follows a marking scheme.

ASSESSMENT GRID

Object No.	Module 1	Module 2	Module 3	Module 4 a	b	c	d	Module 5 a	b	c	Module 6	Module 7	Module 8	Module 9
1	6	–	14	–	–	–	–	–	3	–	–	–	–	20
2	7	16	14	–	–	–	–	–	2	–	10	–	–	–
3	8	–	–	–	–	–	–	–	–	–	–	–	–	–
4	6	–	10	–	–	20	–	15	–	–	–	30	50	5
5	6	4	–	–	–	10	–	10	–	–	10	5	–	–
6	7	16	–	–	–	–	–	10	–	–	25	10	–	5
7	6	–	–	–	–	–	–	–	–	–	10	–	–	–
8	8	10	19	–	–	5	–	10	–	–	5	–	5	–
9	6	14	19	10	–	–	–	–	–	–	5	10	–	–
10	5	8	–	–	5	–	–	–	5	–	5	–	–	15
11	8	16	–	–	10	–	–	10	–	–	10	15	15	20
12	7	–	–	–	–	5	–	5	–	–	–	5	5	5
13	7	–	–	–	–	–	–	–	–	–	10	–	–	5
14	7	–	–	–	–	–	5	–	–	5	–	–	25	–
15a	2	4	–	–	–	–	5	–	–	5	3	10	–	10
15b	2	4	–	10	–	–	–	5	–	–	2	5	–	5
15c	1	4	–	–	–	–	–	10	–	–	3	5	–	5
15d	1	4	–	–	15	–	–	–	–	5	2	5	–	5
16	–	–	24	–	–	–	–	–	–	–	–	–	–	–
Marks Total	100	100	100	100				100			100	100	100	100

Weighting in Marks per Module

All candidates must do Module 1 and any 2 of the remaining 8 Optional Modules, which gives a total of 300 marks ÷ 3 which gives 100%.

N.B.

MODULE 4			MODULE 5		
(a)	Reading	20 marks	(a)	Work on Project	75 marks
(b)	Work produced	50 marks	(b)	Performance	10 marks
(c)	Performance	20 marks	(c)	Discussion	15 marks
(d)	Discussion	10 marks			

MODULE PERCENTAGE GRID

Choice No.	1st Module	%	2nd Module	%	3rd Module	%	Total %
1	1	$33\frac{1}{3}$	2	$33\frac{1}{3}$	3	$33\frac{1}{3}$	100
2	1	$33\frac{1}{3}$	2	$33\frac{1}{3}$	4	$33\frac{1}{3}$	100
3	1	$33\frac{1}{3}$	2	$33\frac{1}{3}$	5	$33\frac{1}{3}$	100
4	1	$33\frac{1}{3}$	2	$33\frac{1}{3}$	6	$33\frac{1}{3}$	100
5	1	$33\frac{1}{3}$	2	$33\frac{1}{3}$	7	$33\frac{1}{3}$	100
6	1	$33\frac{1}{3}$	2	$33\frac{1}{3}$	8	$33\frac{1}{3}$	100
7	1	$33\frac{1}{3}$	2	$33\frac{1}{3}$	9	$33\frac{1}{3}$	100
8	1	$33\frac{1}{3}$	3	$33\frac{1}{3}$	4	$33\frac{1}{3}$	100
9	1	$33\frac{1}{3}$	3	$33\frac{1}{3}$	5	$33\frac{1}{3}$	100
10	1	$33\frac{1}{3}$	3	$33\frac{1}{3}$	6	$33\frac{1}{3}$	100
11	1	$33\frac{1}{3}$	3	$33\frac{1}{3}$	7	$33\frac{1}{3}$	100
12	1	$33\frac{1}{3}$	3	$33\frac{1}{3}$	8	$33\frac{1}{3}$	100
13	1	$33\frac{1}{3}$	3	$33\frac{1}{3}$	9	$33\frac{1}{3}$	100
14	1	$33\frac{1}{3}$	4	$33\frac{1}{3}$	5	$33\frac{1}{3}$	100
15	1	$33\frac{1}{3}$	4	$33\frac{1}{3}$	6	$33\frac{1}{3}$	100
16	1	$33\frac{1}{3}$	4	$33\frac{1}{3}$	7	$33\frac{1}{3}$	100
17	1	$33\frac{1}{3}$	4	$33\frac{1}{3}$	8	$33\frac{1}{3}$	100
18	1	$33\frac{1}{3}$	4	$33\frac{1}{3}$	9	$33\frac{1}{3}$	100
19	1	$33\frac{1}{3}$	5	$33\frac{1}{3}$	6	$33\frac{1}{3}$	100
20	1	$33\frac{1}{3}$	5	$33\frac{1}{3}$	7	$33\frac{1}{3}$	100
21	1	$33\frac{1}{3}$	5	$33\frac{1}{3}$	8	$33\frac{1}{3}$	100
22	1	$33\frac{1}{3}$	5	$33\frac{1}{3}$	9	$33\frac{1}{3}$	100
23	1	$33\frac{1}{3}$	6	$33\frac{1}{3}$	7	$33\frac{1}{3}$	100
24	1	$33\frac{1}{3}$	6	$33\frac{1}{3}$	8	$33\frac{1}{3}$	100
25	1	$33\frac{1}{3}$	6	$33\frac{1}{3}$	9	$33\frac{1}{3}$	100
26	1	$33\frac{1}{3}$	7	$33\frac{1}{3}$	8	$33\frac{1}{3}$	100
27	1	$33\frac{1}{3}$	7	$33\frac{1}{3}$	9	$33\frac{1}{3}$	100
28	1	$33\frac{1}{3}$	8	$33\frac{1}{3}$	9	$33\frac{1}{3}$	100

COMBINED MARKING SCHEME

SCHOOL		CENTRE NUMBER				
CANDIDATES NAME		CANDIDATES NUMBER				
SUBJECT		SUBJECT NUMBER				

	Term 1	Term 2	Term 3	Term 4		Term 5	
Objective	*Teach*	*Teach*	*Teach*	*Teach*	*Mod*	*Teach*	*Mod*
1							
2							
3							
4							
5							
6							
7							
8							
9							
10							
11							
12							
13							
14							
15a							
15b							
15c							
15d							
16							
	100	100	100	200		100	

Total .... out of 300 marks

÷ 3 results in...............% for the Course.

Appendix 4
(Revised) CSE Mode III Drama Syllabus for 1974 Southern Regional Examinations Board

Equal importance will be attached to work in FOUR areas: improvisation; group activity; study and performance of plays; projects on areas of individual interest.

1. *Improvisation*

Creative energy
Response to the idea/situation: characterization; use of information. Operations of the conventions of improvisation; nature and extent of the appropriate communication/shaping.

2. *Group Activity*

The whole group will be expected to offer, and be assessed on, at least two 'group activities', devised and performed collectively. At least one of these will take place in each year of the course.

The subject and conditions of performance will be decided by the group, but it will be performed live, to an audience, and last not less than half an hour.

3. *Plays*

Work on at least one play from each of the following sections:
(a) Chekov — any one-act play
(b) Buchner — *Woszeck*
(c) Sheridan — *St. Patrick's Day*
(d) Brecht — *The Exception and the Rule*

(e) Wesker   — *The Kitchen*
    Orton   — *The Erpingham Camp*
(f) Simpson   — *The Hole*
    Ionesco   — *The Chairs, The Lesson, The Bald Prima Donna*
(g) Albee   — *Zoo Story*
    Pinter   — *The Birthday Party, The Collection, The Dumb Waiter, Short Sketches*
(h) Howarth   — *School Play*
(i) Any other plays which the group may want to do.

Work on these plays will consist of detailed reading followed by:
    design work
    models
    production notes

All candidates will take part, either as actors or technicians, or both, in a performance of at least one play drawn from the categories above; and will be expected to contribute and be assessed on at least one of the following aspects:

(a) Acting
(b) Costume
(c) Set
(d) Lighting
(e) Business Management
(f) Props
(g) Production

in relation to this performance.

4. *Projects*

Each student should keep a file, which will contain:
    (a) written material relating to 1, 2, and 3 above;
    (b) material on topics of individual interest on which they would like to be assessed.

Such topics might include:
    reviews of plays in performance
    scripts written by them
    accounts of work done in other groups than the CSE one: e.g. rehearsal notes or drawings from performances
    tape and video studies, films, etc.
    designs of their own, for exercises outside the syllabus of 1, 2, and 3.

Under this heading, it might also be possible for students to offer dramatic dance or movement material of their own.

Time

All CSE students will be expected to do at least two hours of classwork and two hours of homework per week. Some of this may be taken up with work in a series of optional courses open to them, on the following topics:

1. Dramatic Arts course leading to Guildhall certificates
2. Creative writing course
3. Dance and movement

4. Costume design/making
5. Set design/making
6. Puppetry
   There will be no written examination, but assessment will take place on
four occasions:
   1. End of first year, assessment of first group activity.
   2. Middle of second year, assessment of play production.
   3. Before the end of second year, assessment of second group project.
   4. End of second year, assessment of project work, work on set plays and
      improvisation.
   The marking system for this assessment is given on the appended assessment sheet.

APPENDIX 4

MARKING SCHEME

Category	Sub Category	1st Year Max. Mark	1st Year Actual Mark	2nd Year Max. Mark	2nd Year Actual Mark
Improvisation	Responsibility to Group		10		
	Imaginative energy		25		
	Information/characterisation		25		
	Shaping		15		
Group Activity	Contribution/responsibility to group	5		5	
	Contributions as actors/technicians	12		12	
	Contributions to idea/material	7		7	
	Success of total project	Multiply total by 1·0–1·6		Multiply total by 1·0–1·6	
		(as evaluation of whole group production)			
Plays — Set Plays	(a)		5		
	(b)		5		
	(c)		5		
	(d)		5		
	(e)		5		
	(f)		5		
	(g)		5		
	(h)		5		
	(i)		5		
	Performance		30		
Project	Depends on nature of project in terms of 'objectives'		75		
TOTAL			300		

Appendix 5
Southern Regional Examinations Board
Certificate of Extended Education
Communication Working Party

Drama Modules

(7) *Improvisation*

Aims

That students should work towards:

Facility . . .	in communicating through voice, gesture, movement.
Depth . . .	in shaping, sustaining, giving texture, direction, sense, and character to the material with which they are dealing.
Awareness . .	of others involved, by co-operating and contributing usefully to the activities with others.

Content

The precise nature of the work to be attempted must obviously depend on the nature of each particular group of students and their interests and aptitudes. Some basic guidelines can, however, be laid down:

It is unlikely that any part of the course should be aimed at a performance for an audience.

Candidates should explore a variety of ideas, themes, situations, in a variety of ways.

The skills associated with improvisation should be developed as a part of the course.

Most of the available time will be devoted to group activity, rather than entirely individual improvisations.

Method of Assessment

The teacher will keep a record of the work done during the course. At the end of the course he will write a report on the work of each student and, bearing in mind the criteria given below, grade him for his contribution to the course and the abilities which he has developed and used.

The teacher's grades will be moderated by a visiting moderator who will take a group improvisation session.

Criteria for Assessment
    concentration
    spontaneity
    awareness of environment
    awareness of others
    sensitivity to stimuli
    vocal control
    physical control
    ability to communicate through
        (a) movement and gesture
        (b) speech
    ability to create mood
    ability to explore situations and exploit possibilities
    ability to explain a problem
    ability to see implications
    ability to apply knowledge to new situations
    willingness to take responsibility
    willingness to work as part of a group

The study of this module implies some maturity of approach, critical appraisal and originality on the part of the candidate. The mere representation of the view of others, or of unassimilated facts, is unlikely to prove satisfactory.

(8) Group Activity towards a Workshop Production

Aims
That the group should work towards a live, original performance to an audience.

That the students should conceive, develop and refine the subject for the performance.

Content
The precise nature of the activity to be performed must obviously depend on the nature of each particular group of students and their interests and aptitudes. Some basic guidelines can, however, be laid down:

The skills associated with improvisation should be developed as part of the course.

Students should be encouraged to use a variety of media in the activity.

The group should devise an original activity; decide upon the conditions of its performance; and all should participate in the performance.

The live performance should normally last not less than half an hour.

Method of Assessment
The teacher will keep a record of the work done during the course. At the end of the course the teacher will write a report on the work of each student and, bearing in mind the criteria given below, give a grade for his

contribution to the course, the standard of his work during the course, and the standard achieved in the performance.

The teacher's grades will be moderated by a visiting moderator who will attend a performance and discuss it with the group.

Criteria for Assessment
    inventiveness and imagination
    willingness to work as part of a group
    willingness to take responsibility
    concentration
    spontaneity
    awareness of others
    awareness of environment
    sensitivity to stimuli
    vocal control
    physical control
    ability to communicate to an audience through
        (a) movement and gesture
        (b) speech and possible song
    ability to create mood
    ability to explore situations and exploit possibilities.

(9) *Study Towards Production of a Play*

Aims
That students should study in detail scripted plays.
That students should prepare a play or plays for production.
That where possible the play should be performed.

Content
Two options are available within this module:
EITHER
(a) Candidates should work at two plays from the list given below, or at two plays of similar difficulty, or at two substantial extracts from full-length plays, e.g. *The Royal Hunt of the Sun* Act I; *The Crucible*, Act III. They should prepare and submit a folder of work giving evidence of detailed reading, and also containing design work, models, production notes, etc., which would be necessary for the plays to be staged.

OR
(b) Candidates should prepare and submit a folder of work giving evidence of detailed reading of ONE of the plays from the list given below or a play of similar difficulty, or ONE substantial extract from a full-length play, e.g. *The Royal Hunt of the Sun*, Act I; *The Crucible*, Act III. The folder should also contain design work and/or models and/or production notes, etc. The group should finally present the play as a production for an audience.

    Chekov — any one-act play
    Buchner — *Woyzek*
    Sheridan — *St Patrick's Day*
    Brecht   — *The Exception and the Rule*
    Wesker — *The Kitchen*

Orton   — *The Erpingham Camp*
Simpson — *The Hole*
Ionesco — *The Chairs; The Lesson; The Bald Prima Donna*
Albee   — *Zoo Story*
Pinter   — *The Birthday Party; The Collection; The Dumb Waiter; Short Sketches*
Howarth — *School Play.*

Method of Assessment
  (a) (1) Folder of work etc. This will be graded by the candidates's teacher, bearing in mind the criteria given overleaf. A written explanation must be given as to the qualities in a candidate's work which have particularly appealed to the teacher.
     (2) Oral. Before awarding a grade to the candidate's coursework the teacher should discuss individually with every candidate the course and the folder of work submitted. While no mark/grade will be allocated to this oral, the evidence from it, either to the candidate's advantage or disadvantage, may be used to influence the grade awarded to the folder of work. If this happens, the teacher should append a written explanation to that required under (1) above.
The teacher's grade will be moderated by the Board.

  (b) (1) Folder of work etc. This will be graded by the candidate's teacher, bearing in mind the criteria given below. A written explanation must be given as to the qualities in a candidate's work which have particularly appealed to the teacher.
     (2) Performance. Each candidate will be assessed on the contribution which he makes towards the performance and the quality of that contribution. He should be assessed on *at least one* of the following: acting/costume/set/lighting/business management/props/production.
The teacher's grade will be moderated by the Board.

Criteria for Assessment
  (i) Folder of work:
     awareness of the theatrical potential of a play
     evidence of a coherent interpretation of the play as a whole
     depth and detail of investigation
     imagination and sensitivity of approach
     appropriateness, imagination, possibility, use of colour etc. in models and drawings
     organization and presentation
     accuracy of spelling, punctuation and grammar
  (ii) Performance. Since the contribution of each candidate will often be very different from the others in the group it will be inappropriate to give detailed lists of criteria. Suffice to say that each student should be judged on two areas:
     ability to work with a group
     the quality of his own contribution

At the time of going to press, the CEE has not yet been approved by the Secretary of State. It is therefore certificated as CSE.

Appendix 6

A. Associated Examining Board Outline Syllabus for Theatre Studies at Advanced Level

The course aims at achieving understanding and appreciation of the various materials, forms and methods by which dramatic experience can be embodied and expressed. Drama is studied as an element in general human experience, as a cultural phenomenon, and through the written text. Students will be required to make a study of the theatre in past times and in societies other than their own, and to examine modern and contemporary ideas about the play and its social function. A prominent place is also given to the exploration of techniques (practical skills) associated with the theatre by encouraging the student to make an individual contribution to this field and to participate in a group activity.

The course will be examined through two written papers and a practical. Papers I and II will be of three hours' duration; the practical section will be in two parts supported by a working notebook.

Paper I (Marks 35% of total)

Candidates will be required to write one essay from each of the three sections and a fourth essay from any section of the three, or one question from each of sections 1 and 2 and an assignment from section 3 submitted separately. The material included under sections 1 to 3 is as follows:

1. *Theatre as an Expression of Culture*
   Using as examples the following Key Periods and Developments:
   Ritual (including the Folk Play)
   The Greek Theatre (Aeschylus, Sophocles, Euripides, Aristophanes)
   The Medieval Theatre (*The Castle of Perseverance, The Creation, The Deluge, The Second Shepherd's Play, The Crucifixion* and *Everyman*)
   The Commedia dell' Arte
   The Neo-Classical Theatre (Molière, Racine, Dryden)

2. *Dramatic Theory of the Twentieth Century*
   An examination of the theories of:
   Stanislavsky (*Building a Character* – Methuen)
   Edward Gordon Craig (*On the Art of the Theatre* – Heinemann)
   Meyerhold (*Meyerhold on Theatre*, trans/ed. Braun – Methuen)
   Brecht (*Brecht on Theatre*, trans/ed, Willett – Methuen)
   Artaud (*Theatre and its Double* – Calder and Boyars)

3. *Contemporary Approaches to the Theatre*
   (a) An examination of the recorded work (and, if possible, the experience)
       of at least two of the following:
       The Living Theatre (Julian Beck)
       Theatre Workshop (Joan Littlewood) and Documentary Theatre
       The English Stage Company (George Devine)
       Peter Brook
       Jean Louis Barrault
       Grotowski
       Fringe Theatre, Theatre in Education, Underground Theatre.
   (b) A question may be set asking the candidate to describe and evaluate a
       dramatic presentation, which he has examined in some detail as an
       observer.

Paper II (Marks 35% of total) – Set Texts

Candidates will answer four questions. In Section A they will write one
answer on Shakespeare and one on *either* Chekhov *or* Brecht. In Section B
they will answer two questions on any plays in Sections 1 to 4 other than
Shakespeare, Chekhov and Brecht. Texts for study must be chosen from the
following:

1. *Shakespeare and his Contemporaries*
   King Lear or *Henry IV*, Part 2, *Volpone* (Jonson), *Fuenteovejune* (de Vega).

2. *17th and 18th Century European Drama*
   The Mayor of Zalamea (Calderon), *The Recruiting Officer* (Farquhar),
   The Misanthrope (Molière), *The Servant of Two Masters* (Goldoni).

3. *19th Century European Drama*
   The Cherry Orchard (Chekhov), *Woyzeck* (Buchner), *The Wild Duck*
   (Ibsen), *The Government Inspector* (Gogol).

4. *20th Century Drama 1900–1945*
   Heartbreak House (Shaw), *Six Characters in Search of an Author* (Pirandello),
   Arturo Ui (Brecht), *Huis Clos* (Sartre).
   (b) *Contemporary Drama*
   The Lesson and *The Chairs* (Ionesco), *Death of a Salesman* (Millar),
   Sergeant Musgrave's Dance (Arden), *The Balcony* (Genet).
   There will be two questions on each play. The first question will be
   concerned with the social, political, and cultural context of the play; the
   second question will be specifically concerned with preparing the play for

presentation which will include a consideration of plot, structure, character, dialogue, style, visual statement, thought, etc.

Part III (Marks 30% of total) – Practical Skills

This part will examine the practical skills associated with the theatre, which include participating in a group project and practising an individual skill supported by a working notebook.

The working notebook should record the processes involved that culminate in the demonstration of presentation of the individual skill. This may include photographs, drawings, diagrams, etc., linked and unified by written notes. The notebook must be available for inspection by the moderator on the day of the examination.

The group project should be the realization of an original drama programme that the candidates have created themselves from ideas explored while working on the course. The maximum number in the group is to be fifteen and the examination playing time is to be not less than 15 minutes for small group and not more than 45 minutes for a large group.

The individual skill in which the candidates are required to prepare themselves for examination should be chosen from one of the following:
(a) the analysis and direction of a scene or extract from a play or one-act play;
(b) solo acting of two contrasting published pieces written for the theatre;
(c) a demonstration of the use of lighting or sound equipment;
(d) design and demonstration of puppets;
(e) design and demonstration of masks;
(f) design and demonstration of projected images (slide and/or film and/or shadow) in the theatre;
(g) the submission of a text of an original play; adaptation from another literary form; or compilation;
(h) design and demonstration of costume;
(i) exhibition of designs for a stage setting or stage settings;
(j) or any other appropriate theatre activity or product to be approved in consultation with the tutor and external examiner.
The Skills (c), (h), and (i) to be related to one of the plays studied.
The Skills (d), (e), (h), and (i) are not to be submitted if similar problems are being undertaken in 'A' level Art and Crafts.

Maximum Examination Playing Time
Skill (a) — fifteen minutes
Skill (b) — eight minutes, with a minimum of three minutes for each piece
Skill (c), (d), (e) and (f) – ten minutes
Skill (g) — there is no maximum playing time for this skill. The script, however, should be submitted to the visiting examiner at least six weeks in advance of the date of the practical examination.

Practical Work
The pieces to be chosen by the student in consultation with the tutor and submitted to the visiting examiner at least twelve weeks in advance of the practical examination. The visiting examiner may discuss the candidate's offering with him.
All practical work may be associated with any of the set texts.

B. The Marking of the Group Project

I have tried to evaluate the group projects on the following scale, believing ing that the students should have achieved a level that is *more* than merely sufficient. I have marked them according to a 40 point scale:

40 Clearly understands task through critical/analytical approach, and able to realize it in practical terms – imaginative, relevant, sensitive. Results impressive, unified demonstration. Clearly conversant with the nature of the demand of the activity and able to meet it fully with diligence, competence and group integration.

Superior competence in theatre skills required for the task. Sharp evaluative/critical awareness readily and naturally applied. Real creativity adding dynamism/freshness to what is really well thought out.

Balance of intelligent understanding of all aspects of the task, with ability to work with and for a team. Being able to perceive mistakes and to learn from them. Memorable.

35 Feeling/sensitivity less evident. Performance, though impressive, never fully achieves its potential because of group insensitivity, lack of creative insight or unsparing application, or because these are less sharply in evidence.

Competence in most skills. Sharp evaluative/critical awareness shown in most areas of work. Dynamism slightly less than '40' or not quite so consistently evident, but nevertheless thoroughly well thought out.

Balance of intelligent understanding not so secure at moments when co-ordination is required. As '40' but slightly less memorable.

30 Very good manipulator, very good technically, but feeling is less in evidence or less controlled. Diligence not balanced by insight or group sensitivity and, though achieving a good result, not really memorable.

Higher competence than the norm in all skills. Evaluative/critical awareness consistently applied but less dynamic.

25 Some evidence of facts overlooked or unexplored, but not disastrously so.

Little ingenuity but with great diligence and the capacity for concern for the group. Evaluative/critical awareness only occasionally evident.

Evidence of good understanding and ability to communicate and and work with others but without the vital spark which makes the work memorable.

20 As '25', but with certain basic mistakes resulting through lack of feeling or lack of understanding or lack of effort.

Limited abilities but who, with extreme diligence, inspiration or social sensitivity, achieves the fullest realization of these limited abilities.

A little above the norm in skills. Very little real insight. Only moments of dynamism. Moderately well thought out. Indication of intelligent analysis and real wish to co-ordinate, but lack of perception hampers success.

15 (Pass)

A tendency to 'play it by ear' – but not without success. Of limited ability who has either accepted limitation and proportionately lack of diligence, inspiration, group sensitivity, OR who has raised our otherwise lower standard by extreme diligence.

A *norm* of competence, implying enough interest, aptitude, imagination, sensitivity, intelligence and responsibility to pass muster at the basic skills.

A workmanlike approach, but lacking feeling for subtleties. Reasonable understanding of shape and intent of the material. Reasonable communication with group, but not always aware of difficulties and antagonisms.

10 Major errors of judgement now positively working against the evidence of possible success. Only a superficial grasp of the obvious. Slack. Incompetent.

Unaware of own limited potential – or neglects realization of limited potential; lacks diligence, ingenuity, group awareness; less competence than norm; limitations in ability, imagination.

5 Incomplete, invalid approach, largely irrelevant. No idea of how to use the little sense he possesses. Impervious to the influence of the art form.

Competence so limited as to be able to make only a token gesture in the practical work. Minimal integration.

0 Incoherent, inaccurate, irrelevant, inadequate, totally unsatisfactory.

GORDON VALLINS

Index